THE

Oracle

of Love

THE
Oracle
of Love

How to Use

Ordinary Playing Cards

to Answer Your

Relationship Questions,

Predict Your Romantic Future,

and Find Your Soul Mate

Lee Ann Richards

 THREE RIVERS PRESS · NEW YORK

Published by Three Rivers Press, New York, New York.
Member of the Crown Publishing Group,
a division of Random House, Inc.
www.randomhouse.com

THREE RIVERS PRESS and the Tugboat design are registered trademarks of
Random House, Inc.

Printed in the United States of America

DESIGN BY KAREN MINSTER

Library of Congress Cataloging-in-Publication Data
Richards, LeeAnn.
The oracle of love : how to use ordinary playing cards
to answer your relationship questions, predict your romantic future,
and find your soul mate / LeeAnn Richards.
1. Fortune-telling by cards.   2. Love—Miscellanea.   I. Title.
BF1878 .R48   2003
133.3′242—dc21   2002151244

ISBN 0-609-80894-X

10 9 8 7 6 5 4 3 2 1

FIRST EDITION

For Emerald,

so you will always have a guide

In Appreciation

I want to thank John for being the first to say,
Maybe you should write about the cards.
And I want to thank my girlfriends for their support, especially
Mary Blizzard, who reminds me the rules of writing
and living are one, and Nicole Aloni, who used her chef's knife
to cut a pathway through the publishing jungle.
Thanks to Janice (Jan-Ass), who cracks me up,
La Wenduca, who counsels love, strength, and party hats for all
occasions, and Kathie Collins, who keeps me honest.
I'm filled with gratitude for the gifts of my agent, Julie Castiglia,
my editor, Carrie Thornton, Carolyn and Leigh,
and for Ruth Marvin Webster, funny, warm, Writer Extraordinaire.
Thanks to the folks from the BUT, Wendy's class,
and the Sunday morning group,
all of whom have sustained me at one level or another.

I'm forever grateful to Jimmy Woodard,
whose sensitive hands held my porcelain heart, and to
Jaime Bravo for taking the journey I most admire.

My gratitude also goes to the Swingin' Kings, Motel Swing, Blue
Largo, Billy Watson, Big Daddy, and the rest of the San Diego bands
that boogied me through the writing of this book.

But, above all,
I want to thank my daughter, Emerald,
whose devotion inspires me and fills me with courage.

Contents

THE Oracle

of Love

How This Book Will Help You Find Your Soul Mate

NOT LONG AGO, I STRUCK UP A CONVERSATION WITH THE MAN SEATED next to me at a concert. He asked what I did for a living and I told him I was writing a book about love. He smiled and said, "A reason, a season, a lifetime."

"What do you mean?" I asked.

"People enter our lives all the time," he said. "Some pass through for a reason, some stay for a season, and others remain for a lifetime. You just have to figure out which person has come for what purpose."

Then I smiled, because he'd put in a sentence the intention of this book, which is to sort out the men you meet when you're single: to ascertain the reason you met, to measure the depth of your connection, and to predict how long your relationship will endure.

This book isn't a precise, step-by-step blueprint for finding your soul mate. You can't read it cover to cover, follow its directions to the letter, and then set it on the coffee table late one night and say, "Voilà! I know who zee soul mate eez!" No. It won't work like that.

What it can do, though, is teach you how to apply the wisdom of the cards to your life. It can instruct you in how to grow beyond the defenses and attitudes that have interfered with your relationships in the past and help you to open up to kinder, more generous relationships in the future. It can teach you how to recognize the beauty in a variety of masculine personality types instead of holding on to the one specific type that you recycle through your life, romance after romance.

THE ORACLE OF LOVE has been written to help you to differentiate between the times you function appropriately in relationships and the times you don't. It will interact with your life; it will show you when you're being selfish, miserly, and bratty. It will also identify trust, joy, intimacy, and empathy in you. If you are a willing student, this book will teach you to set boundaries, to be more honest, and to maintain hope and strength while you pick your way through the dating minefield.

What **THE ORACLE** won't do is function as a Band-Aid you can tape over your old wounds, nor will it prompt a shocking epiphany. It won't pat you on the wrist while you swoon with the vapors because the cards said Big Al isn't going to call. What it ought to do is encourage you to rely on your finer, more idealistic side. It should help you to relax and allow your faith in a divine higher power to guide you through the dating process.

Women always ask about their soul mate. They ask questions like:

* Have I already met mine?
* Is my soul mate my husband?
* My ex?
* Will my soul mate ever find me?

My answer to each question is the same: We make many soul-level connections throughout our lifetimes. Women connect with children, parents, and pets as often as with a man. Some women marry half a dozen of their soul mates. It's really just a matter of staying open to the possibility of love and of believing you have the capacity to connect at a deep, deep level.

The first step down the pathway to a soul-quality connection is taken when you abandon the idea that you will live happily ever after with the one flawless man God has set aside only for you. There is no one, perfect, predesignated person who represents your single opportunity for a deep, lasting, spiritual connection in this lifetime. Psychology teaches us that any two people can get along if they're both willing to be honest, be wrong, open up, apologize, and acknowledge their hopes and fears. It's not a great mystery.

After you abandon the notion that a loving connection to someone right for you is a mystical process, you're ready to take step two. This is when you relinquish the idea that Mr. Wonderful is a doctor, 6′2″, blond, blue eyed, drives a new BMW, lifts weights, goes to church and/or therapy, is 100 percent completely over his ex, and never wakes up at night so he'll never hear you snore. No. Your soul mate is probably a little shorter, a little more out of shape, still a tad angry at his old girlfriend, in a career crisis, and has been known to dip into his retirement account to buy a new set of golf clubs, even though he hasn't played in two years.

Many women find it hard to imagine that their soul mate could struggle with the rent or the kids. They like to think that "Mr. Perfect Who Understands Me Without My Saying a Word" would be sensitive to PMS, know how to repair every single broken thing in the house, and never admire another woman's figure.

Women have a tendency to get high on the idea that Prince Charming will "come along, and he'll be big and strong," to quote Billie Holiday. The mythology of our culture teaches us from the cradle that Cinderella will marry the prince. We're taught that Snow White will be awakened from a near-death experience by the chaste kiss of true love. We know that the Little Mermaid will be transformed into a whole, normal person as soon as she tricks Prince Eric into kissing her. No wonder we jump through hoops to make men notice us and buy into the notion that a loving connection to a nice person is something to be earned and a mystical process.

The truth is that a girl has to be honest and take responsibility for her own choices and mistakes. Finding your soul mate is about understanding the unique character of each individual who crosses your path and about selecting the best possible candidate to fill the position as your life partner.

In most cases, your soul mate isn't the person you think he is. If he's not sitting next to you on the couch, zoned out on potato chips and channel surfing in his underwear, while you thumb through this book, then you may have idealized him as gorgeous, affluent, sensitive, generous, and hell on wheels between the sheets. You may even be convinced he was your old boyfriend who still calls once in a while. Maybe sometimes you allow yourself to think, "Oh you foolish girl. You let him get away. Now you'll never establish a transcendent connection with a man." You'll be stuck on the couch with this guy here, night after night, until you choke to death on boredom.

It's my job to point out that your prince is sitting there. He's there night after night, year after year. He brings home his check every week, grunts politely when your mother comes over, and keeps both cars running. It's my responsibility to remind you that at one time, you believed he was the best catch in town, that he would be strong and stable for you, and that he would never run around like your ex did. You once felt a deep passion for the man. I'm here to help you realize that tenderness and romance still exist in him, and if you were to change the way you interact with him, you could unleash his passionate side once again.

♠ ♦ ♣ ♥

The search for a soul mate is a different experience at different stages of life.

Teen girls wonder what the boys in their class think of them. They wonder if they'll get married, have children, or live in a big house. They like to speculate about when the great love of their life will enter the picture. They know this age isn't the time to worry about marriage and a family, but they're curious. They want to know how their life will turn out.

The young woman just getting out of school naturally assumes she'll marry a bright young law school graduate and have children shortly after their wedding, just like her sisters did. She knows she's on the brink of a new, exciting phase of life so she has no real doubts about her future. She just wonders who, how, and when.

The thirty-year-old divorced mother of two toddlers isn't thinking that way. She lost at love. The happy future didn't work out for her. Her main concern is that she make a better match next time. This gal is looking for another chance with a better prospect.

Some women find themselves newly single at forty. These women can doubt their ability to select the right kind of man. They frequently carry the baggage of bitterness and disappointment. Midlife women can be guarded and self-protective. But other women at forty can hardly wait to sink their teeth into the next new guy they meet. Their children are grown and now that they're single again, they find themselves free to play and flirt for the first time in decades. These gals hit the pavement running, as if they just got out of prison.

The older woman who finds herself single may be a widow. Of course she misses her husband and their old life together, but a widow has to accept that her husband isn't coming back. The senior woman may feel ready to share a polite dinner with a lovely man or to see a movie and make a new friend.

Whatever your circumstances are, I will address them in this book because love unfolds at every stage of life—if you let it.

I ask every new client who comes to me if she knows what the purpose of dating is. In response, they mostly sit and stare at me without blinking. Then I say, "I'll tell you what it *isn't!* It's not to make him really, really, really like you! The purpose is to decipher if he's a good, honest, sincere, hardworking guy. It's to determine if he's someone you can respect." Dating isn't supposed to be about sex or about carving more notches on the strap of your Louis Vuitton handbag to mark how many millionaires you went out with. It's supposed to be a safe, structured opportunity to ascertain a man's character, personality, and values.

♠ ♦ ♣ ♥

My intention in writing this book is to help each female reader find a male best friend who will make her laugh; one who likes kids, feels comfortable stretched out on her couch, and knows how to kiss the back of her neck in such a way as to make goose bumps dance across her shoulders.

The second intention of this book is to help women in established relationships to strengthen their connection. The book will remind them of the passion they felt in the beginning of their courtship, which will help them endure a period of separation, financial difficulty, or poor health.

If your goal is to get high, and stay high, on a cineplex-quality Grand Romance with flashy cars and trips to Paris, my book won't help you. But, if you're willing to take responsibility for your choices, it can hook you up with a good human being who shares your values and enjoys your company.

These pages will teach you how to be a better romantic prospect for a better grade of man, which means they will teach you how to conduct your half of a romance with less bitterness, manipulation, need for control, or superficial gestures of love. The cards will help you read the character of the new men you meet. They'll show you where you went wrong in the past, what you can do to change your present situation, and what will happen in the future as a result of the actions you take today. The cards will remind you that the Universe has a plan for you, and that it's an arrogant act of vanity to interfere with this plan just because you've lost faith in the process.

Contained in each of our psyches is an entire deck of playing cards. We're all born with the same fifty-three philosophical principles coded into our DNA. Those principles are played out in every life. All experience will come to all of us and none of us will escape any of the lessons depicted by the cards. No matter how hard we try to avoid it, we're all going to visit the Stations of the Cross marked Death and Isolation as well as True Love and Contentment.

You don't have to be raised by five generations of Indian mystics to be a successful intuitive reader. All you need is a good working knowledge of the cards, a little experience, and faith in your own instincts.

Through the practice of using this book, you will bear witness to all sides of the fabric of life. You will see love lost and won. You will see chaos and confusion, order and clarity. Your friends and lovers will break your heart and heal you. Your faith in humanity will be both challenged and confirmed.

In working with the playing cards, you will learn fifty-three wildly varying principles of life as set out centuries ago by the ancient Gypsy culture of Europe. These principles will bring hope and comfort to your life while they enrich your spirit. They can help you grow into the kind of woman who has the relationship skills to form a permanent, soul-level connection with a wonderful man.

How to Use the Book

Begin by holding a question in your mind. Shuffle the cards while you think about your question. Then lay the cards into a pattern.

Most patterns, or spreads, will describe your current situation, comment on the events in the recent past that brought you to ask the question, and reveal the most probable resolution to your dilemma.

HOW TO READ THE ORACLE

* First, follow the instructions on pages 16–17 to mark your cards.
* Next, form a question. Try to be as specific as possible. Vague questions like "What does my future hold?" aren't very productive. "Will I get married to Harry next year?" is better.
* Select a spread and follow the directions.

HERE ARE SOME TIPS

✳ If a card falls Reversed, read the opening paragraphs about the card and skip to the Reversed section. The Upright section won't apply to your situation. If the Reversed section horrifies you, read the Upright part to see if turning the card around would make you happy. If it would, then ask, "How can I Upright this card?" and pull a card for advice.

✳ The meaning of a card varies depending upon where the card sits in a spread. Let's use the Ace of Hearts, the card of permanent emotional connections, as an example.

  ✳ If the Ace describes the **past,** it says you were living with your family or were happily married.

  ✳ If it describes the **future,** it says you want to move in with your family or get married.

  ✳ If it describes a **person,** it says he's looking for a marital partner, is married at this time, or will turn out to be your ultimate life partner.

  ✳ When the Ace of Hearts is pulled in response to a **Yes** or **No** question, the answer is yes, regardless of the direction of the card because the Ace is an extremely positive card, Upright or Reversed.

CHAPTER ONE

About the Cards

The History

The precise history of the playing cards is uncertain. Theories about their origin are as varied as books on fortune-telling. Some authors claim they came from China and evolved from Dominos. Many believe they originated in Egypt, while others allege they came from India. One theory says the playing deck was born of the Tarot deck while another says they emerged separately for gaming purposes.

Every writer on this subject ends up filing a similar disclaimer that goes something like this:

"To the best of my knowledge, and based on my research, the following appears to be the most likely history of the playing cards."

What follows here is my opinion, based on my own research.

My investigation shows the Gypsies brought the Tarot to Europe from Egypt centuries ago. (The word "Gypsy" is a corruption of the word "Egyptian.") The history of numbers teaches us that the Egyptians adopted mathematics from the Sumerians. The Egyptians were so impressed with mathematics that they turned it into a minor religion and a tool for divination to create the science of numerology. They also tracked the stars in the heavens to create the science of astrology, which was the forerunner of modern astronomy. Egyptian numerology and astrology combined to create the Tarot.

Here's how:

* The number of each playing card corresponds to that number's traditional numerological message.
* One astrological element (Earth, Air, Fire, or Water) governs each of the four suits of the Tarot.
* The message in each number is colored to reflect the interests of the suit.
* The combination forms the meaning of each card.

The Egyptians assigned the science of card divination to Thoth, the god of inner knowledge, or intuition. Religious Egyptians believed inner knowledge was the only true knowledge and that Thoth was the custodian of all mystical secrets.

The tradition of the Tarot spread to the Middle East through trade between the Egyptians and the Sumerians, who were a part of the vast Ottoman Empire. Around 1200 A.D., the Crusaders adopted the cards in the Middle East and carried them to the capitals of the European continent. As the Crusaders wound their way through the major cities of Europe, Gypsy fortune-tellers astounded and amused the reigning monarchs. Eventually, every ruler adopted a Tarot card reader as a part of his staff. Foretelling the future became popular among the aristocracy and clergy, and courtesans used the Minor Arcana of the Tarot to invent games of chance. But, as gambling got out of hand and Gypsy fortune-tellers rose to positions of influence, the cards underwent periods of disfavor.

For centuries, the Tarot cards alternated between acclaim and passionate prohibition by the heads of church or state. Card divination has enjoyed a long roller-coaster ride of acceptance and rejection since it first arrived in Europe.

I believe that during a period when gaming was legal but divination was not, the Major Arcana of the Tarot was dropped to create the playing card deck. A trimmed-down deck would have made it possible for the Gypsies to be in possession of the cards without the threat of persecution for telling fortunes. The structures of the Tarot deck and the playing card deck are so similar that they surely must have evolved from one another. Here's what I mean:

A Tarot deck has 78 cards:
* 22 picture cards called the Major Arcana
  (the Greater Secrets)
* 40 numbered cards called the Minor Arcana
  (the Lesser Secrets)
* 16 Court cards decorated with portraits

The playing deck has 53 cards:
* One of the Major Arcana cards—the first, known in the Tarot as "the Fool" and in the playing deck as "the Joker"
* 40 numbered cards
* 12 Court cards decorated with portraits

The 22 Major Arcana cards of the Tarot describe 22 different philosophical principles. The meanings of the Major Arcana string together to describe a journey through life that begins in birth and travels through marriage, children, prosperity, power, and death, and ends with wisdom and maturity. The forty numbered cards, called the Minor Arcana, describe ideas and functions. They don't depict fated, unavoidable events. Instead, they foretell smaller matters. They describe problems and opinions or moods and preferences. The sixteen Court cards illustrate individuals at various stages of life.

The playing deck articulates the same philosophical journey as the Tarot. The twelve Court cards describe individuals at the same stages of life as the Court cards of the Tarot, except by trimming the Court cards from sixteen to twelve the playing deck has edited out one of the intermediate stages.

Both the Tarot and the playing deck divide the numbered cards and the Court cards into the same four groups, called "suits." Although the suits of both decks govern the same aspects of life, they have different names.

* The **Hearts** of the playing deck correspond to the **Cups** of the Tarot.
* The **Clubs** of the playing deck correspond to the **Wands** of the Tarot.
* The **Diamonds** of the playing deck correspond to the **Pentacles** of the Tarot.
* The **Spades** of the playing deck correspond to the **Swords** of the Tarot.

Disputes exist over the exact significance of each playing card, but there has been a remarkable consistency in the meanings of the Tarot cards over the centuries. The earliest illustrations of Tarot cards depict images of the Hanged Man and Wheel of Fortune that are consistent with the images used today. But, the playing cards are not so fortunate.

Some scholars believe the playing deck and the Minor Arcana of the Tarot have the same meaning. Those practitioners use the traditional Tarot card interpretations for the Minor Arcana to define the playing cards. I believe the playing deck retains the Major Arcana and therefore has deeper, broader meanings than can be found in the Minor Arcana. However, the messages of the Major Arcana seem to arrive in the playing cards in a haphazard manner, which is probably a result of being passed down from one generation to the next in an oral tradition. I find that half, or the Upright version, of a philosophical point will show up in one card while the other half, the Reversed version, will appear in another. I also believe the piecemeal distribution of the philosophical points of the Major Arcana is at the root of disputes over the interpretations of the playing deck.

Regardless of which rendition of playing card history you choose to believe, one thing is certain: the ancient interpretations remain fresh today because humanity continues to wrestle with the spiritual and philosophical issues that challenged it centuries ago on the banks of the Nile.

The Suits

Two ancient disciplines are the basis for playing card interpretations:

Numerology, which explains the meaning of the number on the card

Astrology, which explains the meaning of the suit

♠ ♦ ♣ ♥

Every card in the deck is broken down into two parts, a number or person (the Court cards) and a suit. The deck is divided into four suits or categories, each of which contains ten numbered cards and three Court cards. The message of the number or person shifts to reflect the interest of the suit.

For example, Fours are cards of constructive, physical effort. When the emotional suit of Hearts influences the Four, it becomes the card of caretaking and describes our efforts to nurture. But, when the practical, material suit of Diamonds influences the Four, it becomes the card of physical labor and describes our efforts to make money.

The following chart shows the correspondence between the suits and their astrological counterparts.

	HEARTS	DIAMONDS	CLUBS	SPADES
ELEMENT	Water	Earth	Fire	Air
ASPECT	Emotional	Physical	Social	Intellectual

Each suit governs a different aspect of life as follows:

HEARTS: Heart cards address our feelings and the emotional connections we make throughout our lifetimes. They represent intimacy, romance, permanence, pain, joy, love, and lust. The King, Queen, and Jack of Hearts describe our family members, spouses, lovers, and children. They include the zodiac signs Cancer, Scorpio, and Pisces, and correspond to the element of Water.

DIAMONDS: These are the cards of the material and physical. They seek stability and describe our efforts. The Diamonds portray our health, money, labor, and our basic need for food, shelter, and clothing. The King, Queen, and Jack of Diamonds represent employers, students, professionals, and entrepreneurs. They include the zodiac signs Taurus, Virgo, and Capricorn, and correspond to the element of Earth.

CLUBS: The Clubs are the cards of our culture. They oversee our intuition, our spirituality, our ethics, and our sensuality. Clubs describe the way we navigate our society. The King, Queen, and Jack of Clubs represent our peers, friends, movie stars, and what we call "the Beautiful People." They include the zodiac signs Aries, Leo, and Sagittarius, and correspond to the element of Fire.

SPADES: The cards of the mind define our problems and solutions. They govern our outlook and attitude. Spades urge discriminating thought and depict our daily struggle with anxiety, patience, boundaries, and power. The King, Queen, and Jack of Spades represent doctors, therapists, writers, scientists, and government officials. They include the zodiac signs Gemini, Libra, and Aquarius, and correspond to the element of Air.

The Numbers

The numbered cards in the deck describe a journey through life that begins at birth with the Joker and reaches maturity in the Nines. The Tens represent the completion of the journey and the beginning of a new cycle.

Each number in the deck incorporates the lesson or message of all the numbers that came before it, and expands on that information to create a new principle. For example, every Three contains the knowledge and experience of the Joker, Ace, and Two. In this fluid blending of one lesson into the next, we see the meanings of the numbers grow and deepen as they progress.

The numbers on the cards correspond to the numbers of numerology. Numerology as a science was adopted from the Egyptians by

Pythagoras around 600 B.C. Pythagoras wrote, "Evolution is the law of life." He believed everything in the Universe was subject to predictable, progressive cycles. His means of measuring those cycles were the numbers one through nine.

Pythagoras taught that numbers have a significance apart from the values denoted by figures. Numbers represent qualities; figures represent quantities. **Numbers operate on the spiritual plane, while figures are for measuring things on the material plane.** He taught that with a comprehensive knowledge of the meaning of numbers, one could understand the orderly progression of all life cycles.

The journey through the numbers unfolds in the following order:

THE JOKER REPRESENTS THE NUMBER ZERO: Since his number has no content, he is the soul of newborn innocence. The Joker has neither history nor plans. He's pure spontaneity. The Joker is the first card in the journey through the numbers and as such, has no knowledge of the world. He describes the beginning.

THE ACES REPRESENT THE NUMBER ONE: Aces symbolize the masculine, yang, principles of raw energy, progress, and creativity. They define the essence of the suit and represent the highest possible achievement within the arena governed by the suit.

THE TWOS: After the individual brilliance and accomplishment of the Aces, the Twos turn away from the self. The Twos describe the way in which we seek union. They represent the feminine principle of receptivity, the yin, which seeks to connect two distinct entities.

THE THREES: Once we connect with others, we expand to include one more person or thing. The Threes expand the partnerships established in the Twos.

THE FOURS: The Fours represent solid action and introduce stability through effort. The Fours are practical, productive, systematic, and constructive.

THE FIVES: Action breaks free with the Fives. The Fives depict our struggle for autonomy or separateness. They are the cards of our willingness to fight for our beliefs or to break away from those who oppose them.

THE SIXES: Peace reigns with the Sixes because the greater picture is seen. The Sixes restore our faith in humanity and in the future. Therefore, the Sixes stand for harmony and comfort.

THE SEVENS: Once we find peace in the Sixes, we turn our attention to perfected thinking. A period of reflection can manifest as self-absorption, anxious rumination, or revelation. Every man sees things in his own way and protects his interests with the Sevens.

THE EIGHTS: The Eights are cards of warmth and heart. They are philosophical, generous, modest, and represent the need to satisfy the soul.

THE NINES: The Nines integrate effort with wisdom and determination. They are the culmination of all the cards that came before them.

THE TENS: The Tens are doorways. They represent the end of one cycle and the beginning of another.

The Court Cards

The Court cards are decorated with pictures of Kings, Queens, and Knaves. Unlike the numbered cards, which represent ideas and functions, the Court cards describe the people we encounter as we function in the arenas depicted by the suits.

Remember, each suit corresponds to an aspect of life:

* **Spades** govern our intellect and correspond to the element of Air.
* **Hearts** describe our emotions and correspond to the element of Water.
* **Clubs** rule our social and cultural endeavors and correspond to the element of Fire.
* **Diamonds** represent our money, our bodies, and correspond to the element of Earth.

For example: The Spades represent the Air signs of the zodiac: Gemini, Libra, and Aquarius. We encounter the King, Queen, and Jack of Spades when we go to a doctor and therapist or when we read and write. Spade people are chatty, clever, and witty, but they can also be cold, aloof, and indifferent.

One of the primary attributes of the Court cards is their system of rank. The Kings are the highest, the Queens fall in the middle, and the Jacks are the lowest. This order allows for such considerations as age, power, and experience. Skill and achievement in the aspect of life described by the suit builds through the ranking structure of the Court cards.

Unless the person receiving the reading indicates otherwise, the genders of the Court cards are read as depicted. Queens are female and Kings are male. Court cards represent either gender. Nonetheless, when the King of Diamonds is pulled to define a woman, she functions as the head of her household and the primary breadwinner in her family. When the Queen of Hearts describes a man, he provides daily care for young children. Anytime a Court card appears to represent a person of the opposite gender, the card will describe his or her external circumstances and is not meant as an assault on the masculinity or femininity of the individual.

Diamonds, for example, govern our physical bodies, our basic need for food or shelter, and our finances. Therefore, the Jack of Diamonds, who ranks lowest, is a young person with no work experience. He's a student who attends a trade school or college in preparation for his future career. The Queen of Diamonds is the middle card. She integrated the lessons of the Jack during her college years. Therefore, the Queen describes a person with an established career in middle management who earns a nice living but dreams of a bigger house and a nicer car. The King is on top. He represents the application of brains, experience, and effort to the business world. The King went to college, paid his dues to middle management, and climbed the corporate ladder. Now, he's at the peak of his profession. He enjoys complete financial stability while he indulges his taste for lucrative side ventures like real estate or stock market investments. The King of Diamonds is the most affluent individual in the deck.

Each Court card represents a specific level of achievement within the suit.

In the intellectual suit of **Spades,** the purpose of the young Jack is to keep an open mind. He sees new and different points of view. He builds to the bright Queen, who's clever and witty. She thinks psychologically, has a healthy attitude, and is able to counsel others by sharing her knowledge. The Queen progresses to the King, who has a mind of genius proportions with clear, detached reasoning and uncluttered, dispassionate judgment.

In the emotional suit of **Hearts,** the Jack is a sexy, romantic, emotionally shallow flirt. He grows into the Queen, who introduces vulnerability, intimacy, the need to nurture, nest, and love others. In the King, we see commitment, permanence, protection, emotional strength, and depth of attachment.

In the social suit of **Clubs,** the Jack is modest, friendly, and loyal. He evolves into the Queen, who entertains, holds court, and dazzles with her beauty, style, and charm. The King lives the perfect lifestyle. He has the "right" job, home, toys, and memberships. He's sexy and handsome, glamorous, famous, elegant, stable, accomplished, and very popular.

As a woman, I'm represented by all four of the Queens because a different version of the four feminine principles is drawn out of me by different circumstances.

* I'm a Queen of Hearts when I function as a mother, sister, or wife.
* I'm a Queen of Diamonds when I use my education and stick to my budget.
* I'm a Queen of Spades when I write, discriminate, and counsel.
* I'm a Queen of Clubs when I decorate my home, entertain my friends, buy cosmetics, and make love.

In the same manner, all men are all four Kings.

Jacks aren't gender specific. We're each the best friend (Jack of Clubs), learning new things (Jack of Diamonds), a romantic lover (Jack of Hearts), and sometimes we're inclined to be spoiled, selfish, or willful and to act out inappropriately (Jack of Spades Reversed).

The ranking structure of the Court cards also depicts each stage of life: Jacks represent young people in their twenties, Queens are the flowering and expanding thirties, and Kings are forty-plus.

Whenever a Court card represents a relationship, or describes the outcome of the spread, the person represented by the card will either control the alliance or have the final say in the resolution to the situation.

Reversed Cards

Throughout this book, you'll see constant references to the cards being read Upright and Reversed. These two terms, "Upright" and "Reversed," refer to the position of the card on the table. "Upright" means the hearts on the face of a Heart card are pointing upward. On the "Reversed" cards, the hearts are pointing downward. In the average deck of household playing cards, it's hard to tell if they're pointing up or down. Therefore, I suggest you mark your deck in some way to determine in which direc-

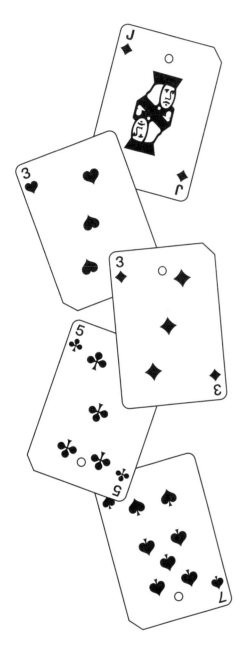

tion the card is pointing. The following are ideas for how to mark your cards.

I should probably mention that I don't believe life is preordained, I believe in free will. Therefore, I trust it's possible to overcome the issues with which we struggle. I believe it's possible to Upright our Reversed cards. In fact, I'm convinced we're obligated to try to. So how do you Upright a Reversed card? You simply ask the Universe to show you what it will take to turn it around and pull a few cards for guidance.

How to Mark the Cards

While playing cards don't look like they have an Upright or Reversed direction, they actually do. The cards contain even and uneven quantities of icons that render them Upright or Reversed.

I suggest that you mark your cards to help you determine their direction. But, you should examine each one closely before you mark it. Here are two ways to mark them:

* Clip off the top right corner of each card.
* Punch a hole in the top of each card.

Feel free to invent your own way to mark the cards because any method will work.

I also suggest that you write on your cards. I know several readers who collect exotic decks of Tarot cards. The variety of graphic images they see confuses them so they write on their cards. You should write on yours, too, because while you're learning the meanings of the cards your notations will work as a prompt for the card's broader, more elaborate message.

All you have to do to write on your cards is refer to the Cheat Sheet on pages 270–271. Copy the brief one- or two-word descriptions on each card, including the "Yes" and "No" answers. The "Yes" and "No" answers are also found in the final sentence on the final page of each essay about the card.

As you expand your knowledge and experience of card reading, you ought to add notes of your own.

I love seeing cards with words scribbled on them, holes punched in them, and their corners neatly clipped. It means the person who owns the deck really cares about her cards and is using them. It means she wants to comprehend the wisdom of the ancients and will give a great reading.

The Timing

Every client asks, "How long?"

I'd like to file a mild disclaimer about time. It's a funny issue. "When?" is certainly a vital thing to know, but it's a vague element and difficult to determine. That's because, as spiritual beings, we have the ability to draw people and events closer to us or to push them away. What if a Gypsy fortune-teller were to say "Your true love will cross your path in six days," and you needed to lose ten pounds. Well, you can see how the six-day time span could be a problem. Some psychic part of you would push the encounter out into the future just to give yourself a chance to get to the gym. But, if the Gypsy crone said "Six years," you might find a stretch of time like six years an eternity and pull the guy into your life sooner. It's hard to be precise when it comes to timing because we have free will.

A timing question is normally asked as a secondary question. First, the client asks a question about her pregnancy, marriage, or in-laws and then she asks "When?"

There are as many different ways to decipher time, as there are readers. I've listed my favorite methods below.

✳ The Gypsies believed the fifty-two cards (minus the Joker) symbolized the fifty-two weeks in a year. Their theory was that each of the four suits correlated to one of the four seasons (spring, summer, autumn, and winter), one of the four weeks in a lunar month, the four parts of a day (morning, midday, evening, and night), and the four stages of life (infancy, adolescence, adulthood, and old age).

Traditionally, the Ace of each suit rules the first week of its corresponding season. Kings rule the second week, Queens rule the third week, Jacks rule the fourth week, Tens rule the fifth week, and so on, with Twos ruling the last week in each season.

The first week of a cartomancy year begins with March 1. The Ace of Diamonds is the first card in the deck so it rules this first week. The Two of Spades is the last and lowest card in the deck. Therefore, it rules the last week of the year, which is the week of February 22 to February 28.

(The extra day in a leap year is under the rulership of the Joker.) The simplest way to answer the question "When?" is to pull one card.

Each season of the year, week of the month, portion of the day, and phase of life is attributed to a suit as follows:

DIAMONDS: spring — first week — morning — childhood
CLUBS: summer — second week — midday — adolescence
HEARTS: fall — third week — evening — adulthood
SPADES: winter — fourth week — night — old age

If you pulled one of the Hearts in response to the question "How long?" the answer would be "In the fall." If you had asked, "What phase of my life will be the happiest?" the same card would say "Adulthood." If it was the first day of the month and you asked, "When will he ask me out?" and pulled a Club, the answer would be "Next week."

✳ If the above system is too vague and you want a specific date, draw one card and compare it with the Birth Card chart on page 273. If you selected the Four of Hearts, the chart would provide five options: March 12, June 25, July 8, November 2, and November 15.

Drawing one card and comparing it with the Birth Card chart is a great way to pick a wedding date but a terrible way to determine when the claims adjuster in the next cubicle will invite you to lunch. A "When will he ask me out?" question needs a more flexible answer.

✳ The method I use the most often to determine time is complicated. But I use it because I'm more comfortable predicting a window of opportunity than an exact date.

I shuffle the deck and fan it into an arch. Then I ask my client to pull two cards. I'm looking for two numbered cards. If she hands me a Court card, I ask her to concentrate harder and pull another until I have two numbered cards. Let's pretend she handed me the Three of Clubs and the Nine of Spades.

Here's how I use the two cards:
   ✳ I compute the difference between the two numbers.
   ✳ In this case, Nine minus Three equals six.

The cards are saying that the event will take place in three to nine months (or hours, weeks, days, or years—we'll figure that out later). The cards say the event won't take place any time before three months. Nor will it take place after nine months. The distance between the two cards is six. So the most precise prediction is the number six. But six what? Is it months? Maybe it's hours, days, weeks, or years?

The increment of time is determined by another procedure. To find the increment, I ask my client to select one card and place it on the table facedown. This card will verify if the quantity of time is to be measured in hours. Then I ask for another card to represent days, another for weeks, and another for years. I turn all the cards over at the same time. Then I examine the group of cards to determine which one is the most positive. The highest ranking, most positive card describes the amount of time that applies to the number six.

Let's say my client pulled the following cards:

* The Reversed Two of Spades to represent hours
* The Upright Three of Hearts for days
* The Upright Ten of Clubs for weeks
* The Reversed Nine of Clubs for months
* The Upright Five of Diamonds for years

Okay. Let's analyze this.

* Reversed Two of Spades? Nah. The Reversed Two is low ranking and negative.
* Upright Three of Hearts? Very good. This is a happy, fortunate, loving little card.
* Upright Ten of Clubs? Definitely. The Ten is a high number with a message about optimism, new people, and fun.
* Reversed Nine of Clubs? No. The Reversed Nine is about declining values.
* Upright Five of Diamonds? Absolutely not. Upright or Reversed, the Five is the card of war.

The best card on the list is the Ten of Clubs because it contains a positive, uplifting message and was the highest number pulled. The Ten was drawn to represent the number in weeks. Therefore, we have an answer to the question "When?" Our answer is "Approximately six weeks." It might be as soon as three weeks or it could take as long as nine weeks.

Let's review the procedure:

* First, we found a number by establishing the midpoint between two numbered cards.
* Then we found a measurement of time by selecting a series of cards to represent increments of time.

* The correct increment was represented by the highest numbered card with the most positive message.

* Timing is the most difficult part of fortune-telling because it's the least accurate and most complicated. Measuring how far into the future is a very advanced aspect of card divination. I know dozens of Readers and I don't know of one who gets the timing right every time, including myself.

Mostly we Readers close our eyes and allow our minds to wander. We pick up images and analyze them. Is it cold? Is it raining? Are the people in my vision wearing coats? Is it summer? Are they at the beach? What kind of trees do I see out the window? Are there leaves on them? Is there a Christmas tree in the room? What do I feel on the surface of my skin? Am I hot and clammy or dry and itchy? Are my arms covered by a sweater or am I wearing a sleeveless blouse? Sometimes our intuition is the best and most accurate method we have for the measurement of time.

"Yes" or "No" in the Deck

Once you give yourself a few readings, you'll learn about the secondary questions that arise naturally from the original question. A person usually asks about the main problem first and then the smaller, subsequent questions come up as the reading progresses. A great number of those secondary questions can be answered with a simple "Yes" or "No" response.

Secondary questions are asked like this:

* "The reading says we'll get married, but will my dad pay for the wedding?"
* "So someone at the party will ask me out. Do I already know him?"
* "When he breaks up with *that woman*, will he call me?"

At the end of the section about each card, I've included a brief note to answer the "Yes" or "No" question. Here's how you find the "Yes" or "No" answer:

* When the secondary questions begin to flow, shuffle the cards and spread them into an arch, facedown. (Or use the leftover cards already on the table if you haven't finished your original spread.)
* For each "Yes" or "No" question, pull one card straight toward yourself.

* Turn the card over by folding it from right to left.
* Look up the card in the book and refer to the final sentence on the final page to find your answer.

Cards were designed to explain the positive and negative influences in your life. Some cards are bad regardless of their Upright or Reversed position and other cards are always good. Still others are positive in one direction and negative in the other. Therefore, it's common to find a positive card that says "No" when it's Reversed, and sometimes an ominous card says "Yes." Each card is a different combination of positive and negative influences and the "Yes" and "No" answers reflect those influences.

When you approach the oracle to ask a simple "Yes" or "No" question, the card you select will provide the answer but will also explain why the answer is "Yes" or "No." After you satisfy the question, don't move on too quickly; stay with the moment long enough to accept what you've been told. You may need to shift gears in order for the concept to sink in. If the "Yes" or "No" question was asked as the bottom line to your dilemma, read the entire essay about the card. Once you examine the card in depth, you will understand the greater message in your answer.

Even professional Readers struggle to answer the "Yes" or "No" questions that are an inevitable part of every reading. I've seen more than one cut the cards into three stacks and search for the Aces in order to divine the "Yes" or "No" answer by their direction and location. More often, they switch to astrology, numerology, or runes. Some rely on logic and intuition while others begin another elaborate spread.

Readings are easier when you have quick access to the "Yes" or "No" answer.

The Details

The following are a number of small but important pieces of unrelated information rarely included in books on fortune-telling. But, the entries are significant if you want to read for other people.

CLIENT VERSUS READER: Throughout this section, I've chosen to use the terms "client" and "Reader." The Reader is the person who reads the book, chooses the spreads, lays out the cards, and interprets their meaning. The client is the person who asks the questions and receives the answers.

HOW TO SELECT A SPREAD: Read all the spreads in the book. Then select three that appeal to you. Choose them for their variety, but start with three easy ones. Don't begin with an advanced, complex spread like Window to the Soul or the Lovers Destiny. You can graduate to more complicated layouts later.

At the beginning of a reading, examine your three-spread repertoire to determine which layout serves your question best. You can't find an answer to a question like "When will I fall in love?" in the "Yes" or "No" section. But, you might choose the Heart's Desire or use a timing technique. (See page 32.) If you don't know which spread to choose, pick the Lover's Pyramid because it's a good one to practice on.

You don't have to confine your questions to romance. The spreads included in this book are designed to answer questions about love, but they'll serve other topics too. You can ask about the sale of your house, your stock investments, or your cousin's health. You can ask the cards anything. If you want to ask about your relationship with your new business partner, use the Lover's Pyramid even though the relationship is not a romance. The spread will reveal how you look at her, how she looks at you, the truth about the partnership, and what will happen to your new venture.

HOW TO TURN THE CARDS OVER: This is more important than it seems. If you flip the cards from top to bottom, you'll turn the card upside down and Reverse its meaning. Always turn the cards from right to left, the way you turn the pages of a book. Never let your client flip over a card because she may not know about the Upright and Reversed positions and will turn them around. Ask your client to leave the card face down on the table and turn it over yourself.

HOW TO SHUFFLE: This may be the most challenging part of card divination. In my classes, my poor students grit their teeth, set their jaw, and furrow their brows in concentration. Most students strong-arm the cards into submission. But shuffling isn't arm wrestling. It's supposed to be natural and effortless. Try to relax your hands while you shuffle and don't force the cards to do anything they don't want to do. Here's my method.

   * Lay the deck on the table and pick up half of it with your left hand.
   * Pick up the other half with your right hand.
   * Lay both halves of the cards on the table in a V shape. The point of the V should be facing away from you. The open wedge should be toward you.

* Set the inside corner of one half on top of the inside corner of the other. Make sure the two pointy corners overlap.
* Place your thumbs against the inside edge of each half and your fingers around the outside edges.
* Now pick up the halves and drop them loosely, by fanning the cards with your thumbs. This is a calm, dropping gesture meant to allow the cards to drift out of your hands and into a fluffy, disorderly stack with the inside, overlapping corners woven together. It probably won't go very well the first time, but don't worry. Start over again and remember that there should be no tension in your hands and the cards shouldn't bend or bow when you drop them.
* After you allow your cards to drift into a big messy pile, lift them up onto their side. Form a fence shape with your hands and hold your blended cards inside the fence.
* Let the cards use your fence to settle back into one stack again.
* Repeat.
* Before a reading, shuffle the deck between three times and ten times.

HOW TO PREPARE FOR A READING: This can be a controversial issue. I know of Readers who prepare themselves by meditating for thirty minutes before they meet with a client, and I know other Readers who drink a glass of Chardonnay. It's up to you.

The best way to approach the oracle is to sit at a quiet table, in a straight-backed chair, with both feet flat on the floor. Allow your hands to rest in your lap while you take a few deep breaths and focus your attention on the center of your forehead.

Keep your mind open and your body relaxed. Stay calm and breathe. Now pick up your cards and shuffle with your eyes closed. (Don't worry. You'll work up to blind shuffling.) Divine energy will naturally surround you and mix into the cards. Let go of your expectations, ego, and ambitions. Simply ask the Universe for guidance while you shuffle. When the cards are well shuffled, open your eyes and lay out a spread.

HOW TO FLESH OUT A READING: The most obvious way is by asking more questions.

Friends and clients can be a little shocked by their first readings. The cards bring up such personal information that they become uncomfortable. New clients tend to blush and look down when they hear unsettling news. Dozens of questions race through their minds, but they're often too stunned to ask them. A good Reader will ask the questions for her client. If you're a natural gossip, like I am, posing the sticky questions will be easy.

Let's imagine your roommate hasn't heard from the man she dated all last summer. He hasn't called since school started and she's already sent him two e-mails that he hasn't answered. Now she wants a reading. Let's say you used the Past—Present—Future layout and found out he reunited with his old girlfriend. Now let's picture your roommate sitting in stunned silence with giant tears rolling down her cheeks. As you can see, she doesn't have the strength to ask the questions tearing her up inside. But, you can ask them for her.

Try these:

* Is he ever going to call me again?
* Why not?
* Why does he love her more than me?
* Does the Universe have another man in store for me?
* When will I meet him?
* Will he be the one I marry?

The kindest thing you can do for a friend going through a breakup is to ask the hard questions for her. Getting the questions out and getting them answered can be helpful and healing.

Another way to expand a reading is to use extra cards. More cards will elaborate on a theme or fill in a blind spot. Don't be afraid to toss extra cards all over the table.

To expand the reading and make it a deeper, more satisfying experience for your client, ask the embarrassing questions for her, toss extra cards on the table, extend beyond the outcome card, pull cards of timing, and look up the "Yes" and "No" answers at the end of the essays about the cards.

CARDS YOU DON'T UNDERSTAND: Well, clearly you should go back and reread the text on any card that doesn't make sense to you. But, if you're in the middle of a reading and don't relate to a particular card, simply close your eyes and say to yourself, "Please say it again," and pull another card to replace the first one. Even professional Readers reject a fuzzy card and replace it with a clear one.

THE BOTTOM CARD: This is the card shuffled to the bottom of the deck. It's a very important card because it tells you **what the reading is about.** If you have a spread laid out in front of you and you've already tossed extra cards all over the table, but you still don't know if you're talking about her new job or her old boyfriend, pull the bottom card. It'll clarify everything. I never do a reading without looking at the card on the bottom of the deck.

ALL REVERSED CARDS: Sometimes, every card in the spread is upside down. This occurs frequently in small spreads, such as Past—Present—Future or the Path to Love. When this happens, read all the cards as Upright but delayed. Don't try to decipher the length of the delay. Just warn your client that the amount of time may feel beyond what seems reasonable.

THE CONNECTION BETWEEN THE READER AND THE CLIENT: Each Reader is merely the sum total of her life experiences. Therefore, your friends will think of you as a good or bad Reader depending upon how well you share their understanding of life.

Don't be hurt if you gave your friend a reading she didn't like. If during the fortune-telling process you blurted out, *"Hello! He's married! What do you expect?"* and your girlfriend thought you were insensitive (maybe even a bit judgmental), apologize for the blurting but stick with your reading. Somewhere in her heart, she knows you're right. Don't take her reaction personally. The Universal spirit wanted her to hear the message, and she did.

If you feel uncomfortable reading for a client, *terminate the reading.* If she begins to withdraw or bristle, tell her you're finished. Never participate in a tense Reader-client connection. If you persist with your reading, your client will think you're a "bad" Reader, which isn't fair. You're not a bad Reader, the connection's bad.

PRESSURE FROM THE CLIENT: Don't succumb to it. Clients often want you to supply them with information the deck won't surrender. As a result, you may be tempted to *extract* it from your cards. A Reader can throw out card after card in an attempt to please a pushy client, but still get nowhere.

I've developed a generic statement to use when this happens. I say, "I am not being shown that information at this time," which is the truth. The Universe would make the information apparent in the original spread if she were supposed to receive it. Maybe the exact piece of data is something she'll figure out on her own, learn to live without, or uncover at another time. Always remember that the reading is not about you. It's about her. The Universe will give her as much information as it wants her to have. You're only a relay station.

READING FOR YOURSELF: In the beginning, most of your readings will be for yourself. You'll sit at home on a quiet Saturday night with a glass of wine or a box of Girl Scout cookies and your old deck of cards from the kitchen junk drawer. You'll shuffle the deck, spread out the cards, and look up their meanings in the book. It'll be relaxing and fun.

After a few months of working with this book and deck, you'll have all your cards marked. Then, you'll be ready to read for a friend. (But, most of your readings will still be for yourself.)

Later on you'll be proficient with the cards, own several additional books about how to use them, and be a regular source of free readings for your friends. At this point, your ability to read for yourself will change. You will no longer be able to do it.

Every professional Reader reaches a level where their personal readings become inconsistent. To be accurate, you have to be objective and your ego can't be involved. The chances of finding an accurate answer are darned slim if a professional Reader asks a personal question and the answer really matters to her. Don't lose hope. Once you get to this stage, card reading becomes a trade-off. You'll win every game of Concentration you ever get into, but someone else will have to tell your fortune.

HOW LONG IS THE READING GOOD FOR? The rule of thumb is "Until the next reading."

If a client gets only one reading in her lifetime, the cards will speak to her entire life. If a client calls every three days for a reading, the cards will cover only that three-day time span.

I counsel my clients never to get more than one reading a month unless they're in crisis. Some folks go once a year, on their birthday, as a yearly gift to themselves. Most people who frequent psychics get a reading two or three times a year. When I worked for a large metaphysical store with half a dozen Readers, I would get two or three readings a week from my coworkers if we were slow. Now, I work at home and only get one or two outside readings a year.

If you select a spread designed to cover a specific period of time, like the Heart's Desire or Secrets of the Heart, make the time span clear to your client so she knows how long to wait before her next reading.

DID I GET THE READING RIGHT? In general, no psychic card Reader can get the reading 100 percent right. At best, she can get it 70 or 80 percent right. Never expect to do much better yourself, and don't expect the professional Reader you frequent to do better either.

I like to cross-check my readings. If the client says, "I don't believe that's possible. You must be wrong," I close my eyes, float my hand an inch or so above the cards, think to myself, "Did I get it right?" and pull one more card. Then I refer to the "Yes" or "No" answers. The card will tell me if I answered her question correctly. If I got it wrong, I ask the client to pull three cards to describe the part of the reading I got wrong. Then I reexamine that portion of the reading.

ENDING THE READING: When the questions stop flowing or your client has used up her time allotment, the reading ends. At this point, I like to say a couple of things.

First I ask my client to "Please pull three cards as a postcard from God." These three cards will either confirm some aspect of the reading we just shared or introduce a new topic we didn't think to ask about. I consider the postcard from God to be my gift to the client. I am giving her an extra slice of my time because I know that in coming to see me, she took a step forward in her life. The postcard is my thanks for allowing me to participate in her forward motion. It's also my way of supporting her commitment to her spiritual journey. I do it to affirm her understanding of life and the workings of the Universe.

After the postcard, the real ending has arrived. At this point, I thank my client for allowing me to enter her energy field. I say, "It has been a pleasure to be in the vibration. I am going to leave you now," and I stop.

CHAPTER TWO

The Spreads

Past—Present—Future

Past—Present—Future is a good spread for questions about ongoing situations that are bogged down or in a crisis, questions like:

* "What will become of our relationship?"
* "Will my ex start making his support payments?"
* "Will the man I secretly love ever develop feelings for me?"

Traditionally, you're supposed to pull one card each for the past, present, and future. But, I use four cards because I want to know what event will link today's circumstance to the future.

TO LAY OUT THE SPREAD

* Shuffle the cards and spread them into an arch.
* Slide four cards out of the arch at random and move them into positions one through four in the order they were drawn. Leave the cards facedown on the table.
* Turn over the card in position one (on the far left) by turning it from right to left the way you turn the pages of a book. This card represents the past.
* Look up the card in chapter 3, the section on the interpretations of the cards. This position describes the circumstances or events that prompted you to consult the oracle.
* Next, turn over the card on the middle-left, in position two. This card represents the present. It describes your feelings or the circumstances surrounding you.

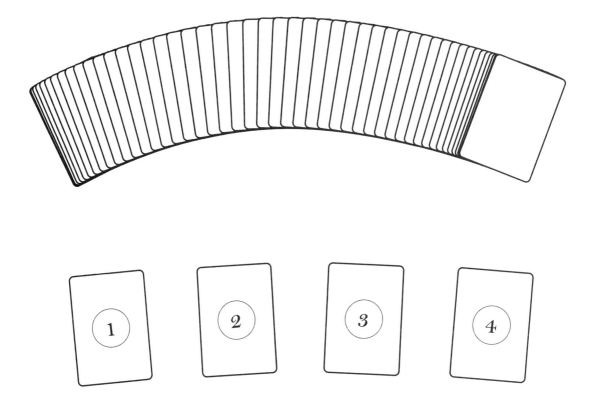

* Turn over the card on the middle-right, in position three. This card foretells the next major incident or phase that will occur in regard to your question. This event will take place prior to the resolution of your problem.
* Turn over the last card on the far right, the one in position four. This card describes the future. It foretells the long-term, final resolution of your question.

After I look at the client's four cards, I like to pull four of my own and place them on top of hers. My cards add depth and elaborate on her statement. The meanings of the two cards blend into one definition. If you don't understand the two-card message in one of the positions, pull more cards to explain it. But, don't automatically throw extra cards on the basic spread if the original four were sufficient and their message was clear.

If both cards in one position are Reversed, read them as Upright, but delayed. Double Reversed cards counsel patience and are a warning that the unfolding of the event or phase will feel unreasonably slow.

TO INTERPRET THE SPREAD

Let's imagine your girlfriend comes over to your house upset with her husband. Let's pretend they had a horrible fight and he stomped out three days ago. This isn't the first time, either. She wants a reading because she's tired of the way he always ends their arguments by walking out in a huff, which leaves her standing in the middle of the living room fuming and sputtering. She doesn't think she can take it anymore. She wants to know what's going to happen to her marriage.

Let's say she selects four cards and you move them into the four positions, in the order they were selected.

THE PAST: THE REVERSED FIVE OF DIAMONDS. The Reversed Five is the card of open fighting. That sounds about right. You don't need more cards to understand the meaning of the card in this position.

THE PRESENT: THE UPRIGHT ACE OF CLUBS. The Ace of Clubs is a card of soul communion and a loving spiritual connection, which doesn't sound like the current condition of her marriage. The Ace also stands for the ministry, but not always the clergy. A ministry is formed when a person speaks his personal truth and people choose to follow him because the way he understands it is the way they understand it, too. In this case, the card probably refers to a counselor with an established following, possibly one at their church, but not necessarily. Let's pretend you asked her to pull another card and lay it across the Ace. Let's say she selected the Upright Three of Spades. The Three is the card of interference. It describes a third person who steps between two others. Clearly, the two cards combine to suggest a round of marital counseling.

NEXT: THE UPRIGHT SEVEN OF HEARTS. The Seven of Hearts is the card of intimacy. It describes our ability to share our hopes and fears. Communication at this level can be risky and frightening, but the benefits of vulnerability are incalculable. The Upright Seven is the link to the future. The Seven in this position tells me they'll pour their hearts out to the shrink and to each other. As a result, they'll both feel heard, understood, and much closer as a couple.

THE FUTURE: THE UPRIGHT KING OF HEARTS. The King knows his own heart. He's aware of how much he loves his woman. The King of Hearts in the outcome position says her husband will draw closer to his true self and his true feelings. He'll develop the communication skills to tell her when he's overwhelmed or needs a break. She'll develop respect for his saturation levels and learn how to back off when she ought to. As a result of the new intimacy they gain through counseling, both of them will choose to stay in the marriage. As her husband grows to feel loved and emotionally fulfilled within the union, she will be more able to recognize his affection for her. They will both be much happier.

The Heart's Desire

The Heart's Desire was used by the medieval French to predict marital prospects. Today, it's still the best way to uncover your own prospects.

TO LAY OUT THE SPREAD

* Shuffle the deck several times and cut it into three stacks with your left hand.
* Place the stacks side by side as shown in the diagram.
* Turn over the stack on the left marked 0–2 Months and spread it into an arch.

* **Search through the arch for the King and Queen of Hearts and the Nine of Hearts.**
* The King of Hearts represents an emotionally strong, committed man who loves openly. He stands for the one who adores you. Therefore, he'll take the necessary steps to make you his wife.
* The Queen of Hearts is a woman in touch with her feelings. Because she knows her own heart, her love is uncomplicated and permanent. This card represents you.
* The Nine of Hearts is the card of true love. It describes the climactic moment when your eyes lock with his across a crowded room, and you recognize that you are twin souls. In an established relationship it foretells the achievement of cherished goals such as an engagement or the birth of a child.

TO INTERPRET THE SPREAD

For this spread, the meanings are the same regardless if the King, Queen, and Nine are Upright or Reversed.

THE KING AND NINE TOGETHER: It would be wonderful to find the King and Nine in the first stack. This placement means you and your soul mate are already in love or will fall in love during the next two months.

If you don't find the King and Nine in the first stack proceed to the second stack, the one in the middle marked 3–7 Months. Turn it over and spread it into an arch. If both cards are in the middle stack true love will find you in three to seven months.

Should the King and Nine fall into the third stack, the one on the right marked Nine or More Months, a considerable delay is seen. Every time the King and Nine cards arrive together it's your fate to fall deeply in love with a man who loves you equally, but if the cards are in the third stack it's going to take at least a year, maybe longer.

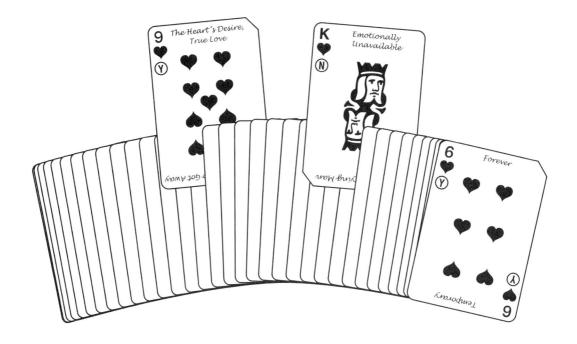

THE KING AND NINE IN SEPARATE STACKS: Should the Nine of Hearts and the King of Hearts fall into separate piles, there's still hope. First find the Nine. Then find the King.

When the Nine is alone in the first stack, look for the King in the second stack. When you find him there, it means you already know this man and already adore him, but it will take three to seven months for your King to fall in love with you. If the King appears in the third stack, you already know him and already love him. If you are willing to wait a long time, he can be yours someday.

When the Nine is alone in the second stack, patience is required. If the King is in the first stack, he's already near you and already in love with you, but you haven't noticed him or don't take him seriously. If the King is in the third stack, you'll notice him in three to seven months and fall in love with him on sight, but then you'll wait for him to notice you. This could take as long as a year.

When the Nine is alone in the third stack, don't bank on things working out too well. If the King is in the first stack, he's an old boyfriend who still calls. If he's in the second stack he'll enter your life in a few months and fall in love with you, but you won't return his feelings for a long, long time, perhaps years.

Here are some tips:

THE QUEEN: The King represents the object of your affections and the Queen represents you. Always notice where your Court card falls in the spread. If all three cards appear in the same stack, you'll feel happy and fulfilled as the romance develops. When the Queen appears in a stack before the stack holding the Nine and King, you will be lonely until you meet your man. When the Queen appears in a stack following the Nine and King, you will process your emotions slowly, drag your feet, and feel ambivalent about the union.

SURROUNDING CARDS: Pay attention to the three or four cards preceding the Nine. They describe the events that will occur just prior to the moment the King and Queen fall in love. The three or four cards following the Nine describe how the romance evolves.

   The two or three cards on either side of the King will elaborate on his circumstances, character, and attitude toward you both before and after he catches you. The cards surrounding the Queen describe how you will feel about the love affair as it unfolds.

TIME: If you count the cards in the arch you can measure the amount of time until you fall in love. Notice where the Nine falls.
* If it's in the first stack at the beginning of the arch (on the left), you're already in love and you know it. Halfway through? You'll be together one month from now. At the end? Two months.
* If the Nine is in the second stack at the beginning of the arch, you'll fall in love in three months. In the middle? Five months. At the end? Seven months.
* Don't try to gauge time with the third stack. It represents some arbitrary point in the distant future that can't be calculated.

The Path to Love

This spread was designed for "What will happen?" questions like:
* "What will happen on my blind date?"
* "If I accept the job and move to Denver, what will happen to my relationship?"
* "If I leave my husband, will I ever remarry?"

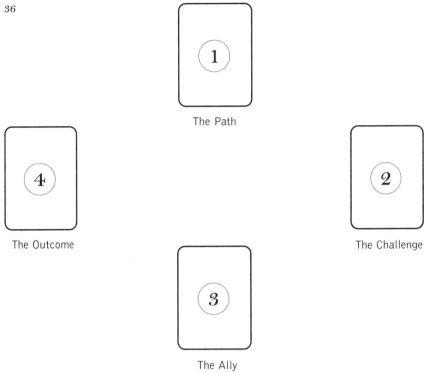

TO LAY OUT THE SPREAD

* Shuffle the deck several times and spread it into an arch.
* Pull four cards at random out of the arch. Leaving them facedown, move them into the pattern shown above in the order they were selected.
* Turn the cards over one at a time by turning them from right to left the way you turn the pages of a book.
* Turn to chapter 3 and read about the cards one at a time, in order. Apply the meanings of the cards to the meanings of the positions of the spread.

POSITION ONE: THE PATH. This spread is designed to be a journey that begins when you step onto the path. The card in this position defines the trail itself. It represents your goal or direction or describes the person or event that has drawn you onto the pathway.

POSITION TWO: THE CHALLENGE. This card describes the greatest obstacle to a successful resolution to your question. It articulates your fears and anxieties, an individual who opposes you, or an irritating, uncomfortable aspect of the journey. This card represents a natural, annoying by-product of your decision to step onto the path.

POSITION THREE: THE ALLY. The card in this position describes the people, circumstances, or influences that will support your journey. It identifies the individual or event that will come to your assistance. The card can represent a group, a specific person, an external circumstance, or a deeply held belief.

POSITION FOUR: THE OUTCOME. The final card describes how the journey will end. This card reveals the resolution to your question. It also foretells how you will feel about the result.

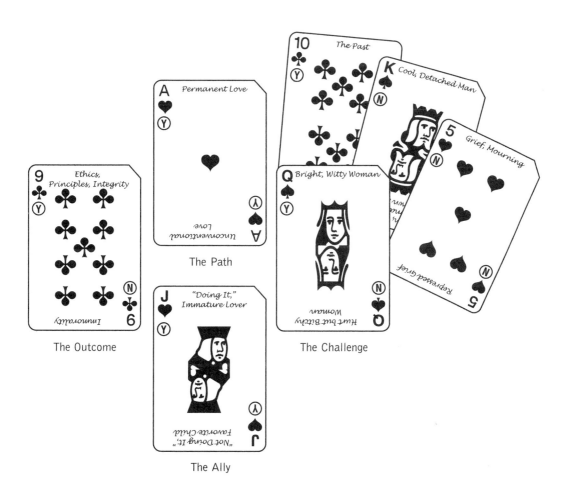

The Outcome

The Path

The Ally

The Challenge

TO INTERPRET THE SPREAD

Let's imagine you went to dinner with a new man last night. It was your first date and you had a wonderful conversation about your goals over dessert. You told him you wanted to get married and have kids someday. He said a couple should see the world and establish their careers before they have babies. And you said, "Exactly!"

You learned that his life goals and romantic ambitions mirrored your own. You woke up excited about your conversation so you made a cup of coffee, pulled *The Oracle of Love* off the shelf, and sat down to give yourself a reading. You want to know, "What will happen with this guy? Will we fall in love, get married, travel, work hard, and then have kids? Or will we date for a while and separate? Or will he even call me again?" You want to know if this new romance will fizzle out or if he's "the One"?

Let's say you shuffle the cards, spread them into an arch, select four at random, and move them into their positions.

Let's say the card in position one, **The Path,** turns out to be the **Upright Ace of Hearts.** The Ace is the card of a permanent emotional connection. It's the card of marriage partners and family members. The Upright Ace says that you seek to be married and are wondering if the new man will go the distance with you.

Let's say the card in position two, **The Challenge,** is the **Reversed Queen of Spades.** The Reversed Queen is bitter, hurt, and verbal. The challenge to a happy future with this man is the angry Queen. Does your new boyfriend have an evil ex-wife? What's his mother like? Or does the Queen represent you? Are you still bitter about your last breakup? The Queen of Spades is usually an Air sign. Are you a Libra, Gemini, or Aquarius? Is his ex? How about his mom? The Queen in this position makes it clear that a bright, articulate woman who hides her pain behind bitter comments is the greatest obstacle to your dream of marriage.

Position three is **The Ally.** Let's pretend the card in this spot is the **Upright Jack of Hearts,** the card of sex, passion, and romance. Your ally in this matter is the remarkable physical attraction between the two of you.

Let's assume the **outcome** card in position four is the **Upright Nine of Clubs.** The card says if you concentrate on your own life and your own goals, without getting caught up in his life and his goals, this little romance could build into something solid and traditional. The Nine of Clubs describes a conservative, ethical alliance that's an improvement over your past relationships. It says this man isn't a prude, yet he has no interest in seducing you. He intends to date you in a polite manner until he ascertains your moral fiber. The Nine advises you to allow him to advance the union at his own pace. He'll move it forward in appropriate increments at appropriate intervals.

The greatest problem you will encounter in your romance is the wounded woman. Let's imagine you throw three more cards on the Reversed Queen of Spades to figure out who she is. Let's say you pull the **Reversed Ten of Clubs,** the **Upright Five of Hearts,** and the **Upright King of Spades.** The Reversed Ten of Clubs represents the past and the Five of Hearts is the card of extreme disappointment. The King of Spades is an Air sign man.

The past, pain, and an Air sign man? Perhaps the woman represented by the Reverse Queen of Spades is you. Your former fiancé was an Aquarius (Air sign) and you're a Libra (Air sign). The three extra cards are trying to explain that the greatest obstacle to your happiness is your own emotional baggage. They say your fear of another painful breakup (like the one you endured two years ago) is the main obstruction to a full partnership with your new guy.

Let's summarize:

* The Ace of Hearts in position one says you're looking for a permanent relationship with a family-oriented man.
* The Jack in position three describes a romantic, passionate connection.
* The Nine in the final position says your fears and doubts will ease up over time. The two of you will grow closer, you'll marry, and over the years your affection for one another will deepen.
* The Queen in the obstruction position says you have to get a handle on your tongue and your old wounds. Your personal issues are the greatest obstacle to your mutual happiness.

Secrets of the Heart

I love this spread and use it often. First, it describes your relationship or problem the way you explain it to your friends and family. Then it describes the same thing a second time, only this time it reveals how you *really* feel about your relationship. The first version is the publicly acceptable rendition. The second one is the truth.

TO LAY OUT THE SPREAD

*   Shuffle the cards and set them to the side.
*   Pull four cards off the top of the deck and lay them face down in a row.
*   Pull another three cards off the top of the deck and place them beneath the four to form a second row of three cards.
*   Pull two more off the deck and place them in a row beneath the other rows.
*   Pull one final card and set it by itself beneath all the others, to create a pyramid shape.
*   Slide the card off the bottom of the deck and place it above the spread.

THE BOTTOM CARD: This is the card off the bottom of the deck. It tells what the reading is about. When you shuffled the deck, you brought this card to the bottom of the pack as surely as you brought the others to the top. It's an auspicious card. If you want more information about this card, pull extra cards from the bottom of the deck to describe it. The meanings of the rows are as follows:

THE TOP ROW: The four cards in the top row provide a superficial description of the situation. They describe the version that you share with your friends and family. This rendition is the socially acceptable one.

THE SECOND ROW: This line reveals the truth. This is private information. It divulges how you really feel, what you fear, or what you secretly want. It shows what you *don't* share with the people in your life.

THE THIRD ROW: This row predicts the future. These cards describe the next major event that is destined to occur in regard to your situation.

THE FINAL CARD: The last card is the outcome card. This single card reveals how your problem will be resolved and explains why.

TO INTERPRET THE SPREAD

Let's say your girlfriend comes over because she heard you bought this book and wonders if you could help her with a tiny little personal matter. You know, just for fun.

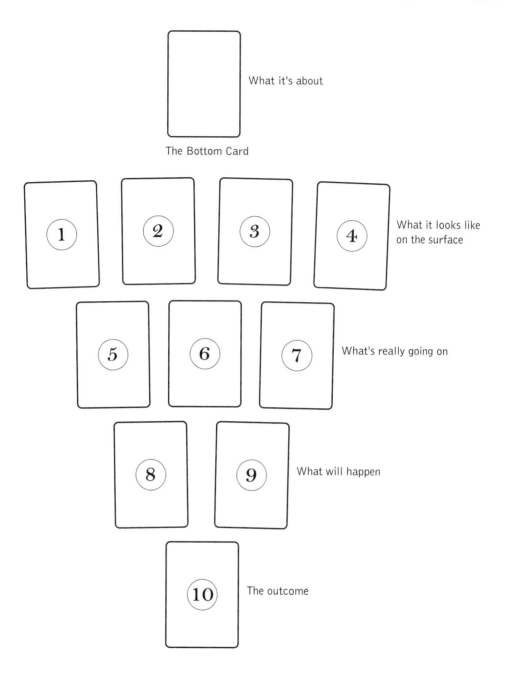

The Bottom Card — What it's about

What it looks like on the surface

What's really going on

What will happen

The outcome

Let's say you ask her what she wants to know and she says, "Well, since the company moved Jason to Washington, I haven't heard from him very much. I'm not complaining, you understand. I know his work is important. I'm just wondering if he'll return home soon." Let's say you nod your head and give her a sympathetic smile while you shuffle. Then, you lay out the

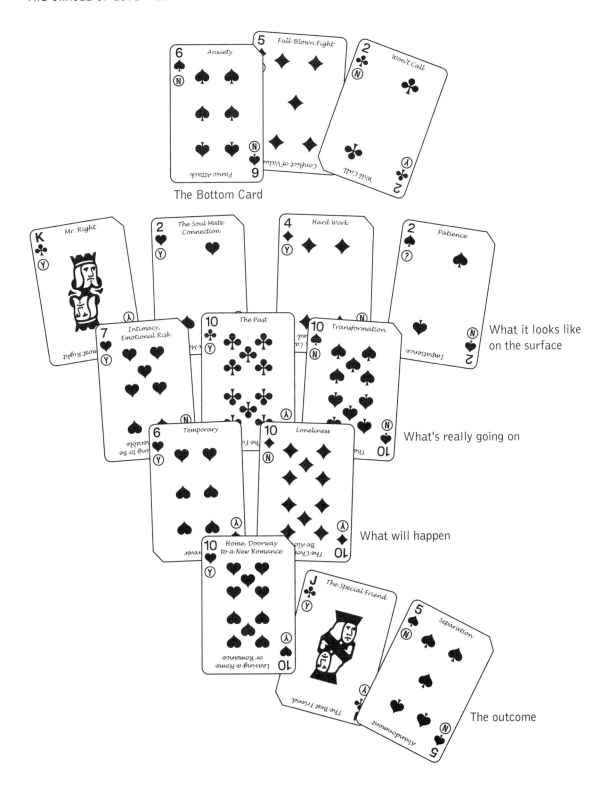

The Bottom Card

What it looks like
on the surface

What's really going on

What will happen

The outcome

spread and turn over the **bottom card,** and it's the **Upright Six of Spades.** Hmm, you say to yourself, that's the card of anxiety. She said she was "just wondering," but she's really quite anxious. So you pull two more off the bottom: **Reversed Two of Clubs** (hasn't called), **Reversed Five of Diamonds** (huge fight). You smile at her and politely don't mention that you already know he hasn't called because they had a big fight.

Let's say you turned over the **TOP ROW** and those four cards were:

* **The King of Clubs Upright** (Mr. Wonderful)
* **The Two of Hearts Upright** (her soul mate)
* **The Four of Diamonds Upright** (work)
* **The Two of Spades Upright** (the card of waiting)

The public version of your friend's story appears to be that her boyfriend's a great guy and her perfect match (King of Clubs and Two of Hearts). She's waiting around while he works hard (Two of Spades and Four of Diamonds). That sounds like the story she told you, but you already know he hasn't called since their argument.

Let's see what the **SECOND ROW** says.

Let's imagine those cards are:

* **The Upright Seven of Hearts**
  (telling the truth despite your fears)
* **The Reversed Ten of Clubs** (backward in time)
* **The Upright Ten of Spades** (no way)

The second row is painting an entirely different picture.

The Seven of Hearts is the card of risking ridicule or rejection (or your partner's anger) and telling the truth anyway. The Reversed Ten of Clubs is a return to the past—in this case, I would imagine Jason's return home from Washington. And the Ten of Spades is the card of the word "No." These three cards string together to say he told her the truth: He's not coming home. He's staying in Washington.

Let's imagine you say, "It appears you had a fight because he's decided to stay in Washington. You haven't told anyone. You still have hopes he'll change his mind, but he hasn't called since your fight and the cold-shoulder treatment is beginning to scare you." Let's say you nailed the reading and she begins to cry as she whispers, "What's going to happen? I thought we were getting married."

Let's pretend you turn over the **THIRD ROW:**

* **The Reversed Six of Hearts** (temporary)
* **The Reversed Ten of Diamonds** (loneliness)

You tell her she will be alone for a while. Eventually, she will make new long-term plans for herself.

Then you flip over the **OUTCOME** card:

* **The Ten of Hearts Upright** (the card of a move to a new home or a new relationship)

The final card can be read two ways. The first way shows her moving to Washington. The other interpretation shows her giving up on Jason and moving on to someone new. Let's say you ask her to pull two more cards to clarify the Ten of Hearts and she selects the **Reversed Jack of Clubs** (the lover who's also your best friend) and the **Upright Five of Spades** (the card of separation).

You have to tell her Jason will stay in Washington and she'll meet a new person. She'll be alone for a while before she meets the next one, and Jason will remain her friend.

Under these circumstances, I would reshuffle and lay out a new spread for her. She needs another reading about the new love who will enter her life.

The Lover's Pyramid

You can use this spread to examine the condition of an established relationship or to explore the potential for a new one. The layout explains how you're functioning within the union at this time and how he's functioning, shows the current state of the connection, and predicts the next phase. That's a lot of information from four little cards.

TO LAY OUT THE SPREAD

* Shuffle the deck several times and spread it into an arch.
* Select four cards at random.
* Pull them straight out from the arch onto the table.
* Place them in the four positions illustrated below in the order they were selected.
* Turn over the card in position one, leaving the other positions facedown on the table.
* Read about the card, and then move to the next position.

Always remember to turn the cards over by turning them from right to left the way you turn the pages of a book. If you flip them from top to bottom you will invert the card and reverse its meaning.

The Future

Your Partner   You   The Relationship

POSITION ONE: This card represents you. It describes your hopes and fears for the union and explains how you feel about your partner.

POSITION TWO: This card describes your partner. It shows his hopes and fears for the union and explains how he feels about you.

POSITION THREE: This card represents the relationship. It explains how the alliance functions and expresses your mutual ambitions for your romance.

POSITION FOUR: The final card foretells the next phase of an established partnership or the future prospects for a new one.

TO INTERPRET THE SPREAD

Let's imagine you're reading this book in the lunchroom at work while eating your Lean Cuisine, and the gal from the cubicle next to yours sits down at your table. Let's assume your coworker is a thirty-five-year-old married woman with two children whose school pictures and soccer photos practically wallpaper the walls of her office.

Let's go a step further and suppose you have your personalized deck of playing cards spread out on the table. Let's say she touches one, even picks it up, and asks if you could read the cards for her sometime. You get excited and offer to do it right now.

Now let's pretend she wants to know if her husband is having an affair. Let's imagine she hangs her head and folds her hands in her lap.

"He doesn't seem to desire me lately," she says quietly, "and I wonder if it's because he has another woman."

Let's say you gulp (because answering a question of this sort is a huge responsibility) and wipe the sweat off your upper lip with the back of your hand. Then you ask her to shuffle the cards. When she's finished, you spread the deck into an arch, invite her to slide four cards out of the arch onto the table, and move them into the positions illustrated above in the order she selected them.

Let's say you turn over the card in **POSITION ONE,** the card in the center that represents her, and it's the **Upright Queen of Diamonds.** The Queen in this position says your colleague is preoccupied with money, with her job, his job, and the efficient maintenance of their household. She's probably working two shifts, one in the office and another at home as cook, maid, and mom.

Then let's say you turn over the card in **POSITION TWO,** the one that describes her husband. Let's imagine that card is the **Reversed**

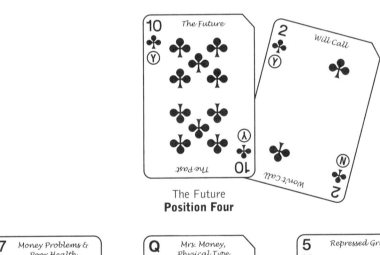

The Future
Position Four

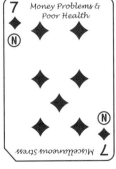

Your Partner
Position Two

You
Position One

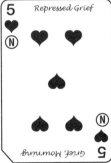

The Relationship
Position Three

Seven of Diamonds, the card of financial and physical distress. So you ask if her husband is broke or sick and she says, "Well, yeah. He lost his job six months ago. His unemployment insurance is about to run out and he hasn't found another job yet. He's pretty worried about money."

Their two personal cards (the affluent Queen of Diamonds and the poverty-stricken Seven) tell you she is the primary breadwinner and her husband is stressed because her earning power exceeds his.

Next you turn over the card in **POSITION THREE,** the card representing the current state of their union. It's the Reversed Five of Hearts, the upside-down card of grief.

The Reversed Five in this position says the loss of his job has disappointed them both. Your coworker feels the strain of her expanded responsibility but hasn't expressed her feelings because she doesn't want to complain. Her husband is disappointed in himself and in the fact that she has to maintain their household until he can find another job. He doesn't express his disappointment because he doesn't want to appear as if he lacks confidence in his future.

How will this situation be resolved? Let's pretend you turn over the **FINAL CARD** and it's the **Upright Ten of Clubs.** The Ten is the card of going forward into the future with optimism and good luck on your side.

Imagine you ask her to select one more card to explain how the good luck will come into play. She draws the **Upright Two of Clubs,** the card of a phone call.

As it turns out, her husband will get a job. It will be a good one and a lucky break. He just has to wait for the call to come through.

So was he having an affair? I don't think so. I think he was avoiding her because he felt emasculated without a paycheck. Their relationship will get back to normal as soon as her husband goes back to work.

Window to the Soul

So much of fortune-telling is spying. Window to the Soul is the ultimate peek into the psyche of your partner. Use it when you haven't seen your lover for a while or when you've met a new romantic prospect. The spread covers a two-month period and is designed to answer the question: "What's going on in his life right now?"

Select another spread if you want to know the depth of his passion for you. This one is better for examining the circumstances that will surround him for the next two months and his emotional response to them. Choose this spread when you want to know what the major points are in your man's life. But make no mistake: you're definitely spying.

This is how the cards will look once they're laid out:

TO LAY OUT THE SPREAD

* Shuffle the deck several times and spread it into an arch, facedown.
* Select nine cards at random by pulling them from the deck one at a time.
* Stack the nine cards facedown, in the order they were selected.
* Place the first card (the one on the bottom of the stack of nine cards) on the far left side of the table.
* Pull the remaining eight cards off the bottom one by one and arrange them on the table to form an arch.
* Now, select another nine cards the same way. Stack them on top of each other facedown, also in the order they were chosen.
* Place the first card from the second stack (the one on the bottom) on top of the first card from the first stack, which is the first card in the arch, the one on the far left. Place the second card on the other second card, the third on the other third, and so on until all nine of the second cards are placed on top of the first nine.
* Turn over the pair of cards on the left in positions one and ten by turning them from right to left the way you turn the pages of a book. Leave the other cards facedown.

* Read the two cards in position one as if they were one card by blending their meanings together.
* Examine the two cards in each position before turning over the next pair.

The following list describes the meanings of the positions. The two cards in each spot rule one area of life. They tell how the person you're spying on will function in regard to that area for the next two months.

1 AND 10: The person with whom he will spend the most time.

2 AND 11: The one he loves the most.

3 AND 12: What is draining his energy or wearing him out.

4 AND 13: The solution to that problem.

5 AND 14: His *real* problem.

6 AND 15: The solution to that problem.

7 AND 16: What shocks him.

8 AND 17: What his heart truly longs for.

9 AND 18: Something pleasant that will occur in the next two months.

TO INTERPRET THE SPREAD

Let's say you married your high school sweetheart right out of college and had two kids by the time you were twenty-eight. Let's imagine that at thirty your husband left you for his secretary. Now you're thirty-two and have reentered the workforce, where you met a district sales manager who's forty, divorced, with two kids of his own a bit older than yours.

Let's pretend you've been dating the sales manager for a month now and you've never known such simpatico. It's as if you share one brain and one heart. Your two boys adore him and he actually met your ex once while you were exchanging the kids and they were mutually friendly. You're crazy about this guy and you wonder if he feels the same way about you.

The problem is that you remember how much you loved your husband in the beginning; how you trusted that your marriage would survive the test of time and how fervently you believed your ex was your soul mate. You thought you would be together for the rest of your lives. A tiny part of you is still bitter about your divorce and afraid to make another mistake. You bought this book, marked your cards, and chose the Window to the Soul because you wonder about the depth of your boyfriend's feelings for you and how well your lives might fit together.

POSITIONS 1 AND 10 ~ The Person with Whom He Will Spend the Most Time. The two cards in this position are the **Upright King of Spades** and the **Upright Four of Diamonds**. The King is a hard-nosed taskmaster and the Four is the card of work. He'll be spending a lot of time with his demanding boss.

POSITIONS 2 AND 11 ~ The One He Will Love the Most. The beautiful **Queen of Clubs** and the sexy **Jack of Hearts** have fallen into this position. The Jack represents physical attraction and the Queen is a very appropriate woman. I think he'll love *you* the most for the next two months.

POSITIONS 3 AND 12 ~ What Is Draining His Energy or Wearing Him Out. The **Reversed Nine of Diamonds** (the card of ambition) and the **Reversed Six of Diamonds** (the card of the natural flow) clearly state that he's tired of waiting for his career to take off. He's beginning to wonder if he set his goals too high and if he should revise them.

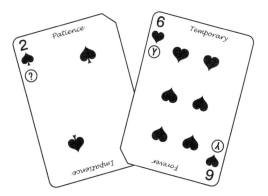

POSITIONS 4 AND 13 ~ The Solution To That Problem. The **Two of Spades** (the card of patience) and the **Reversed Six of Hearts** (the card of temporary situations) are asking him to be patient about his career and to realize that this phase won't last forever.

POSITIONS 5 AND 14 ~ His *Real* Problem. The **Upright Seven of Diamonds** (the card of financial distress) and the **Upright Four of Hearts** (the card of caretaking) describe a broke, stressed-out man who is overwhelmed by the prospect of being responsible for so many people. He's worried about finding the money to provide for his children and yours.

POSITIONS 6 AND 15 ~ The Solution To That Problem. The **Upright Queen of Diamonds** (Mrs. Money) says you're a practical, hardworking, ambitious woman who doesn't plan to quit her job the day after the wedding. The **Upright Two of Hearts** (the soul mate card) says he loves you. The solution to his sense of being overwhelmed is to recognize that you're a team player. You ought to reassure him that you're used to supporting your kids and plan to provide for them until they're out of college.

POSITIONS 7 AND 16 ~ What Shocks Him. The **Upright Nine of Spades** (surprise) and the **Upright Three of Hearts** (joy) combine to say that he's amazed he found someone he really cares about. He thinks you're warm and loving and is blown away by how much fun you have together.

POSITIONS 8 AND 17 ~ What His Heart Truly Longs For. The **Upright Ace of Spades** and the **Upright Eight of Hearts** say he longs for a second chance at marriage. His life goal is to find a mature, intelligent, competent woman who is his equal and a true companion.

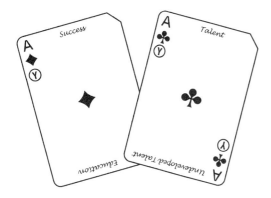

POSITIONS 9 AND 18 ~ Something Pleasant That Will Occur over the Next Two Months. The **Upright Ace of Clubs** is the card of building a following, making a sale, forming a spiritual connection, and buying an engagement ring. The **Upright Ace of Diamonds** is the card of success through endurance. Sometime over the next two months, the man in your life is going to make a sale, and it's going to be a big one. As a result, he'll buy you a ring and make a plan for a life with you.

It's obvious that this man holds you in high regard. He thinks you're beautiful and sexy and is astonished at how swiftly he's developed feelings for you. He has anxieties about his career and his ability to support such a large household. He'll make a big sale in a few weeks, which will be good news. He needs evidence that he can provide for a large family. In finally seeing some of his financial goals realized, he will feel more optimistic about going forward with you. In addition, he'll come to understand that you're a good life partner for him because you would never allow him to take responsibility for your kids by himself.

"Let's Pull a Few Cards on It"

I work a lot of parties: Christmas, New Year's, Halloween (in full Gypsy costume), weddings, and showers. This spread is great for parties.

The object of the game when working a party is to keep the readings light, move a lot of people through rapidly, and give them a reading without their asking a question. Rarely do they approach the Gypsy fortune-teller at a party with a specific problem. They've usually had a glass of wine and are looking to be entertained. I suggest you try this spread when several of your friends want readings.

TO LAY OUT THE SPREAD

* Ask your friend or guest to shuffle the cards.
* Then spread the deck into an arch.
* Ask her to pull three cards at random and leave the cards facedown on the table.
* Then, ask for one more card. Place it above the others.

This fourth card tells you what the question is about (money, love, health, etc.).

✳ Turn the cards over one at a time working from left to right.

Let's imagine I'm entertaining at a Christmas party and a pretty young woman sits down at my table, sets her wineglass on the corner, smiles brightly, and pulls four cards.

I smile back and begin her reading by examining the card in **POSI-TION FOUR,** the one resting above the row of three cards. The card in this position describes what she wants to know. For fun, let's say the card is the **Reversed Jack of Clubs,** the best friend who serves another function in her life, like boyfriend. This card tells me she wants to know about her best friend/boyfriend.

Next, I flip over all three cards and examine them individually before reading them collectively.

✳ Let's imagine the card in **POSITION ONE** is the **Reversed Five of Spades,** the card of abandonment.

✳ The card in **POSITION TWO** is the **Upright Eight of Diamonds,** the card of equality and balance.

＊ And the card in **POSITION THREE** is the **Upright Four of Clubs,** the card of commitment.

These three cards combine to explain her circumstance concerning her best friend/boyfriend. It appears the young couple has mutually agreed (Upright Eight of Diamonds) to abandon (Reversed Five of Spades) one another. They are totally, mutually committed (Upright Four of Clubs) to this course of action. It appears that our girl is in pain (abandonment is painful) but has resolved to follow through (the Four), because they have mutually agreed (the Eight) that separating is the thing to do.

This leaves me with a few questions, like why? And is this arrangement permanent or temporary? The Jack of Clubs contains such a won-

derful message of friendship and love that it makes me wonder how their connection could have come to this.

Therefore, I'm going to pull three cards of my own and place them on top of her three. I will read the two cards in each position as one philosophical concept by blending the two meanings together. This elaborates on the problem/question/issue and offers me more information.

My three cards were:

* **POSITION ONE:** the **Reversed Five of Hearts,** the card of repressed grief.
* **POSITION TWO:** the **Reversed Ace of Diamonds,** the card of an education.
* **POSITION THREE:** the **Upright Six of Hearts,** the card of Forever.

When I cover the Reversed Five of Spades with the Reversed Five of Hearts, the two Fives combine to deliver a message of undiluted abandonment and grief. This girl is pretending she's okay about the separation but she isn't. She's at a party; she's dressed up and smiling brightly, but another part of her is in mourning.

My second card, the Reversed Ace of Diamonds, covers the Upright Eight of Diamonds. These two cards provide a reason for the separation. The Reversed Ace of Diamonds is the card of education. This young couple has separated in order to go to graduate school, probably in separate cities. The mutuality of the Upright Eight tells me they're both in school.

My third card is the Upright Six of Hearts, the card of Forever and Ever Till Death Do Us Part. Her third card, the Upright Four of Clubs, is the card of commitment, the card of staying together. These two cards combine to say their love will endure the separation.

It's a party, so I don't want to upset my pretty client and I don't want to make her mascara run. All I'd say in this situation is, You're separated from your boyfriend and he's your best friend in the world. You're being strong and not giving in to your feelings of abandonment, but it's tough. Don't worry. He loves you as much as you love him and you'll be back together when you've finished school. You two are equally committed to one another and your love will endure this trial.

She'll probably pick up her wineglass and say, "Tell me something I *don't* know," and flounce off to join her friends, but she'll remember her reading from the party. In her bleakest moments she will recall that the fortune-teller said they would stay together, that their love would survive the test of separation.

Use this spread when you have no particular question in mind, or when a friend just wants to sample the psychic experience.

I like to use this "pulling a few cards" technique when my best girl-friends call and ask questions like:

"What does he really think of me?"

"Why didn't he call?"

"How did he think I looked last night?"

You get the idea. This spread is an ideal choice for those nervous questions that drive your friends crazy, are embarrassing to ask, and can't be answered with a simple yes or no. "Just pulling a few cards on it" is casual and informal, but it's also penetrating, accurate, and fun.

The Traditional Gypsy Spread

This spread is the ultimate playing card spread. It describes you or your problem, shows what brought you to your current state of mind, and predicts the natural resolution to your dilemma. But, if you don't like the way things are going to end up, the spread reveals a route to a different destiny. The layout shows how you can intervene on your own behalf and activate an alternate fate by watching for specific events in the immediate future. Those events are the guideposts to your second option.

This layout dates back to medieval Europe and may seem simple, but 7,921,834,931,684,532,415,560,000 variations are mathematically possible so the likelihood of duplication is infinitely small. Select the Traditional Gypsy Spread when you need guidance or when you have to make a decision.

TO LAY OUT THE SPREAD

* Shuffle the deck and spread the cards into an arch.
* Select 15 cards at random.
* Move the cards into positions 1 through 15 in the order they were selected.
* Leave the cards facedown on the table.
* Turn over one wing of three cards at a time.

The spread is interpreted as follows:

CENTER CARDS: THE PRESENT. Numbers 2, 1, and 3. Card 1, the center card, is the most important card in the spread because it represents the

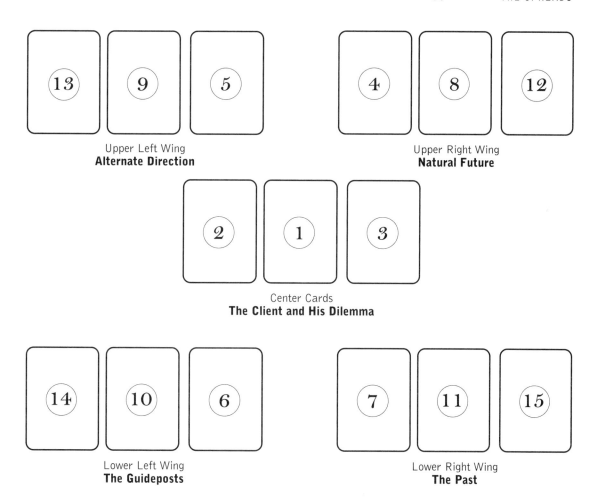

Upper Left Wing
Alternate Direction

Upper Right Wing
Natural Future

Center Cards
The Client and His Dilemma

Lower Left Wing
The Guideposts

Lower Right Wing
The Past

present and pinpoints your situation or problem. Cards 2 and 3 add details, depth, and color to card 1.

LOWER RIGHT WING: THE PAST. Numbers 7, 11, and 15. The three cards clustered in the lower right corner drive the reading. They combine to describe the events of the immediate past that prompted you to consult the oracle or brought you to the situation described by the center cards.

UPPER RIGHT WING: THE FUTURE. Numbers 4, 8, and 12. The cards in the upper right corner of the spread describe the answer to your question. The card in position 4 represents the first step toward the resolution of your problem. That step will lead to a second incident as represented by card 8. Card 12 tells the outcome to your question should you allow the events in your life to unfold naturally, without interfering in them.

Let's recap:

*   The center cluster represents you or your question/problem/issue.
*   The lower right wing explains what occurred in the past that prompted you to consult the oracle.
*   The upper right wing describes how your problem will be resolved if you allow nature to take its course.

Maybe you laid out the spread, read the cards in the upper right wing, and don't like the way things will turn out. Maybe you'd like to interfere with your destiny. The cards in the upper left wing offer an alternative resolution to your problem and the cards in the lower left wing show how to access that second option.

UPPER LEFT WING: ALTERNATIVE OUTCOME. **Numbers 5, 9, and 13.** The cards in the upper left corner of the spread represent your alternate destiny. This second direction can be a big improvement or a big disaster compared to the natural resolution through the upper right wing. You ought to be forewarned that if you choose to pursue the second direction over the first one, the experience won't feel normal. You'll need courage and self-discipline if you're to steer your fate away from its natural flow.

LOWER LEFT WING: THE GUIDEPOSTS. **Numbers 6, 10, and 14.** If the upper left wing offers a more attractive solution to your problem, you should examine the cards in this wing with great care. These cards represent actual events that will transpire in the near future. These events may not be momentous in themselves, but they are the points around which your fate will turn. If you're able to recognize the guidepost events when they occur, you can use them to shift your destiny to the other direction.

♠ ♦ ♣ ♥

When you choose the Traditional Gypsy Spread to examine an issue or to answer a question, the challenge is to discern if the natural direction is superior to the alternative direction. Readings can go either way. Frequently, a change in direction will result in loss or frustration, but just as often staying on course will result in a negative outcome.

I insist you throw additional cards on any card or wing you don't understand. Just toss extra cards all over the spread because they always help to clarify an idea, concept, or event.

TO INTERPRET THE SPREAD

Let's imagine your sister is thirty years old, married, with a six-year-old boy and a baby girl on the way. Let's say she lives in a two-bedroom condo and works out of her home across the street from your condo. Now let's pretend that your sister's over at your house having coffee. You offer to give her a reading so she shuffles the cards and you lay them out into the Traditional Gypsy Spread.

CENTER CARDS: THE PRESENT. Numbers 1, 2, and 3:
> CARD 1—the Upright Four of Hearts, the card of caregiving and nurturing. It describes a child or children under the age of ten.
> CARD 2—the Upright Five of Diamonds, the card of a conflict of values. The person represented by the Upright Five goes over and over something in their mind. They analyze it from every conceivable angle. The couple represented by the card is locked in a disagreement.
> CARD 3—the Upright Three of Diamonds, the card of routines and legal obligations.

"Well," you say, "I guess you two are fighting about the new baby, aren't you?"

She says, "No. Not at all." So you draw an additional card and place it above the Five. That card is the Upright Ten of Hearts, the card of a move to a new home.

"Are you and Paul talking about moving?" you ask.

"Well, I am," says your sister. "I think, with the baby coming and my home business doing so well, we need a bigger place. Paul doesn't agree. But I wouldn't call it a *fight*."

LOWER RIGHT WING: THE PAST. Numbers 7, 11 and 15:
> CARD 7—the Upright King of Spades. This card describes Paul. The King is an Air sign man and Paul is a Gemini.
> CARD 11—the Reversed Nine of Diamonds, the card of diminished expectations.
> CARD 15—the Reversed Eight of Hearts, the card of generosity Reversed, which indicates a lack of generosity.

A **Permanent Love** / Y / *Unconventional Love*

2 ◆ **Physical Proximity, and Travel** / Y / *No Proximity, Travel* / Y

4 ◆ **Hard Work** / Y / N / *Unemployed, Lazy, Overworked* / N

Alternate Direction

3 ♣ **Lies** / N / *Gossip*

9 ♥ **The One Who Got Away** / N / *Desire, Love*

6 ◆ **The Natural Flow** / Y / Y

Natural Future

5 ♥ **Repressed Grief** / N / N / *Grief, Mourning*

Q ◆ **Mrs. Money, Physical Type** / Y

10 ♥ **Home, Doorway to a New Romance** / Y

5 ◆ **Conflict of Values** / N / N / *Full-Blown Fight*

4 ♥ **Young Child, Nurturing, Humanitarian** / N / N / *Codependent*

3 ◆ **Legal Marriage, Routines** / Y / N / *Legal Divorce, Lack of Structure*

The Client and His Dilemma

8 ◆ **The Art of Living, Balance & Equality** / Y / N / *Unbalanced, Inequality*

6 ♠ **Anxiety** / N / N / *Panic Attack*

7 ♥ **Intimacy, Emotional Risk** / Y / N / *Unwilling to Be Vulnerable*

The Guideposts

K ♠ **Cool, Detached Man** / N / *Mean, Strict, Emotionally Shut-Down Man*

9 ◆ **Expectations Too High, Ambitions Too Low** / N / *Ambitious Expectations*

8 ♥ **Nothing to Give, Score-Keeping** / N / Y / *Second Marriage, Strength & Hope*

The Past

"Paul doesn't plan to use up your savings on a new house, does he?" you ask.

"No," she responds. "He doesn't think we can afford a new place. He doesn't think I'll continue to earn at my current rate after I have the baby. I think I *can* continue after the baby comes, but it would be a lot easier if

I didn't have to work in that tiny alcove. I don't know what to do. We need to move and Paul won't listen to me. He thinks the baby can sleep with us for a few months and then the two kids can share a room for a few years. I disagree. Paulie Jr. needs his own room and so does the baby. I've worked hard to get where I am and I'm finally making good money. I don't plan to quit. What do the cards say? Will I continue to earn as much as I am right now? Will Paul agree to move?"

UPPER RIGHT WING: THE FUTURE. Numbers 4, 8, and 12:

> CARD 4—the **Reversed Three of Clubs**, the card of lying or denial.
>
> CARD 8—the **Reversed Nine of Hearts**, the card of settling for a reasonable facsimile.
>
> CARD 12—the **Upright Six of Diamonds**, the card of the natural unfolding of events.

Let's imagine that you scowl and say, "I can't read the Six of Diamonds by itself. Draw another card." Let's say she draws the **Reversed Five of Hearts,** the card of the tears she *won't* shed because she thinks to cry would be self-indulgent.

"Well," you sigh. "You won't like the outcome. You won't be honest with Paul or yourself [Three of Clubs] and you'll decide to settle for what you already have [Reversed Nine of Hearts]. Your disappointment is inevitable [the Six and Five together], but you won't share your true feelings with Paul because you won't want to look like a crybaby. This isn't good. Let's see if the Universe has something better in store for you."

UPPER LEFT WING: ALTERNATIVE OUTCOME. Numbers 5, 9, and 13:

> CARD 5—the **Upright Four of Diamonds**, the card of hard work, of earning in direct proportion to the amount of effort one is willing to expend.
>
> CARD 9—the **Upright Two of Diamonds**, the card of negotiation. It's the "You scratch my back and I'll scratch yours" card.
>
> CARD 13—the **Upright Ace of Hearts**, the card of marriage and family.

"Oh, my," you say to your sister. "This direction is ten times better than the other one. You'll have all the work you can handle [Four of

Diamonds], you and Paul will reach some kind of compromise [Two of Diamonds], and everything will work out great [Ace of Hearts]. The Ace also says Mom and Dad will bail you out if you have problems with the down payment or with your mortgage. If you go this way, you'll get the new house and everyone will be happy. Let's see what you have to do to activate this direction."

LOWER LEFT WING: THE GUIDEPOSTS. Numbers 6, 10, and 14:
> CARD 6—the Upright Seven of Hearts, the card of intimacy.
> CARD 10—the Upright Six of Spades, the card of anxiety.
> CARD 14—the Upright Eight of Diamonds, the card of the Art of Living.

"The cards in this row predict an event in the near future. I think that event will be a conversation [Seven of Hearts]. All you have to do to convince Paul to buy a new house is to have another talk with him about your career ambitions, your desire to contribute equally to the mortgage [the Eight of Diamonds], and your fear [Six of Spades] that he won't take your feelings on the matter into account.

"It looks to me as if you should keep working, ask Mom and Dad if they can help out if you should run into trouble, and talk to Paul again. Paul will cooperate with you [Eight of Diamonds] because he's completely devoted to the family and wants to make all of you happy [Ace of Hearts]. You'll get the new house, but you'll be the one who has to make up the difference in the mortgage payment [Four, Nine, and Eight of Diamonds]."

"Thanks," says your sister as she exhales a huge sigh of relief. She hugs you good-bye and waddles back across the street to have another talk with her husband.

The Cycle of Passion

The following spread examines your relationship over a twelve-month period. Every New Year's Day I give myself a reading using this spread. Then I sit back and watch as the reading unfolds over the course of the year.

TO LAY OUT THE SPREAD

* Shuffle the deck and spread it into an arch.
* Slide 12 cards out of the arch at random and move them into positions 1 through 12 in the order they were drawn.

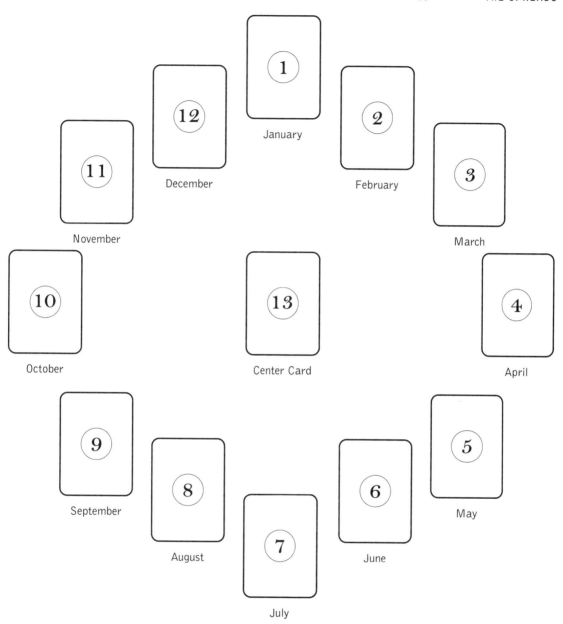

The 12 positions represent the 12 months of the calendar year.

* Leave the cards facedown on the table.
* Select one more card in the same manner and place it in the center, in position 13. (Or, if you would prefer, you can use the card off the bottom of the deck as the thirteenth card. Your choice; either card will do.)

TO INTERPRET THE SPREAD

* Turn over the middle card first and look up its meaning in chapter 3.
* Then, turn over the card in position 1.
* This card represents the current month, even if the day you give yourself the reading is the thirty-first.
* Read about the card in chapter 3.
* Proceed around the circle of cards. Turn over each month by itself and read the section on the card before you proceed to the next month. Continue until you've turned over all of the cards.
* The card in each position describes the single most significant event that will transpire in regard to your relationship during that month.
* Toss additional cards on any that you don't understand or that require more clarification.

If you're married, this spread will help you to examine the various phases your relationship will pass through during the next twelve months. If you're single, this spread will describe your dating experience month by month. The spread predicts how a brand-new romance will build or diminish as the year progresses.

♠ ♦ ♣ ♥

Imagine it's the prime date night of the year, New Year's Eve. Your two best girlfriends are dating and happy with their progress. One has the fresh bloom of a new romance on her cheeks and the other is seeing three men at once. "Three-man girl" is invited to a charity dinner and dance at the country club with a handsome teacher. "New-serious-relationship girl" is driving up to the mountains and spending a cozy, romantic weekend in a cabin with her boyfriend. You're sitting home alone, reading this book. You've been trying to meet someone, but the men you meet are losers, married, gay, too old, or too young. You got out the cheesecake and this book to celebrate New Year's Eve and selected the Cycle of Passion because you want to know if you will meet someone this year. Let's say you pull twelve cards and they are:

THE CENTER CARD. The **Reversed Jack of Clubs,** the card of the best friend who's also your boyfriend. Well, you say to yourself, that's perfect

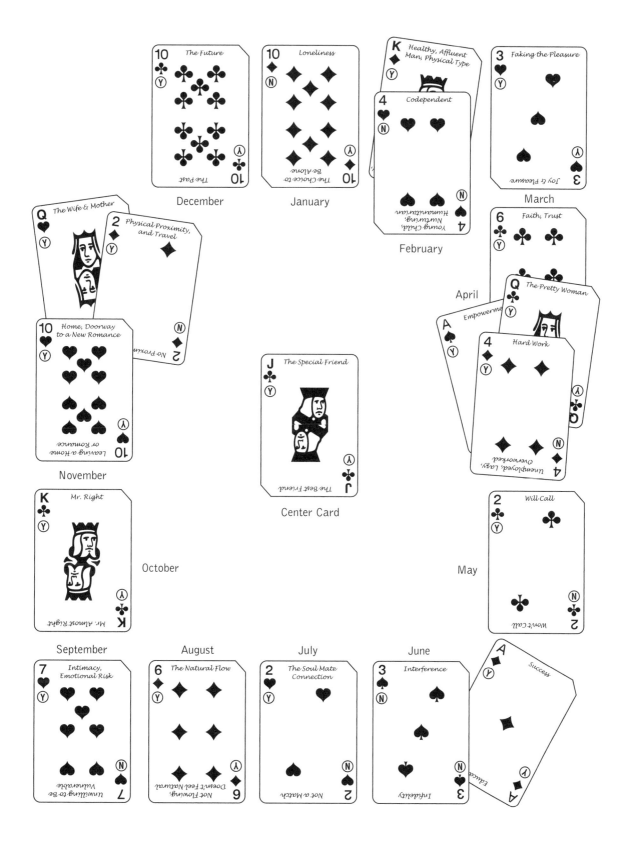

because that's what I'm looking for. I need someone I can hang out with who likes the same things I like, someone I can talk to and laugh with.

Remember, all the other cards in the spread will relate back to the center card, or each monthly card will be a commentary on the center card.

POSITION ONE: JANUARY. The **Reversed Ten of Diamonds,** the card of loneliness. The Reversed Ten in this position says you'll pass the entire month feeling alone, unloved, and as if there is no escape from the grinding boredom of your isolation.

POSITION TWO: FEBRUARY. The **Reversed Four of Hearts.** In this case, the card stands for aching and longing. "For what?" you wonder as you pull another card. You draw the **Upright King of Diamonds,** the card of your favorite physical type. It's perfectly clear that you'll be aching for a tall blond with a mustache. Sigh. February will be another long, boring month.

POSITION THREE: MARCH. The **Reversed Three of Hearts.** The card of making yourself go out with your same-sex friends despite how little interest you have in dressing up just to make idle conversation with the boring men you meet at cocktail parties. The Reversed Three is the card of faking it until it isn't fake anymore. Despite your attitude, in March you're going out on the town with the girls.

POSITION FOUR: APRIL. The **Upright Six of Clubs,** *the card of a date!* You pull two more to describe the date and they're the **Upright Ace of Spades** and the **Upright Queen of Clubs.** The Queen of Clubs? You pull another to define the Queen. It's the **Upright Four of Diamonds,** the work card. Oh, you say, that's Sherry from work. Sherry knows about 700 single men and I've been begging her to fix me up. Obviously, Sherry is about to come through.

POSITION FIVE: MAY. The **Upright Two of Clubs,** the card of a phone conversation. Looks like you and the new guy will give your cell phones a workout.

POSITION SIX: JUNE. The **Upright Three of Spades,** the card of interference. You toss another card on the Three to see what the interference will be and pull the **Ace of Diamonds.** Business demands. Okay. You can live with that. At least it's not another woman.

POSITION SEVEN: JULY. The **Upright Two of Hearts,** the soul-mate connection and your *birthday month!* This alliance deepens in July. It becomes extremely romantic. You can expect flowers and a mushy card. Cool.

POSITION EIGHT: AUGUST. The **Upright Six of Diamonds,** the card of natural progression. August will be a mellow, easy month as your union moves forward.

POSITION NINE: SEPTEMBER. The **Upright Seven of Hearts,** the card of intimacy. This is the month you'll share your fears, anxieties, hopes, and dreams. By September he'll open up about his feelings for you. You'll respond by telling him how you feel too.

POSITION TEN: OCTOBER. The **Upright King of Clubs,** Mr. Wonderful. He's going to be positively charming in October. This is the month you'll meet his friends.

POSITION ELEVEN: NOVEMBER. The **Upright Ten of Hearts,** the card of moving in together. So soon? You pull two more: the **Upright Queen of Hearts** and the **Reversed Two of Diamonds.** No, it's not a move. With the Two and the Queen it looks like a Thanksgiving trip to Michigan to meet his mom.

POSITION TWELVE: DECEMBER. The **Upright Ten of Clubs,** the card of the future, of new people, new places, new friends, and a happy time. Seems you'll have a date for next New Year's Eve. Let's picture you leaning back on your bed and hugging this book to your heart. It appears that this is the year you will finally meet the right guy!

♠ ♦ ♣ ♥

The first few months of the upcoming year will be lonely, and you'll find yourself pining for a new man. Apparently, your coworker, Sherry, will introduce you to one of her friends in April and the two of you will connect. Your relationship will build politely through the phone call stage and survive a few career demands. In September he'll open up and share his fears and ambitions. After that, it's full steam ahead as he introduces you to his friends and takes you home to meet his mom.

You have a very romantic year ahead of you. This man will indeed turn out to be the kind of best friend/lover that you've always dreamed of meeting.

The Single Card

When I teach classes on how to read the playing cards, I advise my students to pull one card each morning. We call this the Daily Card. I advise you to do the same.

TO LAY OUT THE SPREAD

* Shuffle the cards and spread them into an arch.
* With your eyes closed, hold your hand an inch above the cards.
* Move your hand through the air following the arch shape until you feel a warmth or mild heat rising up from a section of the arch.
* Pull one card from that section and leave it facedown on the table.
* Turn the card over from left to right.

TO INTERPRET THE SPREAD

While you sip your morning coffee, read the text on the card. Then get dressed and go to work. At the end of the day, look at your card again and reread the text. Try to understand how that one single card describes the essence of your day. You will be a Reader when you understand the correlation between the Daily Card and your experience of the day.

I know a brilliant Reader who gives Single Card readings that go on for an hour. She's given me several and they've all been pure, luxurious, and uncluttered. She pulls one card and talks all around it. She covers the philosophy, the lessons, and the character of the individual defined by the card. She examines how the card applies to his or her personality, circumstances, and relationships.

The Single Card is ideal for answering bottom-line questions like:

"Why does he love her more than me?"

"What is his true character?"

The Single Card works best for simple questions that would benefit from a great deal of information. In response to a question like "Why did he leave me?" the **Reversed Eight of Clubs** says that he didn't think your connection was peaceful. One of you wanted more glamour. Glamour-guy thought the other was too simple and unexciting. The

Eight indicates that the man was probably the simple person looking for a quiet partner. He didn't think he could make you happy. This man doesn't want much out of life beyond a good dinner with pleasant conversation. He doesn't aspire to a big house and a new Mercedes. He wants to stay home with the kids and teach guitar on the side. He's a mellow person with peaceful aspirations. You were *way* too dynamic for him and (because of your nature) eventually he would have bored you to tears.

In response to the same question, the **Reversed Three of Spades** suggests that one of you was involved with another person and that person came between you.

The **Upright Jack of Clubs** indicates that he just wanted to be friends. He never thought of your relationship as anything more than platonic. He never developed truly romantic feelings for you.

A Single Card is the most Zen way to give or receive a reading, and it's a delicious opportunity for two people to chew down to the marrow on a fine philosophical point.

CHAPTER THREE

The Cards

IN THIS CHAPTER, I DESCRIBE EACH CARD IN DETAIL. BEFORE YOU READ the body of the essay, read the heading. First, the heading shows what the number means, then what the suit means. The text of the essay describes how the two blend to create the essence of each individual card. I've included a quote when I could find one, and in every instance I've chosen a word or phrase to sum up the card. The heading for each essay looks like this:

Ace of Diamonds

Aces: Achievement
Diamonds: Physical and Material

Preparation + opportunity = luck
SUCCESS

In most cases, a commentary about the card is included after the heading. The commentary explains how the number and suit meld together to create a message unique to the card.

I've divided each essay into two parts: the Upright version and the Reversed version. When you give yourself a reading, every card you draw will fall either Upright or Reversed. Regardless of its direction, you should begin by reading the commentary about the card. Then, you can skip to either the Upright or Reversed section, depending on which way you pulled it.

Both the Upright and the Reversed sections are broken down into three subsections:

Individual
Relationship
Circumstances

Here's how to use the subsections:

INDIVIDUAL: This section corresponds to the Birth Card chart on page 273. You can use the Individual section to ascertain the character or destiny path of any person born on any day. Read both the Upright and Reversed descriptions of the individual to determine his character strengths and weaknesses. This section will also describe how a person who wasn't born on that day is feeling in regard to a relationship or circumstance. Since the Individual section describes different types of men, I used the pronoun "he." When you pull a card to represent yourself, the segment describes how you're functioning within the relationship right now. Except, when you read it, you'll have to switch "he" for "she."

RELATIONSHIP: This section describes an alliance. It tells what will become of a brand-new romance or comments on the current condition of an established one.

CIRCUMSTANCES: You can also use your deck of playing cards to inquire about situations that have nothing to do with romance. When you approach the oracle to ask about your job, car, or home, refer to this section for your answer.

After the subsections, I've included a **NOTE**. The Note is a commentary on the card, a recap of its meaning, or an additional scrap of information that wasn't included elsewhere.

After the Note, at the end of each essay, I've posted the answer to the **"YES" OR "NO"** question. If your question can be answered by a simple "Yes" or "No" response, skip the text and go to the bottom of the essay. Your answer will be waiting for you.

The Joker
THE BEGINNING

A portrait of a court jester decorates the Joker. In medieval European courts, the jester's job was to amuse and delight the reigning monarchs. He made riddles and jokes about the peccadilloes and personalities of the courtiers. His humor cloaked a worldly understanding of court life. He disguised his observations as entertainment, which granted the jester the license to speak frankly when others wouldn't dare. He was the forerunner of our twentieth-century stand-up comics. The jester succeeded or failed in life in direct proportion to his ability to read the character and temperament of the powerful people around him. If he failed, and his words and puzzles struck too raw a nerve, he was banished, or worse.

The Joker represents the part of us that dances dangerously close to the truth, and equally close to ruin.

The Joker is a card of destiny. As it says in the essay about the history of the playing deck, the other twenty-one Major Arcana cards were dropped from the pack, but not the Joker. Therefore, when the Joker appears in your spread, take it more seriously than the other cards. Because, whether it's Upright or Reversed, whether it's addressing an individual or a relationship, it lends a strong element of fate or karma to a reading.

The Joker is the first card in the deck. His number has no content, therefore he has no past, no motive, nor plan. He's a newborn and an innocent. He's pure spontaneity and represents the beginning.

UPRIGHT

INDIVIDUAL: The Joker describes a person filled with youthful innocence. He's playful and naive. His outlook on life is open, fresh, optimistic, and original.

The new romantic prospect represented by the Joker will be just that, a brand-new prospect. You don't know this person but you'll meet him soon because it's *his* destiny to meet *you*. Prepare for his entry into your life by throwing out the rule book. Don't draw any hasty conclusions about someone represented by the Joker. The usual yardstick can't measure this unique soul.

The Joker may have been married before. If so, he would like to marry again. He percolates with optimism as he dances gaily forward in search of a new partner and a new way to live and love. In the Joker you've found a character to whom openness and spontaneity are aphrodisiacs. You can be your most unguarded, playful self with him.

RELATIONSHIP: This relationship began suddenly and seemed fated, as if your paths were meant to cross. The card stands for the handsome architect you met the night your cousin dragged you to a gallery opening. You spotted one another from across the crowded room and you both felt a wave of recognition. He had an open smile and an unguarded gaze. You were attracted to the direct way he looked at you. It was disarming and honest. When he picked his way through the crowd to introduce himself, his voice sounded familiar. The romance represented by the Joker is the classic fated encounter.

When the Joker describes an established alliance, it marks a new phase in the relationship. You may have parted from your partner and believe your connection is broken. But, if you pulled the Upright Joker, it will begin again. Only this time the rules will be different because any relationship represented by the card is unpredictable. Even if nothing as drastic as a separation has occurred, a renovation of your alliance is inevitable. Together, the two of you will sand down your connection and apply a new coat of varnish. Then you'll reposition your life together in new and different chambers of your hearts. The renovation will keep the marriage alive because it will refresh your affection for one another.

The new romance defined by the Joker often finds one party to be an innocent and the other a sophisticated guide in the practice of love. This union will suffer many difficulties, but it will be a happy one nonetheless. As it unfolds, it will constantly renew itself with sweet pleasures for the body, mind, and spirit.

CIRCUMSTANCES: The Joker stands for synchronicity or the cosmic coincidence. If you're inquiring about a job, an apartment, or a car, the Joker says it's your destiny to find what you seek but in an unlikely way. You'll find the apartment one night as you circle the block looking for a parking space in a strange neighborhood. Suddenly, in front of the only available spot, will be a "For Rent" sign. When you call the number, the unit will turn out to have the right number of bedrooms and a remarkable view of the city. You didn't find this apartment; this apartment found you because it was meant to be yours. The job or car represented by the Upright card will come to you in the same way.

REVERSED

When the Joker falls Reversed, his youthful innocence takes on a sinister aspect. He becomes childish and unreliable. He's eccentric, chaotic, and erratic.

INDIVIDUAL: This one is restless, flirtatious, and irresponsible. He's spoiled, willful, inconsistent, and unpredictable. Selfish and immature, he's unable to follow through on mundane tasks. He isn't capable of a full relationship because he isn't capable of settling to any one thing or person. He may be experimenting with a variety of sexual partners or be sexually ambivalent. His finances could be unstable so he may ask to borrow a few dollars. He's a kook and a flake. Your challenge will be to accept him as he is or drop him forever, because you can't change him under any circumstances.

If you pulled the Reversed Joker to describe yourself, be careful. You can't focus right now so you could hurt someone badly. Don't get involved with a new person when you feel the toxic mix of indecision, irritability, and vanity pumping through your veins.

RELATIONSHIP: The established connection described by the Reversed Joker has suddenly changed. While you weren't looking, the rules shifted. As a result, your relationship is now fundamentally unstable. The Reversed position spells out a warning because you don't know where you stand. If you're confused, it's a result of compulsive behavior on the part of your partner. He might have a gambling problem or be addicted to meaningless infidelities. He used to be fresh, idealistic, and positive. But now he's a tease, unable to express his feelings, and emotionally distant.

The brand-new romance defined by the Reversed card is unlikely to go anywhere, because your exciting new partner is an irresponsible child. Don't invest your heart here. Nothing will come of it.

CIRCUMSTANCES: When you pull the Reversed Joker to describe a job, it represents a position selling insurance against alien abductions, breast enhancement cream, or those laundry balls you put in the washing machine instead of soap, which are made out of plastic, filled with water, and are supposed to release the dirt from the clothes electromagnetically. The product or company represented by the Reversed card will be unreliable, or worse.

When it describes a new car, the Reversed Joker says the owner lied about the mileage and the maintenance. In fact, the thing probably didn't even belong to him when he sold it to you. He probably forged his girlfriend's signature on the pink slip. A home? Oh my. Someone paid the mortgage with a kited check, charged the furniture to Grandma's credit card, and pirated the cable TV from the neighbor's unit. Don't get involved.

NOTE

The Joker is an open, fresh card about optimism and new beginnings. Whatever aspect of your life it touches, it promises spontaneity, originality, and fun. This card is different. It's unconcerned with the past and the future; it lives for the present.

Upright, the Joker stands for the hope we find in a new day and a new beginning. Reversed, there's no hope. But take heart, because the nature of the Joker is movement. Sooner or later, he will spin himself Upright and dance away in a new direction. Hang on tight. You'll never *believe* what direction that will be!

UPRIGHT: "Yes, because it's meant to be."
REVERSED: "Absolutely not."

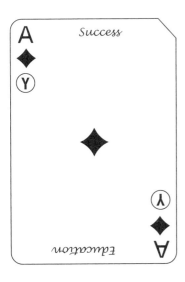

Ace of Diamonds

Aces: Achievement
Diamonds: Physical and Material

"Preparation + opportunity = luck"

SUCCESS

The Ace of Diamonds stands for the whole picture, the accumulated total, or the overview. It represents the sum of our efforts and the inevitable by-product of an education, investments, and experience. The Ace isn't a card of luck; it's a card of planning and persistence.

UPRIGHT

A diamond is composed solely of carbon, a chemical element fundamental to all life. A diamond is carbon in its most concentrated form and the hardest substance known to man. Pressure forms diamonds, but the amount required is incomprehensible. If you can imagine the Eiffel Tower (7000 metric tons) resting on a five-inch plate, you'll get the picture.

The Ace of Diamonds predicts monetary success in direct proportion to a lifetime of careful planning and dogged perseverance. It speaks to years and years of concentrated effort. It's about pushing forward and paying dues despite the strength of the opposition. It's about the squeezing we endure until we emerge clear, crystallized, and unbreakable. The Ace of Diamonds starts out as a lump of coal and endures centuries of outrageous pressure until it's unearthed and sent to Beverly Hills in a velvet box, where it's showcased as a sparkling treasure, perfectly cut and beautifully set.

INDIVIDUAL: The individual represented by the Upright Ace went to school, paid his dues, climbed the corporate ladder, and became president of the company. Now he spends his vacation time stretched out on his yacht in the Caribbean, drinking Mai Tais and listening to Jimmy Buffett CDs. This guy has more going for him than his money. He's a student of life and, at some point, he'll become an instructor at the Street Smart School of Achievement. Eventually, the Ace of Diamonds man will become a mentor.

The new romantic prospect described by the Upright Ace is at the peak of his career so he doesn't have much time to devote to love. He needs a woman with her own profession, someone who's equally absorbed by her own climb to the top. He'll be attracted to a partner whose ambitions and achievements he can respect.

The girl who pulls the Upright Ace of Diamonds to describe the new man in her life should memorize the following:

He would never invite you on the second date if he didn't admire something about your mind, lifestyle, and goals.

There's nothing any woman can do to seduce the Ace of Diamonds man. There is no quantity of low-cut tops or short leopard skirts that could possibly entice him. He, himself, is a master at the art of sexual manipulation. He learned the craft back in the old days, when he was climbing the corporate ladder. This one already knows who you are and what he wants from you. He knew the minute he laid eyes on you. Be confident and be yourself, because he's more interested in your whole person than in your separate body parts.

RELATIONSHIP: The union described by the Upright Ace is an alliance between powerful people. This is the marriage of two attorneys or two doctors. Combined, they earn a ridiculous amount of money. Both have always known they wanted a mate from a prestigious family and an elaborate wedding that would blow away the social register.

The marriage represented by the Ace is old and established. Both halves of this couple come from traditional families that have dominated their communities for generations. When they married, their union represented the bonding of two powerful factions. Both members of this alliance are in line to inherit vast properties. Their sons and daughters are beautiful athletes with scholarships to prestigious colleges, who drive last year's BMW to high school. The Ace of Diamonds couple has worked long and hard on their separate careers, their spiritual lives, their family life, and their relationship.

I should mention here that there's no fall from grace built into this card. The Ace of Diamonds couple isn't greedy and doesn't have a history of ruthless backstabbing. God won't punish them for living a life of privilege and position. These are good, loving people who just happen to be very comfortable.

CIRCUMSTANCES: The car, house, or job represented by the Upright Ace of Diamonds is more than a winner; it's a symbol of achievement.

The Ace represents the luxury vehicle of your dreams, the one you swore you would buy when you made it big. This is a New York apartment with a Central Park view. The Ace doesn't represent a job. Instead, it's a partnership with a prestigious law firm, an advance for the movie of your best-selling novel, or an impressive inheritance.

REVERSED

The Reversed Ace is the diamond in the rough, which makes it the card of education. The Reversed card governs high school, trade school, college, and the more informal institution called the School of Hard Knocks.

Several years ago, I received a call from a man who wanted to book a Gypsy fortune-teller for his daughter's high school graduation party. When I arrived in my Gypsy costume with the puffy white shirt, velvet vest, and purple taffeta petticoat, wearing my big curly wig and twenty pounds of fake jewelry, I discovered the guests were graduating from an affluent private girl's school. Ninety percent of the fortunes I told that night placed the Reversed Ace of Diamonds in a prominent position. As it turned out, a famous Ivy League college had accepted every one of the young women. Their grades were impressive, but I was more awed by their focus. They had no doubts about themselves, their abilities, or their direction. Their expectations were high, and their expectations were their *own*, not those of their parents. Each girl knew who she was and where she wanted to go in life.

INDIVIDUAL: The person defined by the Reversed Ace of Diamonds hasn't climbed all the rungs on the ladder of success yet, although he's in the process. He needs one more certificate to get the promotion, one more year to graduate, or one more teaching credential.

He's a student of life and eventually he'll become a teacher. Sometimes he pursues teaching as a career but more often he's a mentor. There are people who are natural resources for information about life and love. Whether he gets paid for it or not, the man represented by the Reversed card is one of those people.

The new romantic prospect defined by the Reversed Ace of Diamonds is aware he doesn't know enough about love and relationships to make a marriage fly, so he's acquiring some skills. He reads books, attends seminars, and seeks advice in the hope of becoming a better partner. This is a very ambitious person who's accustomed to winning. If you give him enough time, he'll earn his master's degree in loving partnerships. I would never discard a man represented by the Reversed Ace of Diamonds. He's a diamond in the rough.

RELATIONSHIP: The old established partnership represented by the Reversed Ace has decided to expand their knowledge of love and romance. Not because they're a damaged, wounded couple who are desperate to repair their crumbling union, but rather because, as students of life, they enjoy taking notes and facing challenges. These two will be a big success story once they apply the lessons of affirmation, affection, and acceptance they learn at Marriage Encounter. They may even go on to counsel other couples or conduct encounter groups of their own.

The new Reversed Ace romance represents the fertile environment in which you will earn your primary education in "How to Be a Good Partner" or "What to Look For in a Mate." The Ace describes a serious curriculum so, clearly, you must need more relationship expertise or the Universe wouldn't have enrolled you in the class.

When the Ace describes your relationship status, whether or not you think you have anything to learn, you *are* learning. One day you'll look back on your current alliance and say, "That one taught me everything I know about relationships."

CIRCUMSTANCES: You'll need your degree or certification, or to participate in a training program to get this job. Take a class in automotive maintenance before you buy this car, and this apartment building is either located on campus or houses students.

NOTE

The Ace of Diamonds is a strong card with a positive message about growth through knowledge and experience. Upright, the growth is complete and you're sitting on top of life's treasure chest. Reversed, you're a student enrolled in the School of Affluence, or Marital Bliss, or another class the Universe wants you to take.

The Ace of Diamonds represents the pinnacle of material and emotional success. It's the card of having endured the 7,000 metric tons of pressure it takes to crystallize into a bright, glittering gem.

UPRIGHT or REVERSED: The Ace is always a "Yes."

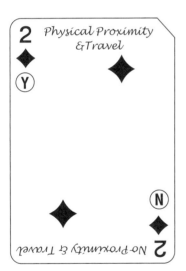

Two of Diamonds

Twos: Union
Diamonds: Physical and Material

PHYSICAL PROXIMITY

The Two of Diamonds is about the need to connect with another human being in a tactile way. This is not a card of physical romance, of sex and passion, but rather of reaching out in person. The card stands for coffee dates, dropping by the house, and flying home for Christmas. The Two is also the Travel card because it represents the effort to be in the same town or the same room with another person.

Besides being the card of proximity, the Two is the card of negotiation and compromise. In medieval Europe, before young lovers could pass their time in each other's chaperoned presence, their parents had to negotiate the terms of their alliance. The Three of Diamonds represents the legally binding marital contract. The Two describes the deal the parents struck before they drew up the marriage documents, including how many cows and bolts of cloth the families would exchange. The Two of Diamonds stands for giving a little and getting a little. It says, "You scratch my back and I'll scratch yours."

UPRIGHT

INDIVIDUAL: The individual defined by the Upright Two is fair minded and pragmatic. He has a worldly understanding of life so he's able to accept limitations. He presses for the advantage in all his dealings because he feels as though he ought to, but he knows when to quit. Once he's worn his opponent down, he lightens up because he doesn't want to alienate him. He'll make his adversary cry "Uncle," but he'll be a good sport. A Two of Diamonds person is respectful and courteous regardless of whether he wins or loses.

This man has been known to have a pushy side. He may pressure you to sleep with him, move in with him, or marry him. If you understand that his demands are actually negotiations, then he's easier to handle. Tell him relationships aren't business arrangements. They're about two people connecting with their hearts, minds, bodies, and souls. Ask him to have faith in your love and surrender his need to cut a deal. Ask him to allow your spirits to merge naturally. He'll oblige because he knows if he cooperates with you today, you'll accommodate him tomorrow.

The Two of Diamonds lover prefers to see you in person rather than speak to you on the phone. He's physical, sensual, and tactile. He needs to touch you and smell your natural scent. When he falls in love with you, he needs to drink you in with his eyes. He's attracted to the tone of your voice and the texture of your hair and skin. Take his hand in yours when you sit in the movies. He needs the contact; it tells him you love him.

RELATIONSHIP: The couple defined by the Two of Diamonds thinks it's fun to discuss, negotiate, and bargain. They travel a lot too. When they do, they go places where they both have interests. For example, they might fly to New Orleans because he has to see a client. Her roommate from college lives in the French Quarter so she goes along and it's a win-win trip. These two don't crowd one another. They know how to compromise or trade for what they want.

The Two of Diamonds relationship is in constant motion. No request is answered with a simple "Yes, dear." If she asks to see a movie, he says, "Of course, darling. But first I want to hit a couple of buckets at the driving range." And that will be their deal. First they'll go to the country club and then the movies. While he hits a few balls, she'll scan the newspaper for movie schedules. After the movies he'll suggest coffee, but she'll want a piece of cheesecake. So that's their next deal. They'll drive the extra mile to the coffee shop with the good cheesecake. This for that. That for this. Although it's a bit exhausting, it isn't a bad way to live.

If you pulled the Two of Diamonds to describe your new love, you will fuse or pull apart in proportion to the amount of time you spend together. Your alliance will fade without sufficient amounts of touching, smelling, and listening. So much so that sometimes the Two represents a long-distance romance where both parties struggle to see the other as often as possible. Regardless of the manner in which it's conducted, the union's most marked quality is the way these two broker everything from how much syrup to put on the waffles to who rides shotgun.

CIRCUMSTANCES: When pulled to describe a car, the Two of Diamonds says you can get a better price if you bargain. A job? It will require a lot of travel, but you can upgrade your compensation package if you're willing to negotiate.

If you draw this card and you do nothing else, at least go to the physical location and look at the house, office building, or auto. Its whereabouts or appearance will supply the additional information you need to decide whether or not to rent, buy, or work for it.

REVERSED

The Reversed card doesn't make time for frivolous luncheons or unproductive movie dates. It no longer finds value in a happy medium, either. In this position, the Two stops negotiating and becomes cemented in its own point of view.

The Reversed Two is still a card of travel, but only the long-distance kind.

INDIVIDUAL: The man represented by the Reversed Two of Diamonds isn't around much. He either lives far away, travels constantly, or has quit coming over to see you.

He isn't flexible either. It's his nature to adopt one perspective to the exclusion of all others. He has a "Take it or leave it," "My way or the highway" attitude toward life and love.

The new romantic prospect described by the Reversed Two has quit calling and asking you out. You should accept that your romance is over because he won't withdraw to reflect on your relationship, change his mind, and ask to come back. The Reversed Two man doesn't compromise and he never changes his mind.

RELATIONSHIP: Either the duo described by the Reversed Two of Diamonds travels together, is locked in a stalemate, or they have quit seeing one another.

If they travel together, their relationship is all about the countries they visit and the languages they speak. They spend their time planning their next vacation or pasting photos into the album from the last one.

If they aren't travel agents working for the same cruise line, these two are polarized. They can't discuss their issues or make plans because they're stuck in their separate perspectives and neither is willing to move to the middle ground.

The Reversed Two pair is either planning a trip together or they've stopped going out. Sometimes the decision not to get together is temporary and sometimes it's permanent (it depends on how old the relationship is), but it's rarely sad or painful. The decision to terminate their visits was just another deal they hammered out between them.

CIRCUMSTANCES: The Reversed Two says Don't negotiate. It wants you to stick to your price or your terms. If the new organization won't meet your financial needs, keep looking for a group that will. If you know how much you want to pay for an apartment or a car, don't succumb to a hard sell. Instead, drive down the street to the next apartment building or the next car lot.

NOTE

The Upright Two of Diamonds foretells a trip, predicts a compromise, or wants two people to sit down together, in person. The Reversed card is unyielding. It still travels, but it doesn't negotiate.

UPRIGHT: "Yes."
REVERSED: "No."

```
┌─────────────────────────────┐
│ 3    Legal Marriage,        │
│        Routines             │
│ ◆                    ◆       │
│ Ⓨ                           │
│                             │
│            ◆                │
│                             │
│                      Ⓝ      │
│ ◆                    ◆       │
│ ∂ɹnʇɔnɹʇS ɟo ʞɔɐˈ7          │
│ ˈǝɔɹoʌᴉᗡ ˈ1ɐbǝ˥        Ɛ   │
└─────────────────────────────┘
```

Three of Diamonds

Threes: Expansion
Diamonds: Physical and Material

THE RULES

Like the skeleton beneath our skin, or the wood frame behind the stucco, the Three of Diamonds represents the infrastructure of life. It corresponds to our disciplines, routines, and obligations. The Three stands for the frequency with which we wash the car, hit the gym, and see the dentist. It's the card of mortgages and auto loans.

The Three also describes the policies and procedures we accept as proper social conduct. The card dictates no white shoes after Labor Day and no loud stereos in the apartment building after ten.

My friend Janice and I were having coffee the other day. Our conversation turned to the inevitable difficulties that arise when an unattached person selects his or her romantic partners from within the same social circle. We agreed there's a polite but unspoken code of conduct that allows a new couple to form and coexist comfortably in close proximity to any former lovers. We also agreed the responsibility for the comfort of all three people belongs to the ex no matter how wronged she may have been in the breakup.

Take me, for instance. I once dated a man whose ex-wife invited me to her home for their daughter's birthday party. I politely accepted her invitation despite my obvious reservations about being in my new boyfriend's ex-wife's home. When we arrived, she made me feel comfortable by gaily introducing me as Good Old Steve's Wonderful New Girlfriend. She made a point of smiling warmly at me and completely ignored Steve all evening. As a result, I relaxed and the three of us were able to interact without the subtle, disruptive tension that usually exists between a former wife and a new girlfriend.

Janice and I mapped out how the comfort level is established. It's a two-part procedure:

1. The ex makes a small, distancing gesture toward the old partner (ignores him).
2. Then, the ex invites the new lover onto the playing field by making a small, accepting gesture designed to acknowledge the new union (handshake and smile).

These two steps create a way for the past and present lovers to be in the same place at the same time.

The boyfriend ought to be heads-up enough to introduce the two women in his life so they can dance out the ritual described above. But if he isn't, the ex has to offer a handshake and smile as a metaphorical "handing over" of the old partner to the new partner's care. It's a symbolic passing of the torch. The new lover can't approach the ex because if she did, it would remove the element of generosity and be a symbolic "seizing" of the torch.

The new girlfriend should respond in a warm and friendly way to any effort of any size that the ex-wife is willing to make. Any withholding of the gesture by the ex suggests that she is still in love with her old partner, or is unable to let go, and signals competition. Without the token of friendship, no matter how small, tension will exist.

Now, I know some of you may feel nauseated by now. I know some of you have been dumped, cheated on, lied to, and haven't seen a dime of child support in ten years. And I know the idea of putting out your hand and smiling at the other woman might make you sick to your stomach. But, someday you're going to have to calm down and accept who he is and what he did. Either you can come back to this passage at that time, or you can face that you drew the Three of Diamonds right now. The presence of the Three in your spread says it's time to think about comfort levels, about how much more pleasant it would be for both you and your children if you could all move easily between your home and his.

UPRIGHT

INDIVIDUAL: The lover described by the Upright Three understands the rules of dating but lacks spontaneity. He knows to take you to coffee on the first date, to dinner on the second, and to make a pass on the third. He's the kind of guy who leaves your apartment promptly at 9:30 because he has to work in the morning. He would never stay over on a weeknight because it would throw off his routine.

The Three of Diamonds personality doesn't cultivate a rich internal life until pretty late in the game. When he's young, he does things the way his parents did. He doesn't question his life choices. He just re-creates the same life his parents lived because that's what feels natural. This guy gets married young because his parents did or becomes a firefighter because his dad and brothers are firefighters. The Three of Diamonds man has to suffer a divorce or two before he begins to examine his heart.

As he ages he becomes a better marital prospect. The more he fails, the kinder, less fussy, and more compassionate he becomes.

RELATIONSHIP: Because the Three represents obligations and the time-honored way of doing things, this is the card of legal, binding marriage. It stands for lawyers, the courts, and legal documents. The Three doesn't speak to the tender, passionate connection between partners who marry; instead, it confines itself to the precisely worded legal contract of marriage, including the prenup.

In the spread of an unmarried couple, the Upright Three represents their dating routine; it's the schedule agreed to by both parties that regulates the frequency of their phone calls, dinners, and sleepovers. The primary focus of this unmarried couple is the pattern of time they have agreed to spend together and apart.

CIRCUMSTANCES: When the Three describes a job, it's a contracted position. The contract will outline the services to be rendered and the fees to be paid for those services.

Should the card describe a home, the most outstanding aspect of the house is the actual purchase of it. The price or terms of the mortgage is its most prominent feature.

When the Three describes an environment, it will be orderly and well maintained, but the interior decorations will lack imagination. The primary focus of the household will be the seating assignments in front of the TV or the rotation of personnel on the dishwashing schedule.

REVERSED

INDIVIDUAL: This free spirit has no schedules, no rules, and no specific routines. He's just a fly-by-the-seat-of-his-pants kind of guy. He's usually divorced, on his way to court, or chronically late. It's not that he's disorganized, it's that he doesn't give a fig for other people's routines or social codes of conduct.

This is also the person described above who doesn't relinquish his ex once the romance has ended. Normally, it's not because he's still in love, but because he lacks the social savvy to know when to step aside. This is the oblivious former lover who rushes up to your boyfriend at a party, throws her arms around his neck, and pulls him aside for a private conversation that excludes you. The Reversed Three doesn't represent a person interested in rekindling the romance. This character just doesn't understand why, if they used to be such close friends and have nice little chats at parties in the old days, they can't continue in the same vein today.

The Reversed Three also describes someone whose divorce isn't final or who is still hammering out a property settlement with the lawyers.

The Reversed Three is the card most likely to represent your own ex.

RELATIONSHIP: When the Three falls Reversed, it's the number-one indicator of legal separation or divorce. The card doesn't speak to the outcome of the proceedings or to the messy, painful emotions connected to the termination of a marriage. It merely addresses the legal dissolution of the union.

In the spread of an unmarried couple, the Reversed Three represents a casual, unstructured, or spontaneous style of dating, except one partner usually finds the informality uncomfortable. This person would like to tighten up his arrangement because he isn't always confident he has a date on Saturday night. He would like to buy tickets to a concert and feel some degree of certainty that his lover will attend with him. He finds it difficult to plan ahead because of his steady's indifference to timetables.

CIRCUMSTANCES: The Reversed Three describes an unreliable work environment. This corporation fires its employees without notice, reneges on contracts, fails to pay their commissioned sales representatives, and is sued with such regularity that they keep a full-time attorney on staff. If you pulled the card to represent your existing job, you may need an attorney of your own to get the next contract.

The house defined by the Reversed Three has some type of legal problem; it's in foreclosure, has liens against it, or is tied up in a lengthy probate. The interior of this home doesn't quite meet most standards for efficiency, either. No one waters the yard with any regularity, so the grass nearly dies before it's resuscitated. No one cleans the dog run or is in charge of dusting. The dishes and newspapers pile up for days.

NOTE

The Three of Diamonds Upright stands for the daily obligations and responsibilities that lend form to our lives. The Reversed card represents a lack of structure or distaste for fixed routines.

UPRIGHT: A crisp, efficient "Yes!"
REVERSED: "Oh, No."

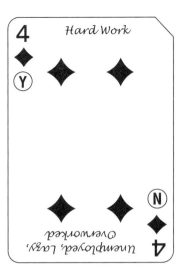

Four of Diamonds

Fours: Effort
Diamonds: Physical and Material

WORK

The Four of Diamonds is the card of effort. It stands for hard physical labor, perseverance, and responsibility.

I once read an article about the amount of time people work in a day and the way in which that amount determines their success in life. The study said the least successful people work 12 hours a day or more. It made an example of a warehouse worker, who said with pride, "I'm the foreman here and I work sixteen hours a day, seven days a week!" The study claimed the twelve-hour-plus guy works so hard that he never completely relaxes and unwinds. He doesn't take vacations or days off, so he develops low-grade burnout. Eventually, he won't be able to perform in a way that reflects his full ability. He'll be too tired.

The article said that people who work eight hours a day never get anywhere, either. The eight-hour guy goes in, does his job, leaves his work at the office, and goes home to his real life. He doesn't work hard enough to outshine his coworkers so he isn't very successful.

It is the person who works ten hours a day, five or six days a week, who is the successful one. He works more hours than are required of him, but he stops in time to avoid overworking. He can go on like this for years at a stretch without wearing himself out. As a result, he earns the most money, receives the most promotions, and banks the biggest bonus check.

The Upright Four of Diamonds represents the ten-hour person and the Reversed card represents the twelve-hour guy. The one who works eight hours a day would only pull the Four to describe whether or not he's working at all. Upright, he is. Reversed, he isn't.

UPRIGHT

The Upright card describes the positive manifestation of our efforts. This is a card of physical strength and concentration. It operates on the premise that if you're willing to put in enough effort, you can manifest any amount of money or love. The Upright Four stands for how hard we work at our jobs and the amount of responsibility we take for our relationships.

INDIVIDUAL: The man represented by the Four is a beast of burden. He takes on hard, physical tasks and receives compensation in direct proportion to the effort he expends. The Four of Diamonds man is a superb provider because he's diligent and persistent. He slaves all day and then goes home to recharge his batteries in the bosom of his family so he can get up tomorrow and do it again. He's a nurturing presence in his household too. He asks each child what he or she did that day, walks the dog after dinner, and dries the dishes just so he can stand near his partner and quietly reconnect with her.

The Four of Diamonds man creates romantic interludes. He understands that if his marriage is to last a lifetime, he has to set aside time for daily passion and conversation.

This man knows that relationships require hard work, and he's willing to do the work. But he's careful not to do more than his share. It's his style to lay down a solid foundation of friendship before he takes the relationship to the next level. By the way, the "next level" is his private domain. The Man of Physical Labor is a patient and tireless lover.

When he marries, the Four of Diamonds man will select his life partner for the way she works at her job, maintains the home, and contributes to the relationship.

RELATIONSHIP: The Four of Diamonds defines the effort we put into our relationships. Upright, it's the "We can work it out, baby, I just know we can" card.

The married couple defined by the Upright Four of Diamonds has constructed one of the most fulfilling relationships in the deck. From the very beginning, from the first day they met, they set out to build a loving foundation for a serious partnership. Over the years they've maintained their union by grooming it with the tools of cooperation and affection. The difference between these folks and those who nurture doomed affairs is that the Four of Diamonds couple *only works where they can profit*. Both parties to this marriage refuse to waste their energy. They measure their efforts into neat level spoonfuls and dish them out where needed to maintain a healthy, even-keeled alliance.

In private, both parties will watch their mate to see if he or she is putting an equal amount of elbow grease into their partnership. It's not that they're a couple of scorekeepers, but rather that force, drive, and results are the basis of their union. They will not stay together if one partner kicks back on the chaise lounge to enjoy the fruits of the other's labor. The hardworking member of this duo will simply pack up his tools and move on to the next person.

The brand-new romantic prospect represented by the card will take you on hiking and swimming dates. He'll buy tickets to sporting events and invite you to drive miniature Formula One cars. The Four of Diamonds man is a physical person and likes physical outings. The two of you will march through the dating process at a hearty pace, with a sense of purpose. As a couple, you can work through any problem that pops up between you.

CIRCUMSTANCES: The Upright Four is a very positive card. If you pulled it in response to the question "Am I going to make any money?" the answer is yes, but you're going to have to earn it. The Four isn't about winning the lottery. It's a nose-to-grindstone card. The Four will pay cash dividends in direct proportion to the effort you put out.

The Four of Diamonds is the card of how hard you work at your job. Upright, there's a lot of work to be done and you are just the muscle-bound soul to accomplish all of it. You can possess any car, house, or job represented by the Upright Four if you're willing to work for it.

REVERSED

INDIVIDUAL: "Lazy" is such a *harsh* word, but I'm afraid it applies to the person represented by the Reversed Card of Effort. This man is the eight-hour guy who's chronically unemployed, fundamentally unemployable, or else his greatest talent is lying on the sofa all day with a beer in one hand and the remote in the other. The Reversed Four man is also the twelve-hour guy who takes on too much responsibility for too long and loses his effectiveness.

The new romantic interest represented by the Reversed card comes in two packages. The first one is the lazybones lover who wanders through his relationship without a plan of action or any particular romantic goal. He's available for the union as long as his partner doesn't require he do anything to sustain it.

The second manifestation of the Reversed Four is the love-aholic who has a history of taking responsibility for every aspect of the relationship. It's his nature to plan all the dates and solve all the problems.

Fortunately, by the time he's defined by the Reversed Four, the second type has usually figured out that he's not supposed to do quite so much, that his partner is supposed to come up with 50 percent of the leisure activities, household chores, and romantic gestures. The man represented by this version of the card has learned to hold back and wait for his partner to step forward and deliver her fair share of the effort. I suspect he committed some icky little crimes of overindulgence before he adopted his current outlook because it's more his style to overdo than to underdo.

RELATIONSHIP: These two are a couple of directionless, emotional dropouts. They have such an informal commitment that their relationship is really nothing more than a vague wandering in and out of one another's beds. They're just informally hanging around with each other.

They may live together or have been prompted to marry by one of their parents, but neither party puts any energy into the union. Neither *feels loved* by their mate and they aren't *in love* either. They don't know if they'll continue to wander together for the rest of their lives, if they'll have a child, buy a house, or wander off with someone else. The truth is, they'll probably have a family when she accidentally gets knocked up and they'll own a house when they inherit one.

The married couple represented by the Reversed card doesn't invest any energy into their marriage anymore. They've long since stopped working on it. Unless they decide to turn the Four around by seeing a shrink, reading a Venus-Mars book, or taking a ballroom dance class, their union will die of neglect.

The brand-new Reversed Four romance is headed for the scrap pile. Neither party will propel the alliance forward.

CIRCUMSTANCES: When the Four falls Reversed, you're out of work or don't want to work. The Reversed card says you hate your job, don't want the job, or aren't willing to take on the job. It says you aren't putting in the effort it takes to find the car/house/job or, if you already know where to find it, you're too lazy to fill out the credit application/rental agreement/résumé.

NOTE

The Four of Diamonds measures effort. When the card is Upright, it represents the healthy amount we invest in our jobs and relationships. When

Reversed, it describes either the lazy, unmotivated slob living inside each of us or else it stands for our inner overachiever.

UPRIGHT: "Yes."
REVERSED: "No."

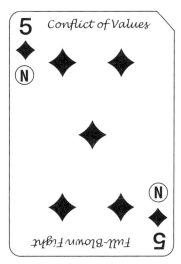

Five of Diamonds

Fives: Conflict
Diamonds: Physical and Material

THE WAR INSIDE YOUR HEAD

UPRIGHT

The Upright Five of Diamonds stands for a mental process that goes something like this:

"I have $1,000. I guess I could pay $500 on my Visa, $100 on my store card, and put $400 into car repairs. Or, I could put $200 on the Visa, skip the store card, just do the brakes for $150, and rent that cabin in the mountains for the weekend. Or, I could save the whole $1,000 until my sister takes her vacation. We could meet in San Francisco at that spa. But then my Visa won't be paid and the car is falling apart. Hmm. Maybe I should put $100 on my Visa . . . ," and on and on, ad nauseam.

The Five stands for the way a person goes over and over and over something in her mind, infinitely back and forth, analyzing it from all sides. It's crazy making.

The process is called "being in your head."

INDIVIDUAL: The man defined by the Five of Diamonds has an old, judgmental tape recording of a parental voice playing inside his head. He believes in the voice so he strives for perfection. His adherence to the tape's strict, unattainable standard leaves him feeling as if nothing he does is good enough. The Five of Diamonds man is preoccupied with rules, efficiency, trivial details, and procedures. He prizes work and productivity over pleasure and relationships because pleasure is something to be *earned*. He's hard on himself and others, and rarely gives gifts or compliments. He's stilted, stiff, critical, judgmental, and overly analytical.

The new romantic prospect described by the Upright card isn't much fun. His idea of a hot date is to debate religious theology over dinner or to argue the merits of overhand versus underhand pitching in women's softball. If you're playing on an underhand team, he'll fight for the overhand perspective. He'll insist that you do things "right," which could mean anything from making the bed with hospital corners to ironing the cuffs *before* you iron the sleeves of his shirt. He's not affectionate or sympathetic and the little rush he gets from sparring with you will irritate the hell out of you.

RELATIONSHIP: Here, equally rigid perspectives manifest as a conflict of values. The established couple represented by the Five of Diamonds may care deeply for one another, but they will hold opposing and inflexible points of view on most subjects. Under the best of circumstances they'll have an ongoing, friendly debate that, over time, will fine-tune their value system.

Under the worst of circumstances, these two will disagree about what is most important in life. She'll believe the list should be marriage, kids, and house. He'll think it ought to be job, friends, and golf. The fundamental difference in the way they prioritize will create a difficult relationship filled with blame, criticism, and complaints. These two will argue about which house to buy, whether to spend their vacation in Paris or the Grand Canyon, and at what age the baby should start preschool.

If you pulled the Five to describe a new alliance, the card foretells a quarrelsome romance. You'll want to watch the boat parade on Christmas Eve because you think it's romantic. You'll tell him you love the reflection of the little white lights on the black water and how warm you feel nestled in his arm in the brisk winter air. But he and his sister want to sit in the basement and look at the photo albums from their childhood, drink eggnog, and reminisce, just like they do every Christmas Eve. You'll argue that it's more important to spend the holidays as a couple.

If you choose to stay with the new man represented by the Upright Five of Diamonds, expect to bicker over every single detail of your life together.

CIRCUMSTANCES: Any situation described by the Upright Five of Diamonds is uncomfortable, disagreeable, and argumentative. You'll fight with the landlord, go to war with the car dealer, or threaten to quit if you don't get a raise. Under these circumstances hold out for what's important and surrender what you think you can live without.

REVERSED

When the Five falls Reversed, the voice inside your head is obsessing. It's building a lawsuit, cataloging faults, and listing crimes in preparation for a huge defense. When the physical, argumentative Five spins upside down, it becomes the card of rage.

INDIVIDUAL: The Reversed five describes a man who's contentious by nature. He gets high on the cleansing white heat of his own indignation.

When you first meet him, he'll seem like a reasonable soul, if something of a perfectionist. As you grow closer, he'll offer to help you by pointing out your flaws. He'll give you advice on how to improve your personality, your home, job, kid, investments, friendships, car, wardrobe, and diet. He'll tell you he's only correcting you because he cares about you and loves you. But his need for control will escalate. One day you'll wake up to realize your home has become a prison and you're married to a temperamental control freak. You and the kids will feel battered by his relentless judgments and criticism.

Should you kindly take his hand in yours and tell him living with a dictator is unpleasant, Mount Vesuvius will erupt.

This relationship will not endure. By the time you're hiding the leftover grocery money in the safe deposit box your mother got in her name so you can finance an escape, you'll believe he's the meanest son of a bitch alive.

RELATIONSHIP: This marriage is nothing but a series of attacks. These two don't have the skills to resolve their conflicts so they try to destroy one another. They're a violent couple prone to screaming outbursts in public places, which they punctuate by throwing drinks. These two have used their keys to scratch "Asshole" and "Bitch" onto the hoods of one another's cars. They slam doors, throw plates, and set fire to each other's clothes. They're the couple who shows up at dances on the arms of new, more attractive dates. They sit at tables on opposite sides of the room where they bristle and glare across the dance floor and lay big wet kisses on their escorts. They'll cause a scene in the parking lot, which will force their new lovers to defend them.

If you pulled the Reversed Five to describe a new romance, *Ohmigod!* I don't think anybody bought this book so they could marry into a mess like this. Don't accept any more dates with this man. Better he should be a little ticked off now than really angry later on. Besides, the chances are good that you're the new girl he's dating to fuel his hot-blooded breakup with someone else.

If you're already married and you pulled this card, well . . . you guys are having the big one. Pull more cards to see if there's a way to resolve your disagreement. You may need counseling to build up your skills if you hope to settle a conflict of these proportions.

CIRCUMSTANCES: The Reversed Five represents the landlord who didn't replace a washer in the faucet and the drip, drip, drip has rusted the sink. You're afraid he won't refund your deposit because of the discoloration. So you show your friends the bathroom and make them promise to testify in small-claims court, send registered letters requesting the landlord repair the faucet, and take Polaroids of the damage.

If you pulled the Reversed Five to describe a car, house, boat, or job, don't buy it, rent it, sail it, or agree to work there. You'll be sorry if you do.

NOTE

The Five of Diamonds is the number-one indicator of a disagreement. When Upright, the conflict is low-grade and although it's annoying and a serious head trip, you can resolve it.

When the Five falls Reversed, the situation is out of control. This is the card of name calling, finger pointing, chest thumping, and letters from lawyers. The upside-down Five says you'll want to slit somebody's tires or throw a brick through their front window. It also says you'd better hope the other guy doesn't get to you first.

UPRIGHT or REVERSED: A great big "No!"

Six of Diamonds

Sixes: Faith
Diamonds: Physical and Material

Let go and let God.
—AUTHOR UNKNOWN

THE NATURAL FLOW

The Six of Diamonds couples faith with the physical. It's the card of man's struggle to conform to God's will, which is a breeze for some people and life's great challenge for others.

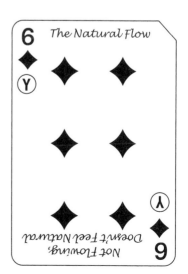

Take surfers, for instance. Surfers never know what to expect until they arrive at the beach. Corporate surf dogs call the surf report for current info on their favorite break, but the hard-core surfer never does. Surfer purists walk outside at 6 A.M., stand on the cliff, and let the waves tell them what to do. They trust in their mother ocean and in their private relationship with the power, grace, and beauty of nature. They know they could lose their board in the shore break or catch the ride of their life, and they know a power greater than their own will decide which way it goes.

The Six tells us the Universe has a divine plan and our role in that plan is to simply relax into it. The card represents the organic unfolding of events. So much so that the Six is really just a phrase, or rather, just *half* of a phrase. "It's perfectly natural that _____" is the phrase, but you'll need another card to fill in the blank.

When the Six is drawn sandwiched between other cards it's read as the word "naturally." It represents the unforced course of events that will link the first card to the second. For example, when it falls between the Three of Hearts and the Joker it says, "When you go out with your friends [Three of Hearts], it's perfectly natural [Six of Diamonds] to meet a new romantic prospect [Joker]."

UPRIGHT

The Upright Six of Diamonds is the card of natural rhythms.

INDIVIDUAL: This person is in tune with the cycles of life. He's aware the cycles are inescapable, that they're the hand of fate and the will of God. He trusts the ups and downs of fortune to follow one after the other as surely as sunrise follows sunset. His understanding of this fundamental truth is his special gift.

If you pulled the Upright Six to describe your new love interest, you've met an uncomplicated man who will respond to you without a hidden agenda or ulterior motive. He knows you will grow closer together or further apart as you are meant to. Instead of snatching life's offerings, he allows good fortune to glide toward him in its own time. To those who are bogged down in strategy, whatever this man does seems original. He's comfortable in his own skin.

RELATIONSHIP: Your attraction to this relationship was unavoidable. You have floated into each other's lives as easily as water trickles into the little cracks and crevices in the sidewalk. Your connection has developed just as freely. Your marriage was or will be pure inevitability.

The Six adds nothing to an established connection except to comment on the way it functions year after year. This relationship adapts. It dips and bends like a rivulet that splashes off rocks, splits around trees, and puddles into gullies, flooding them and flowing onward. This couple shifts their individual needs to suit the needs of their relationship. Because of its fluidity, this marriage endures.

CIRCUMSTANCES: When the Six is drawn, I often just say, "Of course." In answer to the question "Will I get the apartment/job/car/dog?" I say, "Well, of course you will," because the Upright Six of Diamonds is the card of the unavoidable unfolding of events.

REVERSED

The Reversed card feels uncomfortable and sometimes that can be a good thing. There are circumstances under which we ought to go against our basic instincts. Occasionally the most relaxed approach leads to undesirable consequences. When it does, we need to step back and try a new direction. If you seek to change an aspect of your life, to reverse the way you usually do things, the Reversed version of the Six will be a very appropriate card. But, you will feel uneasy because breaking old habits is unsettling.

INDIVIDUAL: This person doesn't mesh easily with others. It's not that he doesn't like people, it's that he isn't on course. He's not in touch with the universal flow. As a result, he moves along in fits and starts, uncomfortable and self-conscious. He doesn't have a spontaneous bone in his body. He would never take his hands off the bike handles or close his eyes and fall backwards off the high dive of life. In relationships, he hesitates and loses the moment.

If you pulled the card to describe a new romantic prospect, he'll be the last person on earth you ever thought you would go out with. Even after you date him for a while he'll still seem unlikely.

RELATIONSHIP: This new alliance won't unfold the way you planned. In fact, the relationship may seem so unusual that you might struggle against it. Try to relax and realize you're involved in a romance unlike any you've experienced before. Expect it to go in a direction you never thought a relationship could go. Try to view this as a good thing. Try to release your grip on the steering wheel and let the relationship drive itself.

The established partnership described by the Reversed card is in an odd phase. The connection isn't easy and natural right now. It isn't flowing. These two can't seem to get on the same page emotionally, which isn't necessarily a bad thing. It's just a little out of the ordinary. Pull another card to see how this phase will work out.

CIRCUMSTANCES: When you draw the Reversed Six to describe a situation, it won't contain any synchronicity. There will be none of that "This feels meant to be" quality you're accustomed to feeling when something is right. If you pulled the card to ask about a new apartment, you won't live there because it isn't in the cards for you.

NOTE

The Six of Diamonds invites you to sit back and watch your life unfold in God's time, in His way. The Reversed card sends the same message, but says the experience won't feel comfortable.

UPRIGHT: "Of course."
REVERSED: "Yeah, but not like you'd think."

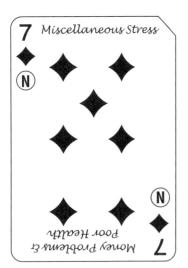

Seven of Diamonds

Sevens: Tension
Diamonds: Physical and Material

STRESS

The *American Heritage Dictionary* defines stress as "extreme difficulty, pressure, or strain," which pretty well sums up the Seven of Diamonds too. The Seven is a card of compression and restriction. It puts the squeeze on you.

Upright, the Seven represents a temporary condition. This is the card of insufficient funds and annoying little aches and pains. When it falls Reversed, it describes excruciating poverty or a permanent physical handicap. The Upright card gets on your nerves, but at least it's temporary. The Reversed card is everlasting and life altering.

UPRIGHT

When Upright, the Seven stands for generic stress and miscellaneous difficulties. The card represents standard annoyances like your in-laws' annual summer visit, the way your bad knee hurts most of the time, and that cramped after-Christmas feeling when your credit cards are charged up to the max.

INDIVIDUAL: The Seven of Diamonds individual drives an old clunker of a car, has mac and cheese for dinner twice a week, and his kids wear hand-me-down clothes to school. He endures chronic allergies, owes $60,000 in student loans, and drinks too much coffee.

If you pulled the Upright card to describe your new boyfriend, listen to him talk about money. If he sounds like he's been in his current condition for more than a year, expect to go on discount dates. This means at best, he has a coupon or will suggest you go Dutch. At worst, he'll invite you to dinner but you'll have to sit through the time-share sales pitch before you can eat. This is the guy who doesn't want to pay for drinks so he'll slam down a couple of vodkas at his place before he picks you up. He'll invite you to the movies and then lie about your age at the ticket window. He'll claim you're under twelve or over fifty-five. He has trouble with his woman because once he becomes involved, he borrows her car or lawnmower or starts dropping by at dinnertime. When he takes her out on Friday night he claims he "forgot his wallet" or "can't break a hundred," so she winds up paying.

The new romantic prospect defined by the Seven of Diamonds isn't anybody's idea of a knight in shining armor. In fact, a girl would have to have prosperity issues of her own to consider a second date with such a certified tightwad.

RELATIONSHIP: The Seven of Diamonds is the card of poor health and often describes an unhealthy relationship. This alliance doesn't nurture either party. In fact, it draws out their sickest, most neurotic tendencies. The established couple represented by the Seven of Diamonds is impoverished emotionally and materially. They have a chemistry between them that manifests as money problems or illness. It's not uncommon for one member of this duo to be sick and the other to function as his or her nurse. I mean, literally, one person may be pushing the other around in a wheelchair.

These two will blame each other for their condition, but their real problem is the nature of their connection. Should they find some money, instead of paying back their parents or landlord, they'll spend it on new stereo equipment. They don't understand that fortunes are built by saving, trimming the overhead, and doing without new clothes, expensive haircuts, and top-of-the-line cell phones. Their condition could escalate to a bankruptcy without a serious shift in the way they think and function. The Upright Seven of Diamonds condition is fixable. With discipline and patience this couple could mend their credit rating and break their cycle of poverty.

The brand-new alliance defined by the card will be unpleasant. You won't date this man more than a few times. He'll turn out to be so cheap that you, too, will cry poor as a way of protecting your own assets. Politely pass on the romantic prospect described by the Seven of Diamonds because you didn't buy this book to help you find a tense, unhealthy situation like this one.

CIRCUMSTANCES: The Seven of Diamonds' apartment will grate on your nerves. It will be dingy, dark, and depressing. A pet described by the card needs an expensive operation, the car will cost you more to repair than you paid for it, and the job pays minimum wage. Keep looking.

REVERSED

The Reversed Seven of Diamonds is the card of ruinous debt, chronic illness, and physical disability. It describes an extreme brand of difficulty well beyond the variety that ordinary mortals can cope with.

INDIVIDUAL: The person defined by the Reversed Seven is under tremendous strain. He struggles every day of his life just to put enough gas in his car to get to work—that is, if he's physically able to work. He does daily battle just to keep the lights turned on. When he goes to the Laundromat he has to choose which clothes to wash because he can only afford two loads. He drives the oldest, most wasted car on the road, rents a tiny place in the worst part of town, and holds a permanent garage sale in his driveway to supplement his disability check.

The person represented by the Reversed Seven of Diamonds isn't cheap. He would love to pay once in a while, to see a movie, to buy new clothes, or to stroll along the boardwalk eating ice cream with his favorite girl, but he can't. His financial picture is far too desperate to justify an extravagance like ice cream.

If the Reversed Seven person isn't drowning in financial difficulties, he lives with an arthritic back, diabetes, or goes to dialysis three times a week. The health issues attributed to the Reversed card are chronic, ongoing, and probably not 100 percent healable. They can be brought under control or managed, but they are in no way casual or temporary. When the Reversed Seven represents a man who can't perform sexually, his problem is physical, not emotional, and he should see a medical doctor.

The new romantic prospect represented by the Reversed card is unhealthy, destitute, or both. He can't afford to date or isn't well enough to date.

RELATIONSHIP: The relationship represented by the Reversed Seven is crumbling because of illness or financial difficulties. These are the folks who answer the phone and claim they don't speak English or hang up on their bill collectors. If the landlord comes to the door, they hide in the back of the house and pretend they aren't home. Their life together is horrible, but they'll never part. They can't afford to.

The brand-new romantic interest represented by the Reversed card can't support a basic lifestyle and can't afford to date you. Throw more cards on the Reversed Seven to see if he can upgrade his job, find a new doctor, or apply for assistance from social services. Perhaps after his life stabilizes he'll be a better romantic prospect. For now, his situation is all-consuming and he isn't available for a breezy summer romance with you.

CIRCUMSTANCES: Any condition defined by the Reversed card will result in an injury, a financial loss, or both. The car represented by the card will be too expensive even if it's free, the job won't pay a dime, and the apartment will be so beat up that you'll never get the smell out of the carpet. No one prospers under any circumstance represented by the Reversed Seven of Diamonds. This is the card of bankruptcy.

NOTE

The Upright Seven of Diamonds is a stressful little thorn of a card, but if you're diligent, you can work through it in a relatively short period of time. When the Seven appears Reversed its punishing effect will penetrate all the way to your core, and may last a lifetime.

UPRIGHT or REVERSED: A huge "No!"

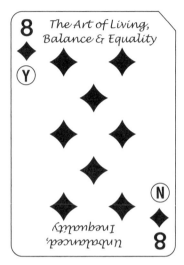

Eight of Diamonds

Eights: Philosophy
Diamonds: Physical and Material

BALANCE

I always see this card as being a disk balanced on the pointed top of a pyramid. The disk is divided into narrow slices, like a pie. If I place a pebble on one slice of the pie, the disk will topple over. But, if I put pebbles on two slices of the pie in direct opposition to one another, the disk will balance itself. If I select two more opposite slices and place pebbles on both of those . . . and then select two more and then two more . . . I will create stability for my disk. Eventually I will have so many pebbles on my disk I can even take one off, creating an imbalance, but the disk won't topple.

The slices of the pie represent the various aspects of the life we live. If I put a pebble on the slice marked "work," I should put one on "play." If I place one on "relationships," I need one for "privacy." The slice marked "spirituality" balances "materialism." We need pebbles for the elderly and children, for football and the opera.

The active pursuit of a pebble for every slice of the pie of life is the art of living.

UPRIGHT

INDIVIDUAL: The lover described by the Upright Eight of Diamonds is a balanced person. His life is full and filled with love because he devotes equal time to each of his emotional facets. He participates in his children's schoolwork and sports activities. He sets aside time for his wife: time to see a movie, eat dinner, or take a walk alone together without the kids. He invites his mother to lunch and plays tennis with his buddies from high school. He preserves a slice of time for himself, too: time to read, tinker with his car, or study yoga.

The new romantic prospect defined by the Upright Eight of Diamonds will never obsess over you. He's too grounded, too aware of the importance of his other relationships. This guy is "present" in each moment of his day. When he leaves your doorstep, he leaves you behind. Which doesn't mean he doesn't think of you or doesn't love you, and it doesn't mean he's unfaithful to you. He isn't cursed with a short attention span or a need for flattery. Quite the opposite. He believes your love is mutual and has enough confidence in your union to turn his back on it while he nurtures his other emotional connections.

RELATIONSHIP: The brand-new relationship defined by the Eight will develop into a healthy one because it's an add-on to a well-rounded life. Neither person will abandon their friends in order to rotate as a satellite around their new sweetheart. Neither of these two needs a romance to fulfill them because their careers, families, friendships, and hobbies fulfill them. This love affair will only be a charming aspect of an otherwise complete life.

The established couple represented by the Eight understands the need for emotional attachments beyond their own connection. Their front door is open to parents, siblings, ex-wives, stepchildren, friends, and neighbors. This pair is invested equally in their alliance and is equally in love. Their marriage is reciprocal, creative, and soulful because it's simple, sane, and stable.

CIRCUMSTANCES: The Upright Eight of Diamonds is the "Do what you love and the money will follow" card.

The Eight represents a career that feeds both your soul and your pocketbook at the same rate. When pulled to describe your job, it says you are an artist at what you do.

I once had an accountant who appeared to me to be the driest, quietest, most boring mouse of a man. But once I spent time with him and bore witness to his creativity, I realized he was a virtuoso with numbers and his little accountant heart thumped with a passion for his subject. He danced my money away from the IRS by investing it in fine art and second mortgages. Eventually, I learned to recognize the twinkle in his eye and came to understand that he wasn't some tedious little man hiding out in the safety of numbers. He was a rebel and an artist.

REVERSED

INDIVIDUAL: The person defined by the Reversed Eight is out of balance. He either overworks or doesn't work at all. He may be so self-disciplined that he never permits himself a whole Sunday on the couch with the remote and a bag of potato chips.

The new romantic prospect defined by the Reversed card will discard all his friends and family members as soon as he meets you. He has no life of his own and he's hoping you will give him one. He really believes that your love for him defines him, so he'll work overtime to please you.

RELATIONSHIP: Regardless of whether the Reversed Eight describes an established connection or a brand-new one, the association is out of balance. This is an alliance between the prince and the peasant girl, the idle affluent housewife and her impoverished gardener, or the rock star and his groupie.

For regular couples, one person is deeply in love and the other is allowing him- or herself to be worshipped. For one, the sun rises and sets at the whim of their lover. For the other, the romance is unremarkable, but convenient or flattering.

CIRCUMSTANCES: When the Reversed card of balance and artistry describes your job, it says you're just workin' for the money. It says there's no artful skill involved in your work and you're not caught up in the day-to-day thrill of being there. The Reversed Eight says you're just slugging it out for the cash and you need to find something else to do.

The car or home defined by the Reversed Eight isn't giving back to you. This is the car that you groom and fuss over that hardly has the decency to start in the morning. This house springs leaks, grows mold, and chews up a garbage disposal every year.

NOTE

The Upright Eight of Diamonds uses its gifts of equilibrium and mutuality to fashion a full, balanced existence. It integrates every conceivable aspect of life into your reality.

But when the Eight falls Reversed, it stands for an unbalanced existence or a one-sided love.

UPRIGHT: The Eight is a "Yes."
REVERSED: "No."

Nine of Diamonds

Nines: Culmination
Diamonds: Physical and Material

AMBITION

The Nine of Diamonds is the card of your material goals and the explicit fulfillment of them. It stands for every rung on the ladder of success. Its message begins with one foot on the ground, the other on the lowest bar, and a firm handhold on the side rails. Then, the Nine of Diamonds pulls itself up the rungs until it reaches the top, where it sits on the loftiest crosspiece. From this great height a person can enjoy a panoramic, penthouse view, but only those willing to make the climb ever get to see the horizon from such a commanding perspective.

UPRIGHT

INDIVIDUAL: The Upright Nine describes a winner. This man is ambitious, quality conscious, and aspires to the finest life has to offer. He's affluent, self-made, and well schooled in the spiritual laws of prosperity.

The mature man defined by the Nine of Diamonds knows there are many aspects to the good life and that material wealth is only one of them. Primarily, he understands success is a journey and not a destination. He believes a true winner is defined as much by the love he receives from friends and family as by the size of his bank balance. He knows good health, loving relationships, creativity, and spiritual discipline contribute in equal parts to success.

The younger man defined by the card has grandiose plans to claw his way to the top. But, when he gets into the climb, he'll discover that pulling himself up by his fingernails isn't exactly how it works because the climb is an inner game. He'll find the more he relaxes into it, the higher he can ascend. With experience, he'll figure out that the more he struggles, the tougher it is to get anywhere.

If you pulled the Upright Nine to describe a new romantic prospect, this man will be a step up for you. He's the type you always aspired to, the kind you always thought was a "catch." You'll go after him because to marry a man of this quality has been a lifelong ambition. And it *is* a matter of *you* going after *him*. He probably won't think to pursue you because, as a Nine of Diamonds type, he doesn't think to glance back over his shoulder and check who's climbing up the ladder behind him. He's got his eyes fixed on the future. He's looking to fall in love with a woman who's already rich and beautiful. This doesn't mean that unless you were born into the Rockefeller clan or look like Cindy Crawford this man won't fall in love with you. Quite the contrary. He just thinks "rich" and "beautiful" are symbols of achievement. He's looking for a woman with goals, skills, intellect, and heart all tied up in a sexy package. So go ahead and pursue him, but do it with taste and class because this guy isn't going to respond to anything else.

RELATIONSHIP: This couple holds their alliance to a very high standard. They uphold lofty ideals, maintain physical beauty, earn impressively, and are careful to move the relationship forward in appropriate increments.

This marriage is the union of two well-rounded individuals who carved out their positions in life prior to getting married. They both earn fabulous amounts of money and drive matching Lexus sedans, but they aren't finished. Next, they want to have five children, buy a cabin in the mountains, or run for public office. This couple isn't the Neiman Marcus, exclusive country club type. They're more likely to be liberals who take diving vacations to Tahiti or trek to Tibet to meditate with the Dalai Lama for two weeks, right before the annual sales convention in Toledo.

The brand-new couple described by the Upright Nine of Diamonds has high expectations for their relationship. They fully expect to marry and prosper together. I predict the union will proceed just as they anticipate. Neither of these people is foolish, immature, or silly. Neither is inclined to run around, use drugs or alcohol, or quit his job the week after the wedding. This is an ambitious alliance for both parties. Their relationship will flourish both materially and emotionally because the Nine of Diamonds is the card of marrying well.

CIRCUMSTANCES: When the Nine describes a car, home, or job, it'll be the high-profile status symbol to which you've always aspired. It's the new Mercedes sport coupe, the mock-Tudor mansion with the manicured lawn, or the prestigious vice presidency that comes with a corner office, your own executive secretary, and catered luncheons in the corporate dining room.

When the Upright card falls near the Nine of Hearts, the two cards foretell the absolute fulfillment of your most ambitious aspirations regardless of whether they're material or emotional. The two red Nines combine to manifest as very, very big stuff, all wrapped up in a turquoise Tiffany box with the signature white ribbon.

REVERSED

INDIVIDUAL: The man described by the Reversed Nine doesn't believe he has the right to aspire to great heights. Some part of him feels guilty lusting after material gain, but he does anyway. He pooh-poohs obvious symbols of affluence at the same time he doggedly pursues them. He drives an older car (but it has a pricey stereo system) and lives in a modest house (but the kitchen is provisioned with a Wolfe Range, Nova Scotia salmon, and a case of twenty-year-old Scotch). The Reversed Nine describes the closet gourmet or the silent partner.

The average man represented by the Reversed Nine never thought the hottest girl in school would go out with him so he never called her. Most likely, she would have dated him, but we'll never know because he doesn't shoot that high. The Reversed Nine of Diamonds man is embarrassed by success or is convinced that lusting after filthy lucre is a sin; that love and money are distant dreams meant for other, more glamorous people.

The brand-new lover defined by the card won't aspire to getting married, buying a house, or advancing in his profession. He won't sweep you off your feet with a diamond engagement ring or buy you a $300 handbag from Saks Fifth Avenue for your birthday. He's going to wind up with a woman who doesn't expect much out of life. He's going to finally make it legal with the one who waited fifteen years for him to pop the question.

RELATIONSHIP: The love affair represented by the Reversed card won't live up to your expectations. You'll have to lower your standards if you want to continue with this alliance. The Reversed Nine man doesn't have the raw materials it takes to make your girlhood dreams of marital bliss come true. That doesn't mean you can't stay in the relationship, it just means you two won't go to yuppie nirvana together.

Maybe your boyfriend has another idea about how to conduct your romance, and if you listen to him, perhaps you'll discover another way of relating. Maybe he wants to stay home with the children while you build a brilliant career. Of course, that would trash your notion of becoming a sporty housewife with blond highlights and a new Volvo, who takes lunch with the girls at the tennis club. But, these things are negotiable.

CIRCUMSTANCES: Whatever these circumstances are, they won't materialize because you've overshot your mark or bitten off more than you can chew. The house, car, or job represented by the Reversed card is beneath you. You can do better. If you insist on continuing with this project, you'll have to lower your expectations by at least half.

NOTE

When the Nine appears Upright in your spread, it promises fulfillment and achievement on a grand scale. It says you should set ambitious goals and be aggressive. Shoot for the moon. When it appears Reversed, you've shot too high. If you want to proceed, you'll have to lower your standards.

UPRIGHT: "Oh, baby! Yes, yes, yes."
REVERSED: "I'm sorry, but it's just too much to expect."

Ten of Diamonds

Tens: Doorways
Diamonds: Physical and Material

ISOLATION

The Ten of Diamonds is about the wisdom you gain while alone. Solitude allows you to establish routines that feel natural and uncompromising. Tuning in to your own private rhythm determines how often you like to make your bed or do the laundry. Isolation creates organic schedules for eating, bathing, sleeping, and teaches you what your guilty pleasures are. If you aren't pleasing anybody else, what do *you* like to do? Eat ice cream at midnight? Wash the dishes naked? Spending time alone cements your knowledge of yourself as an individual. It's nourishing, valuable, and healing, but a hard thing to do.

UPRIGHT

I watched my mother move from the big, active household of her marriage to the quiet widow's cottage of her senior years and eventually to a new beginning with a loving man. After our father passed away, Mom made a commitment to solitude because she wanted to find her separateness. She wanted to find a more authentic version of herself; a self that wasn't defined by society, a man, or children. Without the experience of being alone to discover her own quirks, her personal likes and dislikes, she would never have come to live the life she enjoys today. Her period of isolation was the challenge that fine-tuned her personality.

The Upright Ten invites you to have independent experiences, and guarantees if you find the courage to go forward alone you will draw closer to your core self. The Ten bestows the gift of self-understanding and promises that once the lessons are learned in seclusion, you will be able to use them to live a more fulfilling life out in the world.

INDIVIDUAL: The individual represented by the Upright Ten of Diamonds is in the process of self-actualization described above. He may appear aloof or be something of a loner, but he'll be wise and humble. This man's life has no emotional clutter in it. He's organized his leftover romances into friendships and holds his chaotic family members at arm's length. Because he's cleared his emotional palette of any foul-tasting residue, his heart is clean and pure.

The new lover described by the Upright Ten expresses his affections with difficulty, through small acts of kindness. He requires a great deal of privacy, but can emerge from his hermit's cell for field trips to restaurants or movie houses. When he does rally for a date he's quick to scuttle back to the safety of his cave. He's a wise counselor and teacher so you can expect prudent guidance from this shy, reclusive soul, but don't look to him for passion, drama, excitement, or flamboyant declarations of his undying love for you. They're not in his nature.

RELATIONSHIP: The established partnership described by the Ten is a somber one. This connection is deep and lasting, but never frivolous. This duo's activities revolve around mundane household tasks and their individual needs for retreat. They are a duty-oriented couple who spends their weekends at the Laundromat or mowing the lawn. At its best, the Ten of Diamonds marriage supports the lessons of self-value, humility, and practicality. At its worst, the union feels dull and prim, like the scholarly connection of two librarians or a cool alliance between the butler and the housekeeper.

The brand-new relationship represented by the Ten of Diamonds won't progress to a passionate romance. You may be able to organize a few phone calls that seem more like counseling sessions than pillow talk or you might meet for coffee once or twice, but that's all. To expect anything more is to set yourself up for a disappointment because, regardless of whether it's old or new, this alliance will leave you home alone, night after night.

CIRCUMSTANCES: The Ten of Diamonds is about the conscious choice to seek your fortune, solo. The card describes the adventure of leaving a prosperous, high-profile law office and going into private practice. Although initially scary, the decision will turn out to be a wise one because you will discover how to practice law in your own style. One day, when you stop by the bank to deposit "the Big Settlement Check," the money will be symbolic of your own private triumph.

The car or apartment defined by the Upright Ten will require wisdom, knowledge, and maturity to appreciate. If you use your head and select it for practical reasons, you'll make a wise choice.

REVERSED

Upright, the decision to be alone is an empowered choice rooted in wisdom and undertaken in a spirit of adventure. When the Ten is Reversed, the isolation is imposed by fate and isn't a pleasure. It's loneliness.

My older sister went directly from home to the college dorm and straight from the dorm into a long, loving marriage. She'd been married twenty-five years when her husband died of cancer. My sheltered, protected sister had independence and autonomy thrust upon her. She lived very far from the rest of the family where her career, her child's education, and her financial commitments kept her isolated. She found herself trapped in a lonely, boring hermit's cave.

The Universe *forced* isolation onto my sister, Ten of Diamonds Reversed, and *granted* solitude to my mother, the Ten Upright.

INDIVIDUAL: The Reversed Ten man is lonely, isolated, and unhappy about it. He's living without a relationship for a while and as a result, life feels dreary or empty to him.

The new romantic prospect represented by the card won't seek a tie with you because he finds you witty and sensual, but rather to ease his loneliness and sense of deprivation.

RELATIONSHIP: The marriage described by the Reversed Ten is a celibate bond between two loners. These two are living in separate cities or their marriage is a match in name only with segregated bedrooms and unrelated routines for eating, working, and parenting. They barely inhabit the same household.

The new alliance described by the Reversed Ten is a temporary arrangement between two lonely people. Their connection doesn't contain enough physical passion or sufficient quantities of romance and tenderness to propel it forward, so it won't develop into a nourishing emotional bond. If these two were to confide in one another about how lonely they are and how their isolation frightens them, perhaps they could turn the card around.

CIRCUMSTANCES: The Reversed Ten of Diamonds represents a grinding, suffocating routine from which there is no foreseeable escape. It's the condition of a military wife who waits patiently for her husband to return from his tour of duty overseas. This situation is bleak, devoid of contact with others, and notable for its relentless boredom.

You will find this car or house by yourself, and then you'll be the only one to drive it or live in it. The primary feature of this job is the way you will work in complete seclusion.

NOTE

When the Ten of Diamonds appears in your spread it's offering you the gift of wisdom gained through introspection. Your perception of the gift as a valuable opportunity or a lonely curse will be determined by your reaction to it. Try to view solitude as something that you need, as something you've sought out intuitively. If you push against the experience, the lonely feeling will tighten across your chest like a seat belt strap. Don't struggle. Instead, embrace your time alone. My mother and sister were released from the hermit's cell and you will be too.

UPRIGHT: "Wisdom. Yes, if you use it."
REVERSED: "No, no, no."

J ◆ Ⓝ
The Student,
New Business

Ⓝ ◆ J

Identity Crisis

Jack of Diamonds

Jacks: Young People
Diamonds: Physical and Material

THE STUDENT

UPRIGHT

As the youngest of the individuals represented by the earthy, prosperous Diamonds, the Jack is the heir to their legacy. His destiny is to uphold his family values and grow into a money-making King or Queen. Toward that end, the Jack is a student. He goes to school because education is the first step toward affluence.

INDIVIDUAL: The Jack of Diamonds is youthful and physical. Oriented toward the outside rather than the inside, he's an extrovert and a know-it-all but popular nonetheless. He has a joyful spirit, is playful, gregarious, and the heart of the party. He has an endless supply of energy and a talent for sports. The Jack shares his opinions freely, but only a fool would take his advice. His intentions are good but he's full of half-baked ideas and promises he can't keep.

The individual defined by the Jack has a need for meaning in his life. Philosophy, religion, poetry, and the concept of true love are important to him, but he gets bored easily. He knows he's in a cocoon, that he's growing and changing, but he's unable to identify in what way. He's tired of waiting for his new life to commence, but like a chrysalis, he'll be released when the time is right. Until then, he has to live with the uncertainty of his present condition.

The romantic prospect represented by the Jack will be slow to expose his inner life to you. He finds it hard to share his budding spirituality and dreams of affluence. Don't force this man to make a decision, to change, or to open up. You might push him away forever. Instead, grant him the time he needs to grow comfortable with you and allow him to open his heart at his own speed.

The man described by the Jack will retain his youthful appearance to the end of his days. He's a Peter Pan, forever young and vibrant, and won't grow old quickly.

RELATIONSHIP: The new romance described by the Jack is a complicated, delicate alliance unlike any you've ever known. This is a fated but temporary connection. You will both learn new things by being together. However, your combined future is unpredictable right now. Regardless of whether or not you stay together, you'll both gain greater depth and insight into the workings of partnerships as a result of your relationship.

Established couples represented by the Jack are eager students of love. They lie in bed at night and read books on male-female communication blocks. They attend couples seminars and visit a marriage counselor. These two are goal oriented. They aren't reading the self-help books for abstract information. They don't care how relationships work in general. They want to know about *their* union, about how to make *theirs* function better. These two have a lot of fun together. They play practical jokes, tell racy stories at the dinner table, and host parties. This couple believes the main reason to get married is to have a playmate for life. They may be on to something.

CIRCUMSTANCES: When you pull the Jack Upright, you're at the beginning of a new enterprise. This can be the circumstance of a retired person who takes a few workshops in preparation for a second career, or it can be an eighteen-year-old on his way to college. The Jack represents new business ventures, new careers, and new knowledge. He stands for internships, junior partnerships, and certification programs that will guarantee a quick raise. If you pulled this card to describe a car, house, or job, the Jack says you ought to buy, rent, or work for the fun, sporty one.

REVERSED

The Reversed Jack is linked with the Hanged Man of the Tarot. The card describes someone who feels upside down, someone suspended between the realities of his current life and his vision of the future, which he has not yet clarified.

INDIVIDUAL: The person defined by the Reversed Jack is having a full-blown identity crisis. He's a student without a school or a businessman without a profession. He's a seeker of the truth and of his true path.

This man's position is a precarious one. He's rejecting traditional avenues to knowledge and striking out in his own direction. He'll meet with outspoken antagonism and even persecution, which may crush his spirit and deprive the world of the good he might do. Any attempt to force him into conventional patterns will be met with opposition. However, if he can recognize that idealism still exists in others he can direct his energy toward concrete goals. What this man needs most is a sympathetic partner to remind him that he's not alone.

The new romantic prospect described by the Reversed Jack is in the process of altering his romantic situation. He's breaking up with a significant partner. He's in the process of letting go and moving on, but the transition is not complete. This man is not available for a full relationship with you at this time. If you like him, be a friend to him. Right now, he needs a sidekick more than he needs a hot and heavy romance.

RELATIONSHIP: The marriage defined by the Reversed Jack of Diamonds may place hefty demands on you. It may force you to change the external circumstances that make up the structure of your life. Your partner could be in a transition and be without a source of income for a while. As a result, you may have to sell your possessions or become the primary breadwinner. You may long to escape from the responsibilities of this marriage but be equally unable to abandon your spouse. Mutual dependency may bring out the worst in you both as you struggle with the roles of victim and savior.

The established couple that pulls this card is in the process of reorganizing their marriage. They may be struggling to recapture the past, but they should stop trying to make sense of their relationship. The way to move forward and to grow as a couple will be revealed to them eventually. For now, they must relax and accept the fact that this is an unproductive phase.

If you pulled the Reversed Jack to describe a new romantic connection, it will be complicated and difficult. Your union will be so strange that you may not recognize it as a romance. This alliance may never get off the ground.

CIRCUMSTANCES: Sacrifice is the essence of the Jack of Diamonds Reversed. Therefore, this is not the right time to make a decision. Accept this current, stagnant phase and do not force yourself or others into inappropriate activity.

NOTE

The Jack of Diamonds represents our unconscious life, where nothing is quite what it appears to be and where we develop the skills to create our conscious life. The Jack is a student of both the divine and the mundane. He's a scholar, an athlete, and he represents the part of us that must be patient and remember to breathe while we wait for our destiny to unfold.

UPRIGHT or REVERSED: The Jack is a "No."

Queen of Diamonds

Queens: Women
Diamonds: Physical and Material

Men, chocolate and coffee . . . the richer the better.
—FROM A NEEDLEPOINT PILLOW ON LINDA LEE'S COUCH

THE PRACTICAL WOMAN

The suit of Diamonds governs the tangible, the concrete, that which we can hold in our hand. It speaks to our basic need for food and shelter, our physical bodies and our money. The Queen of Diamonds is realistic and grounded. She's the Queen of Stability and is usually an Earth sign woman: Taurus, Virgo, or Capricorn.

UPRIGHT

INDIVIDUAL: The Queen of Diamonds views life in the following manner: First, she needs a comfortable, serviceable place to live. Second, she needs plenty of stuff to eat and drink and sit on and sleep in. Third, she needs the money to pay for all this plus the small touches that make life worth living, like classes and trips to the swap meet, or movies and books. She rings up her expenses on the cash register in her soul, where she calculates the price of a basic lifestyle.

So she's practical. She goes out and acquires the best education she can afford. Then she takes the best job she can find. Next, she installs herself in the most well-constructed dwelling available to her. Finally, she opens a savings account. Her goal is to construct a lifestyle sturdy enough to withstand the ups and downs of fortune.

The Queen of Diamonds is a hardworking, stubborn, economical, helpmate of a wife who likes a man with a nice fat paycheck like hers. She's not above marrying for money or security and would find it difficult to divorce an affluent husband. (It would break her heart to give up her tennis club membership.) If the gentleman she loves is a struggling artist, he must actually sell a painting. Because, as much as she admires the people who make beautiful objects, she's not a romantic idealist who believes a couple can live on love alone. She won't marry the man whose credit report reflects a tiny little bankruptcy. She won't tie her money to his unless "the Stain" is *permanently* wiped off his record.

The Queen of Diamonds doesn't like flashy modern furnishings. She thinks that stuff is for Eurotrash playboys. She would prefer to reupholster a traditional, well-built garage sale find. She seeks old-fashioned value in small touches like windowsills and a real brick fireplace (cinder block is so iffy). Hardwood floors are best, as are top-quality bathroom fixtures that perform smoothly and effortlessly.

The earthy Queen chooses her wardrobe from the neutrals: black, white, cream, gray, or brown. She avoids garish colors and prints as ostentatious and embarrassing. No polyester either. She likes the naturals: silk, wool, and cotton. She's an investment dresser. She collects conservative pieces guaranteed to remain in style a long time. She likes clean lines, voluptuous textures, and the posh engineering of hidden zippers. The Queen usually grows up poor, so during her college years she'll be aware of how her monetary situation compares with that of the other students. To appear financially neutral she'll adopt a uniform of tailored blue jeans and crisp white shirts. She doesn't see any reason for the entire student body to know the facts of her financial status, regardless of what they may be. Over time, she loosens up. If you stay in her life long enough, you will watch the smooth, functional hairstyles of her youth get fluffier and fluffier or blonder and blonder as she ages. I don't know why.

The Queen of Diamonds is the Queen of Beautiful Objects, who set her sights on something special long ago. The object stands in her heart as a prime symbol of glamour. It could be a leather jacket or an exotic sports car. My friend Adele says it's a mohair sweater she admired in college. The glamorous object is never described with one word. It's not a jacket; it's a black leather jacket. It's not a car; it's a 1964 British racing green Austin-Healey roadster. Adele rolls the phrase around on her tongue. It's emotional ice cream to her. She loves the flavor of pearl buttons nestled into the cotton candy fur of mohair. One day the Queen of Diamonds will acquire the precious object.

But, inevitably, the acquisition comes too late. When the money finally arrives the moment has been lost. Adele has bought ten mohair sweaters since college, but none has been perfect because the sweaters were an attempt to set aside her reality of being shy at school. They were an attempt to finally be a pretty college ingenue.

When Adele turns her wide, intelligent eyes toward me to ask, "Doesn't everyone live like this?" I have to say "No." The Queen of Clubs was the stylish one who was the first to wear the sweater way back when, and the impulsive Queen of Spades bought it the minute she saw it on the Queen of Clubs. The Queen of Hearts only wants what feels soft and sensual against her skin (mohair might itch). It's the Queen of Diamonds who carries a torch for beautiful, symbolic things.

As the goddess of the physical, the Queen of Diamonds Upright will be a man's precise physical type. If buxom blondes transfix him, the Queen will be the perfect example of that look. If he prefers short brunettes with tight butts, she will be the embodiment (pardon the pun) of that stereotype. Pulling this Queen is not about beauty. It's about fixations on types. It's about superficial, physical attributes found attractive. Does he love ethereal maidens, long-legged and willowy? If he does, the Upright card says she's his type.

RELATIONSHIP: The union defined by the Queen is oriented toward the acquisition of money and position in a healthy way. This is a very sporty and very modern two-career family with matching SUVs and a lovely condo. They spend their weekends in fresh jeans and white, white tennis shoes shopping at a warehouse grocery or hardware store. They usually have a boat, cabin, or recreational vehicle, which makes their lifestyle look fun and casual. These two don't care much about spirituality or charity. They go to church and contribute to worthy causes, but they don't get into the deeper aspect of such things. Their focus is on the installation of a productive routine that will provide a steady flow of cash into their household. Their aim is to live the American dream and they always achieve their goals.

The new romance described by the Queen will begin because of the way you look. This man has a long history of being attracted to your general type. Your connection will flourish or whither at your discretion. You will have total control over the alliance.

CIRCUMSTANCES: The job described by the Queen isn't a job at all. It's a career that requires a good education, an internship, and five years' experience. The Upright card represents a rock solid, middle-management position with plenty of opportunity for advancement. The Queen always has a little money set aside for the unexpected, so it's a card of mild affluence too.

The home or car represented by the card will be contemporary and upscale, but not top of the line. It's not a mansion on the most exclusive ridge in town, but rather a condo in a brand-new high-end complex. This car is new and impressive, but it's an Infiniti, not a Mercedes.

REVERSED

INDIVIDUAL: When she falls Reversed, the Queen of Diamonds is a financial mess. She's deep in debt with the charge cards clutched tightly against her bosom. She's broke and still spending on pointless "necessities" or doesn't want the responsibility for managing her own affairs. She's either overwhelmed by her need for more money or is working two jobs to make ends meet. The Reversed Queen of Diamonds is impractical and frivolous or strapped beyond belief.

The Reversed Queen is not her lover's usual physical type. Perhaps you should pull more cards to see if that's going to be a problem.

RELATIONSHIP: The couple who selects the Reversed Queen of Coins as the symbol of their everlasting love will deal with the downside of money.

These two will spend a great portion of their marriage seated at the kitchen table fussing over bills and complaining about each other's expenditures. Both parties will want the other to take more responsibility for their basic necessities. Neither wants to work hard, economize, or alter their spending habits. These two are critical of one another. Neither thinks the other is much of a catch but feels trapped together by their lack of funds. At best, this is the marriage of two happy shopaholics who are *trying* to do better. At worst, imagine a destitute, middle-aged pair driving away from their parents' house with another of Mom's checks to tide them over until payday.

A second version of the Reversed Queen marriage is the workaholic couple who doesn't make time for love. These two have allowed their careers, their home, and their luxury cars to define them. They like to be seen with the "right" people at the "right" country clubs. Affluence, not affection, holds this match together. Their dinner hour is a business meeting and they write off their vacations. The Reversed Queen couple presents a prosperous facade. They attend upscale cocktail parties where they coo and nuzzle; that is, if their social situation requires "Public Demonstrations of Affection." If their friends are more impressed by the professional approach, they'll quote stock prices and sales figures instead. Either way, behind the scenes these two bicker and blame, and scramble to make ends meet.

CIRCUMSTANCES: In the spread of a financially stable person, the Reversed card reveals temporary money problems or physical illness, including infertility. It shows the need for rest, exercise, and better nutrition. It suggests you find a second job or a cheaper apartment. The Reversed card wants you to create a new budget and pay off your credit cards.

NOTE

The Queen of Diamonds defines the practical, efficient aspect of women. She's the Queen of Economy who puts up jam every summer, buys her wrapping paper at the after-Christmas sales, and makes her kids work part-time while they go to college. She represents the part of us that grew up with a frugal parent and never forgot the lesson of thrift.

As a rule, women feel great when they go into Queen of Diamonds mode. They get pumped up on the endorphins of closet organization and bulk shopping.

UPRIGHT: "Absolutely."
REVERSED: "Oh, if you must . . . but you probably shouldn't."

King of Diamonds

Kings: Men
Diamonds: Physical and Material

MR. MONEY

Have you ever had a big stack of twenty-dollar bills? Whenever I have a thick wad I spread it out the way you hold a hand of cards and I fan the bills at my face as if to cool off with them. I

K ♦ Y

Healthy, Affluent Man, Physical Type

Workaholic, Unhealthy, Financial Difficulties
K ♦ i

smile a cocky smile and imagine walking down Rodeo Drive in Beverly Hills pointing and saying, "I'll take that, and that, and that too." To understand the King of Diamonds, you have to grasp how it feels to have a thick stack of fifties or hundreds. The stack represents power, security, and potential fun because that's what money adds to our lives.

The King of Diamonds is usually a Taurus, Virgo, or Capricorn man.

UPRIGHT

INDIVIDUAL: The Upright King is shrewd, practical, and in a voracious earning cycle. He rarely thinks of himself as witty, sensual, intelligent, talented, or handsome. He's proud of what he earns and what he can buy; he finds his identity through his material accomplishments and acquisitions. He's the King of precious gems, fine art, and luxury vehicles. He's the King of Mutual Funds, Cash Deposits, and Real Estate. He's the King of Physical Labor, too, and often uses his body to earn a living. He can be a construction worker, professional athlete, or singer.

My entrepreneurial Virgo father was bright, worked hard, and worked smart. But he took the knocks normal to independent businessmen. As children, we never realized he had ups and downs. I suppose we thought he earned the same amount every month because he portioned out money as if he did. Mostly, we assumed we were broke. When he died, my mother found stock investments, apartment buildings, life insurance policies, and undeveloped land she never knew existed. It made her angry to have been kept in the dark all those years while she gave herself home perms and sewed her own dresses to save money. I suspect the side ventures supplied the cash my father needed when he was on the bottom of his earning cycle. I also suspect that he was embarrassed, that he didn't want his beautiful wife to know he wasn't on top of his money game.

The Upright King of Diamonds shows his attachment to his family by providing for them. The more he loves his kids the harder he works to put braces on little Suzie's teeth and send Junior to baseball camp. His notion of good parenting is to introduce his offspring to the "right" kind of people, to dress them "well," and send them to the "best" schools. His snobbish efforts are his way of helping his children down the pathway to their own eventual affluence. He's trying to give them a good start in life, and he may very well succeed.

My father loved us so much that he joined our local country club. He took us to family buffet night every Sunday—even his mother came along. He sat at the head of the table and beamed with pride at the status dinner he was able to provide for his household. We found it boring and stuffy, but it was a very sentimental experience for him *because he was paying*.

If you pulled the Upright King of Diamonds to describe a new romantic prospect you should ask yourself if you have the aptitude for this man. He's not a hearts-and-flowers romantic. In fact, once you're engaged, he'll never write another line of poetry again. But, if he loves you, he'll be solid for you and you'll know how he feels by what he does for the family.

If you decide to date the unattached version of the King, here's what to expect:

The Czar of Supply and Demand is a very physical being. As a result, he will only approach a woman he's physically attracted to. Once he's in dating range of her he'll sell himself by marketing his best attributes, which means he'll do all the "right things" (those are the King's quotes) to prove he's the best applicant for the position as her lover. This is normally a clumsy maneuver that can entail a great deal of bragging, name dropping, or ostentatious displays of cash. The object of his affection is supposed to be impressed and to swoon in response. A woman should never declare her attraction to the King before he's flashed his wallet at her. But, once he does, she should give him a very clear indication that she's interested. If she fails to respond at this precise point in the dating process, he'll assume another, more qualified applicant got the job and he'll apply elsewhere. So let him impress you first, and then swoon on cue. Good luck.

RELATIONSHIP: Any time a Court card describes a relationship, the individual represented by the card has control of the alliance. When the King of Diamonds is in charge, you won't have much to say about things. He'll make most of the major financial decisions by himself. You might have a voice in the really big stuff like the purchase of a new home or your own car, but not necessarily. If he gets wind of a good buy on a house in an upscale neighborhood, you may be packing before you even know what color the carpet is.

The primary feature of this marriage is his belief in the deepest part of his soul that all his efforts are for you and the kids, but you may not see it that way. You may see him as always needing to control the money or as not being open about his resources, which you're bound to resent. Try to remember this man has one great redeeming quality: he's sincere.

He really does love you, he really is attracted to you, and he really will be responsible to his family. You can trust that he has your interests at heart, although you may have to remind yourself of this fact many times throughout your marriage.

The duo defined by the King likes money and the power that goes with it. They're affluent *because* of their alliance. They have a strange chemistry between them that manifests as dividends.

This is the couple who never completely allows their children to move away from home. If they do, they attempt to stay connected by buying Junior a condo. This is their way of being a family, which is very controlling. What they would really like more than anything on earth is for all the kids and spouses and grandbabies to live on one great big family compound. Of course, the King of Diamonds couple would be the matriarch and patriarch who own the grounds. If they could make the compound fantasy come true, this couple would be so happy, they'd name the place Shangri-La.

CIRCUMSTANCES: Any situation described by the Upright King will prosper. If pulled to describe your job, the card says you'll earn a lot of money or the position will catapult you to bigger and better things. The home described by the King is expensive, but a good investment. The new car will be a status vehicle. And you'll either get a good buy on it or turn a profit when you sell it.

REVERSED

Whenever I see the King of Diamonds, I picture the card spinning in a circle. The King is rich when he's up and poor when he's down. He'll probably spin all his life. Therefore, when he's in the Reversed position, he should be patient. It's his nature and his destiny to spin around again, but it'll take time.

INDIVIDUAL: When he falls Reversed, the King is "temporarily embarrassed," as my entrepreneurial father used to say when the wheel of fortune turned against him.

The Reversed King is in a down phase, is mismanaging his finances, or may be so indebted that the considerable sum he earns each month is eaten up by obligations before he cashes his check. He's the deadbeat dad, the tightwad, the workaholic, or simply unable to generate enough funds to support an average lifestyle. The Reversed King also represents the physically ill or infertile man.

The Reversed King of Diamonds is not your usual physical type. If you normally date tall brunette firemen with blue eyes, the King will be a short, blond, brown-eyed stockbroker.

RELATIONSHIP: The Reversed card describes the King's darkest aspect. This man honestly believes commerce governs every aspect of life. Therefore, he keeps his wife on a very short financial leash. The lengthening of that leash depends upon how well she meets his physical needs. If she gives him what he wants, he expands her household budget. The Reversed King believes money is the great, bottom line common denominator for all people under all circumstances, and, boy, is he wrong. His sex for sale thing makes for a rotten marriage.

The woman who chooses to marry the Reversed King will wake up one day and ask herself, Am I really this mercenary? Am I selling myself for slipcovers? So she'll pull away; he'll notice, and tighten the leash. She'll speak up, she'll explain; he won't hear. Her words sound like bargaining to him. He likes the game so he'll play hardball and up the ante. She'll try once more, but he'll never get it. This poor guy believes his only real value lies inside his wallet. Because she's cast in the role of financial and sexual subordinate, his wife will dream of cleaning him out in divorce court.

The Reversed King of Diamonds will be voted Most Likely to Have the Messiest Divorce and will insist on a stringent prenup for his next marriage to a much less savvy woman. It's odd to note that once he discovers this vehicle for feminine favors he sticks with it. The divorced Reversed King rarely attempts to change his pattern. Instead, he pushes forward and tries to broker a better marital "deal" next time.

The young King of Diamonds needs to choose his wife carefully. This man requires a lot of love, affection, food, and sex to be happy and comfortable and to provide stability and security for his family. The practical Queen of Diamonds will crack a whip over his head all his married days. She will step right into his "money for favors" game where stalemates and elaborate bargaining procedures will cloud their time together. He needs to wed the loving and nurturing Queen of Hearts. She'll support his efficient efforts and cherish him with a sentimental, soothing fervor. She'll be proud of his successes and kiss away his boo-boos when his card spins upside down. She'll never slip into the money game with him. She'll be happiest when smothering him in sex and food.

CIRCUMSTANCES: The Reversed King is broke, in debt, unhealthy, over-worked, or unwilling to work. The situation represented by the card is the same. This employer has trouble making the payroll, overworks his staff, or doesn't pay the standard wage. This car will spend its entire life in the shop and you can't afford this apartment.

NOTE

JUST A TIP: Never ask the King of Diamonds a question unless you want a direct, unsweetened response. He will only tell the truth, and the truth can hurt. If you can't handle the answer, don't ask the question.

UPRIGHT: "Yes."
REVERSED: "Maybe. Wait and see."

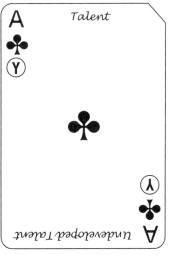

Ace of Clubs

Aces: Achievement
Clubs: Social and Spiritual

Talent is nothing more than a gross lack of inhibition in a real specific area.
—BRUCE MACINTYRE, ART TEACHER,
    JEFFERSON ELEMENTARY SCHOOL

TALENT

The Ace of Clubs is the card of the ministry. An individual forms a ministry when he speaks from his heart and people who agree with his point of view assemble in appreciation. A ministry develops when your feeling for a subject resonates in the soul of the loyal devotee who follows you. The Ace of Clubs represents the ministry of personal trainers, sculptors, accountants, astrologers, salesmen, cooks, or dentists.

The Ace of Clubs further represents your personal sense of truth and the talent you possess to communicate that truth. In order to understand ourselves well enough to communicate our perspective, we have to go inward, scroll down our menu of feelings and emotions, and click onto the one or two items we sense to be the most sincere. This is the process of enlightenment. Once we learn how to read our emotional register we are able to make choices more in tune with our true feelings. As a result, we are able to function from a position of more clarity, honesty, and consistency because we are more authentically ourselves. The process of scrolling and clicking and our ability to be honest with ourselves determine the quality of our relationships and our talents.

Men and women fall in love differently. Women fall in love when they bond sensually. A woman connects with her child as she strokes him, sings to him, and breathes in the sweet, powdery scent of his skin. She listens for his cry, knowing that she stands guard between her newborn and the harshness of life. A woman bonds to her man when she has evidence that her style of femininity appeals to him. Her approach may be stimulating conversation, gourmet cooking, or wild sex, but because he responds to her method of expressing her affection, she begins to love.

A man loves quite differently. He scans his heart for that psychic jolt, that instinctual connection that tells him "She's the one!" He needs to feel it way down deep inside or he can't go forward. A woman will get the flash, but afterward she must feel appreciated for her style of loving. A man will say he wants the same appreciation, but in truth he just needs the flash. Consequently, when you pull this card in response to the question "Does he love me?" the answer is "Against all reason, against all logic, and possibly against the advice of everyone he knows, yes he does, deeply."

UPRIGHT

INDIVIDUAL: The individual defined by the Ace of Clubs has God-given talents. He was blessed at birth with gifts he can't explain. He just knows what he knows. He channels those gifts into works of beauty. He's a musician, writer, dancer, painter, or psychic and his ministry is well developed.

The new romantic prospect represented by the Upright Ace of Clubs has the capacity for extreme honesty, but not the brutal kind. He has the brand with the warm eyes and gentle smile that speaks to his understanding of the human condition. He will simply lay his hand on top of yours and you'll feel grounded and loved because he touched you.

Suddenly, all your clever dating strategies will evaporate. This man will feel strongly attracted to you, but not in a mere sexual way. This attraction emanates from someplace deep inside his soul. And you will feel the same way about him.

RELATIONSHIP: The Ace of Clubs describes a psychic bond. Whether they've been together for a long time or they just met, this couple knows precisely what the other feels from day to day, from moment to moment, even in times of separation. They share a deep, inner connection that feels like something from another lifetime. This is a lasting, spiritual union between two people meant to be together. They could never be with anyone else.

CIRCUMSTANCES: The situation typified by the Ace is lovely, and often takes place in a traditional temple of worship. Catholicism and Judaism fall under the jurisdiction of this card, as do museums, the ballet, and the symphony. The Ace of Clubs governs any environment devoted to conventional means for filling up the soul with the wonder and power of the divine.

The Ace also covers the engagement and the technical buying of the ring. It defines the precious moment when two shining faces peer through the glass and spot the everlasting symbol of their union. This is an ecstatic experience neither of them will ever forget.

REVERSED

The Reversed Ace is logic instead of intuition.

INDIVIDUAL: This person feels the psychic connection but can't put it into words because he doesn't trust in intuition. So he takes action to show how he feels. He does things like fix your car on his one day off, or volunteer to take you to the airport.

If you're wondering if your man loves you, and you can't tell because he's so quiet and not a mushy kinda guy, the Reversed Ace shows the truth. If he does things that aren't convenient for him but are designed to accommodate you, he loves you. If he says he doesn't want to come over Saturday night because it's raining and he doesn't want to drive twenty minutes in the rain, he doesn't love you. He can't say the words yet, but you're being shown. His actions are logical instead of intuitive.

Regardless of whether your alliance is old or new, the Reversed Ace says it would be wise to stand back to determine if your lover will come through as promised. It recommends you examine the evidence if you want to ascertain his feelings for you. This is a good exercise and every woman ought to do it once a month. Sit down with a cup of coffee and make a list of the actions he took over the past few weeks to nurture you or your household. Did he help clean out your mother's garage? Did he pick your kid up from soccer? Did he loan you his truck, drive your grandmother to her doctor, or install the curtain rods? His actions are symbolic of his feelings for you, and every single one is a long-stemmed red rose to him.

RELATIONSHIP: The romance represented by the Reversed Ace is a great one. These two assume the best way to express their love is through thoughtful behaviors meant to support their union. This couple is solid for one another. They call when they say they will, they don't make plans without consulting each other, and they always deliver their share of the rent on the first of the month.

This is a pair who understands their relationship exists solely between the two of them. How their parents, or their friends, or the actors in the movie choose to conduct their romance is of no consequence to these two. They take actions to nurture and support their connection, which just happens to insulate them from outside influences, and that's fine with them.

If you were to make a list of the Top Ten Best Relationships ever, the Reversed Ace would represent most of them.

CIRCUMSTANCES: The Reversed card stands for unconventional temples of worship like Alcoholics Anonymous, New Age spiritualist churches, or *I Ching* meditation groups. The card represents any religion or belief system you were not born into.

NOTE

The Ace of Clubs is a card of enlightenment. Its luminous presence foretells truth and beauty regardless of whether it falls Upright or Reversed or what aspect of life it comments upon. It doesn't add to a relationship, it's the *essence* of relating.

UPRIGHT or REVERSED: The Ace of Clubs is always a "Yes."

Two of Clubs

Twos: Union
Clubs: Social and Spiritual

COMMUNICATION

If you want to understand the Two, you have to picture your-self seated at a desk with the phone tucked under your chin. While you chat, you have to slip a piece of paper into the fax with your left hand and scroll through your e-mail with your right hand. To comprehend the Two, imagine driving from the dry cleaners, to the grocery, to the dentist, to the post office, to the gas station, to the bank, all on your way to pick up the kids at school. Now, if you can do this with the cell phone pressed against your ear, you understand the card.

UPRIGHT

INDIVIDUAL: The Two of Clubs individual lives a life of nonstop minor activity and endless conversation. This one spends his evenings on the telephone, but call waiting and side conversations constantly interrupt him. He seems scattered or unfocused because he never performs one function at a time.

The new lover described by the Two is chatty and spontaneous. He'll call you while he waits in line at the bank. He'll regale you with witty stories about people you don't know between sips of mocha latte while he fills out his deposit form. The man described by the Two of Clubs may not be the most soulful, most romantic prospect you'll ever meet, but he'll be bright, funny, flirtatious, and a lot of fun. Bear in mind, though, that yours won't be the only number programmed into his speed dial.

RELATIONSHIP: This one is an online romance, and it's probably one of several. The whole relationship is just a series of phone calls or e-mail messages.

The Two of Clubs union isn't significant because it hasn't evolved beyond a superficial level. Until such time as another card comes to define it, the connection won't have enough substance to be called a relationship.

CIRCUMSTANCES: This environment is busy, noisy, and propelled by caffeine. The home or car described by the Two is the one you found online. The job is a telemarketing position, a writing assignment, or has something to do with computers.

REVERSED

The Reversed Card is reluctant to run all those errands or to make all those calls.

INDIVIDUAL: The person represented by the Reversed Two is the social butterfly who converses so vaguely that you'll wonder if their talk actually qualifies as conversation at all. This is a vacuous individual who has authored some of the most superficial dialogue ever conducted over cocktails. Their prattle is so light and breezy that it never actually lands on a topic.

The new romantic prospect defined by the Reversed Two will have a short attention span. He'll flit from girl to girl, tell each of them the same lame anecdotes, beg for their numbers, and forget to call.

RELATIONSHIP: The marriage partners represented by the Reversed Two of Clubs may not be on speaking terms. These two aren't connected at a deep, emotionally satisfying level. They don't converse in a way that communicates their dreams and fears. Instead, they exchange bits of information about the kids and the party at the neighbor's house next Saturday.

As a predictor for a new romance, the Reversed Two says he may never call. If he does, he'll leave a message on your machine. In general, this man isn't interested in how lovely, bright, and special you are. He's only interested in another number he can dial when he gets bored. Therefore, he'll call at surprising times, have nothing to talk about, and won't ask for a date. Keep looking. You can do better.

CIRCUMSTANCES: Sometimes the card stands for a call we don't want to make. Like the one to the landlord to tell him you don't quite have the rent yet.

NOTE

If you're consulting the oracle because you want to know if that special someone will call, Upright they will. Reversed, they won't.

UPRIGHT: A small thin "Yes."
REVERSED: Sort of "No."

Three of Clubs

Threes: Expansion
Clubs: Social and Spiritual

LIES, GOSSIP, AND DENIAL

If I was in denial I think I'd know it.
—NAME WITHHELD

The Three of Clubs is the card of gossip, of calling each other up and speculating about the neighbors. The Three is a light, chatty little card that doesn't intend any harm; it only means to spread the news.

My girlfriend Kathie says we can get away with saying terrible things about people if we just add "Bless her heart" at the end. (Not that Kathie would say anything malicious and then try to pour sugar on it, you understand. She's just pointing out that other people have been known to.) For example: *"That poor, misguided Sue Ellen has slept with everyone from the grocery boy to the mayor, bless her heart."* Or, *"Grandpa Joe smelled like a brewery by 8 A.M. every day of his life, bless his heart."* I thought I'd add this morsel because it's an unusual brand of gossip, from the hit-and-run school and a personal favorite of mine.

I once read a book about the evil of gossip. It said gossip is really an expression of our rage. We tell on people because we're angry with them. I have to confess that I do that. If one of my girlfriends hurts my feelings, fails to return a blouse, or flirts with my boyfriend, I make sure I work the anecdote into my next conversation with our other girlfriends. This is a terrible and very petty character flaw of mine, but all my friends do the same thing, *bless their hearts.*

UPRIGHT

INDIVIDUAL: The individual defined by the Upright Three of Clubs loves to chat up new people and be the first to report back to his friends with the gory details. He enjoys reading the *National Enquirer* and watching the entertainment gossip shows on TV. He knows the latest dish on all the celebrities, the status of the famous trials, and the contract disputes of popular athletes. He thinks gossip is entertaining and believes it's harmless, except when the harsh light of examination shines on his own life. Then he overreacts horribly. This person could easily find a career talking about people, which means he could be a reporter or columnist for the society section.

The brand-new romantic prospect defined by the Upright Three is someone you've heard about. He's your cousin's neighbor or he's her boss and you've already heard every detail of the brilliant contract he negotiated with the European manufacturer. Your cousin goes on and on about how dreamy he is. You know how glad she is he's getting a divorce from that horrible woman and is finally free to date you. When she drags you to her company picnic and introduces you to him, you'll already know a great deal about him—more than he could possibly imagine.

RELATIONSHIP: Regardless of whether this union is new or established, the Upright Three of Clubs says it's fodder for gossip. There's something so exceptional about this connection that other people feel compelled to comment on it. Maybe your sweetie is your ex-husband's brother, or maybe he's a Christian minister and you're an exotic dancer. In any event, the Three of Clubs attachment is notable for its hot-topic value.

The new romance defined by the Three may end before it begins because of its tremendous potential for scandal.

CIRCUMSTANCES: Everybody you know is talking about you when the Three appears. The gossip will get back to you in the way children play the "telephone" game. That's the game where kids sit in a circle on the floor and one child whispers a secret into the ear of the child seated next to him and that one passes it on. The secret is told around the circle until it comes back to the first one, who hears his own words distorted into an entirely different message, much to the delight of the whole group.

The Three is a warning not to overreact when you're the object of gossip because the rumor is twisted and exaggerated. The Three wants you to stay calm because your composure in the face of disgrace will pay off for you.

Someone will casually mention the house, car, or job represented by the Upright Card. You will hear about it in passing and if you recognize it as an opportunity, you can be the first to inquire about it.

REVERSED

The Reversed card is the card of lying. But it's also the card of denial because denial is a way of lying to the self. Think of the alcoholic who claims he only had a couple of cocktails before dinner. Or the overweight guy who says, "Gee, all I ate was a piece of chocolate." (Anyone on a diet knows you can't eat *chocolate!*) Or the housewife who turns a blind eye toward her philandering husband and druggie son because she can't face the horrible truth about either of them. The Upright or Reversed position describes the *degree* of the denial, the Reversed card being total la-la land.

INDIVIDUAL: The Reversed Three darkens to describe a malicious gossip. This person is an evil soul who'll invent any story he believes will manipulate a person or situation to his advantage. It's his nature to seduce the person with the power, money, or love he seeks. He just flat out butters them up one side and down the other and will destroy anybody who interferes with the process. Should you catch him in a lie, he'll accuse you of picking on him. He'll snivel and whine and shed a real tear when he tells Mr./Mrs. Powerful how mean you are. This guy will destroy your character by claiming you said or did things you would never say or do and even your friends will believe him. He's a ruthless stinker with an ugly talent.

The Reversed Three also stands for the caustic, catty raconteur in your clique who likes to be the center of attention. He or she has a bitchy, witty style that hurts. This one's clever, but mean.

If the man represented by the Reversed Three asks you out, don't go. He'll lie to you, seduce you, and then brag about it.

RELATIONSHIP: The couple described by the Reversed Three of Clubs presents a false front to the world. They don't tell the truth about their finances, their past, or their families. They'll claim they bought their condo after they sold their old one, but in truth they're renters. If they tell you they're working on a screenplay and drop the names of the famous people they know in Hollywood, don't believe them. They lease their Porsche and they borrowed their beach house.

If the Reversed card describes a brand-new alliance, your new partner isn't telling the truth about his circumstances. Don't get involved in the union represented by the Reversed Three.

CIRCUMSTANCES: The Three stands for jobs in advertising or fiction writing. The novels described by the Reversed card don't contain a shred of personal experience. They're brilliant, original, and completely made up.

The ad in the paper for this car, job, or apartment wasn't entirely forthcoming. Take the car to a mechanic, call the Better Business Bureau about the workplace, and ask the neighbors what the landlord is like. What you hear will disappoint you. Unless you write fiction for a living, the Reversed Three of Clubs presents an entirely dishonest situation. Be careful when you see the card.

NOTE

We're all guilty of gossip, of fibbing a bit, and certainly of a little denial. But you've pulled *this* card and that's significant. When the Three appears Upright, it's a warning to guard your temper and to be cool while you're the object of gossip. Try to hold the truth in your heart and have faith that eventually you will be seen for who and what you are.

When the Three of Clubs falls Reversed, open your eyes and inspect the facts because you're in denial or being deceived. Plus, there's a distinct possibility that you're being overly clever about other people's idiosyncrasies.

UPRIGHT or REVERSED: Either way, this card is a "No."

Four of Clubs

Fours: Effort
Clubs: Social and Spiritual

SELF-ESTEEM

UPRIGHT

The Upright Four of Clubs is the card of high self-esteem, which we don't want to confuse with the sparkly, toothy grin in the bathroom mirror, called vanity. The Four describes a deeply rooted self-approval that is the natural consequence of a belief in one's fundamental goodness, personal values, and standards. The Four of Clubs isn't a card of good bone structure, a hot body, status car, or designer wardrobe. The Four is deeper than that. It's the card of self-assurance and self-respect.

INDIVIDUAL: The individual described by the Upright card is poised, idealistic, and humane. He understands the key to self-confidence is to accept himself as he is, to recognize that he's flawed but love worthy despite his flaws.

The character represented by the Four isn't vain, cocky, or arrogant. He's sensitive, humble, and radiates a warmth and vulnerability that's attractive and seductive without being sexual. This person is friendly, kind, and genuine.

The brand-new lover represented by the card will pull you in with his openness and willingness to expose his heart. He's nice to everyone but he doesn't take up with just anybody. He's not interested in a needy woman who will try to hook his sympathetic side. He isn't attracted to gals who drink, run up credit cards, or fool around with other men.

The Four of Clubs man is aware of how insidious low self-esteem can be, that it creeps into all your affairs and contaminates them. He doesn't need a constant reminder of how awful it is to feel unworthy or incompetent and he doesn't need a boy toy or buxom showgirl hanging off his right arm to feel good about himself. What he does need is a gal with an unshakable faith in her own spirit and abilities.

RELATIONSHIP: The Four of Clubs is the card of commitment. To make a deep and lasting commitment to another, you have to be committed to yourself. You can't truly love anyone else if you don't love yourself.

Therefore, when you pull the Upright Four to answer the question "Will he marry me?" the card says he loves both himself and you, that he's totally committed to the union and will indeed marry you. It also says that he put a lot of thought into the decision to spend the rest of his life with you. He hasn't chosen you because of your money, appearance, or social position. He's committed his life to yours because you're the one he respects the most and gets along with the best. The Upright Four says he believes he made the right choice too.

The brand-new union represented by the Four will be positive, sane, and loving. This connection will go further and do better than you could possibly imagine at this time.

CIRCUMSTANCES: These circumstances are some of the best in the deck and they'll turn out better than you think. Jump at the opportunity to rent, drive, work for, eat at, live in, or brush your teeth with any substance defined by the Upright Four of Clubs.

REVERSED

INDIVIDUAL: The Reversed Four individual hears a barrage of negative, ancient, parental messages echoing inside his head. This person is hard on himself, critical of his own talents and abilities, and judgmental toward others. He suffers from low self-esteem. Under no circumstance does he believe that he's good enough just as he is. He always feels defective or inadequate so he shields himself with a perfect wardrobe, extreme acts of kindness and generosity, or else refuses to participate in romance at all, often for a lifetime. This guy hides behind a barricade of the "right" people, clothes, cars, houses, sugary niceness, or prickly indignation. His issues can turn him into a martyred saint or a condescending, arrogant jerk, neither of which is normal.

Another manifestation of low self-esteem is the need to be right all the time. If the Reversed Four person can prove that you're wrong either by asserting his moral superiority or by shouting you down, his opinion of himself will rise in direct proportion to the amount he puts you down. It doesn't matter if he gets it right, what matters is whether or not you can prove him wrong. If you can't, then he's right by default. Ergo, he's the superior person by default too. Checkmate.

Good luck with the individual whose ego is so damaged that he adopts the superiority game to bolster his self-esteem. This one believes that he's got his issue "under control" and if you don't agree, he'll be happy to straighten you out on that topic too.

In reality, the person depicted by the Reversed Four has a pair of shutters locked closed across the sunshine of his heart. If he were to open those shutters and allow others to feel more of his personal radiance, he would be happier. If he opened up, even a crack, he'd be able to hear the regard and affection that's been flowing toward him all along. Until now he hasn't been able to receive messages of love and support because the shutters have been locked across his heart. A little more friendliness on the part of this individual will make him happier than he can imagine.

Because the new romantic interest defined by the Reversed Four doesn't truly love himself he doesn't have the capacity to love anyone else, including you. In response to the question "Will he marry me?" the Reversed Four says, "No." He doesn't love himself enough to love another person so he won't tie his life to yours. Any commitment he is able to make will be insincere, shallow, or fear based. At best, his idea of engagement or marriage will be shaky and subject to revision. At worst, your romance will just be another in a long chain of brief liaisons with stormy endings because he can't commit.

RELATIONSHIP: The couple described by the Reversed Four of Clubs has their shirts handmade on Bond Street in London. They know of a "brilliant!" little Italian man tucked away in an obscure corner of Los Angeles who handcrafts their shoes. They know the owner of the most chic restaurant in Beverly Hills where they send their salads back if the lettuce isn't crisp or the vinegar has been uncorked too long. They know the lead singer in the band personally and vacation with their famous friends in the south of France.

People who know these two call them shallow, but superficiality isn't their problem. They're preoccupied with prestigious, elitist consumption because when talented, brilliant, famous people accept them, it means they're special, too, which bolsters their self-confidence. Their real problem is the chorus of critical, judgmental voices singing inside their heads. These poor snobs don't believe anything they do is good enough so they surround themselves with people, places, and things that reflect well on them, which makes them feel worthy.

The twenty-year marriage described by the Reversed Four is held together by guilt and shame. Neither of these people actually *wants* to be married to the other, but they stay together because they're afraid to join the singles scene or to lose the high-image lifestyle they've put together. Both parties fear they couldn't create a stylish life on their own or that they're worthwhile people without one, so they stay married and stay miserable.

The brand-new romance described by the card won't go very far. Issues of low self-esteem will cloud even the first few dates, which will manifest as self-denigration, neediness, or bragging and name dropping. You won't be able to get enough from one another emotionally so the romance ought to fizzle out pretty quick.

CIRCUMSTANCES: The car, apartment, or job represented by the Reversed Four will either be "beneath" you or you won't feel you're "good enough" for it. Don't get involved in circumstances represented by the Reversed card. They won't promote high self-esteem.

NOTE

There's a way out for the individual defined by the Reversed Four, but the road to self-love is not an easy one. You have to do the hard stuff, like accept your flaws and learn to silence the mean-talking voice inside your head. It helps to have evidence of your own goodness, too, so I suggest you donate your time to charity. When you read to children at the library, sponsor a school in a Third World nation, or visit an AIDS ward, you make real cash deposits into the self-esteem bank. Instead of buying a glamorous, status dog to flatter yourself and look good to the neighbors, rescue an elderly one from a shelter. Kind acts build self-esteem, not cars, clothes, or the right reservations. I suggest that you contribute where it really counts, where *you* really count. Maybe you could take a shift delivering meals to shut-ins.

UPRIGHT: A greater "Yes" than you may realize.
REVERSED: "No."

Five of Clubs

Fives: Conflict
Clubs: Social and Spiritual

Confronted by outstanding merit in another,
there is no way of saving one's ego except by love.
—Johann Wolfgang von Goethe

COMPETITION

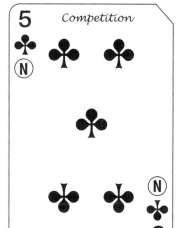

Think of how often we pit ourselves against one another:

We smile at our coworkers as we secretly hope to be the one who gets the promotion. We circle the mall parking lot like vultures looking for a prime spot. Even in the warmth of our own homes, siblings struggle for attention from Mom and Dad, who don't notice because they're busy arm wrestling for control of the TV. Women dye their hair, wear makeup, and starve on salad to be more attractive than one another.

Our competitors are usually close to our age. We may even have an underlying fondness for them or respect their skillful maneuvers. Ordinarily we like our opponents and recognize our similarities to them while we harbor jealousies toward them too.

UPRIGHT

The Upright Five depicts the kind of good-natured competition we feel when our best friend is able to shed a couple of pounds and find a better hairstyle. We're happy for her, but a part of us rises to the challenge and buys a new dress.

Let's say you asked the question "How do I get my old boyfriend back?" and you pulled the Upright Five. The card is telling you to become more of a competitor. Get your hair done, lose some weight, or buy a pretty sweater because you need to beat the competition—which is always another woman. (Hopefully not his mother.)

There's a second meaning for the Upright Five. The feeling of being overwhelmed belongs here. The second meaning is related to the first in that competition is too much for some people. If you were raised to believe competition is impolite, or if you're unable to compete, you may be turned off by rivalry or not feel up to the challenge of it.

INDIVIDUAL: The boyfriend or husband described by the Five always knows where he stands in relation to others. When in love, he measures his appearance, his money, and his athletic prowess against the other men in his social circle. At work, he's the number one salesman because he makes it his business to know everyone's sales figures and he's not content until his are the best. He designs his romantic gestures to outdistance his friend's gestures. He'll fly you to Paris and propose on top of the Eiffel Tower just so no one's engagement story can compete with his.

Another variation on the romantic partner represented by the Upright Five is a man who's easily overwhelmed by the demands of an average relationship. More than two phone calls a week feels like pressure to him and your desire to make love all night is overwhelming. If you like this guy enough to cater to him, plan on a slow pace, sudden disappearances, and to keep a roll of paper towels handy. You'll need the towels to blot his sweaty brow and dab cool water on his wrists during his bouts of emotional claustrophobia.

RELATIONSHIP: These two pepper their relationship with good-natured competition. It's a marriage between lawyers who debate the virtues of butter versus margarine over breakfast. This duo takes turns playing devil's advocate for the sheer pleasure of the exercise.

The new prospect represented by the Five is hard to snag. Other women are interested in him, so you'll have to pull out all your ammunition. Buy a sexy dress, touch up your roots, and practice tossing your mane while you laugh at his jokes. You could use the bathroom mirror to rehearse staring at him, wide eyed, and whispering, "How brilliant. I never thought of it like that." Or you could refuse to compete for a man this way, decide it's an overwhelming task, and go meet someone new.

CIRCUMSTANCES: If you want this house, job, or car you'll have to compete for it. You'll have to send a fruit basket to your loan officer, refer a couple of clients to your prospective employer, or slip the car salesman a fifty to tear up the other guy's application. Even if you beat the competition, you may not enjoy the car/house/job defined by the Five. Owning it, living there, or working for this company may be overwhelming.

REVERSED

When the Five falls Reversed the competition gets ferocious and personal. The Reversed Five of Clubs is the card of jealousy.

INDIVIDUAL: This boyfriend or husband is a nightmare. He's the possessive type who creates an angry scene if you dare to walk out the door in a skirt above the knee. He fires questions at you like:

"Where are you going?"

"Why are you dressed like that?"

"Who are you meeting?"

He becomes enraged if he thinks another man looked at you at the movies. This man is verbal and paranoid, plus he's capable of stalking. He'll follow you to work, to your sister's house, or to church just to be sure you go where you said you were going.

When the Reversed Five describes you, you're the kind of woman who's jealous of her boyfriend's kids. If he has them for the weekend you feel betrayed because it was supposed to be "your time." You're the crazy girl who confronts her man because he wants to shoot pool with a friend on Friday night, or he can't account for an hour of his Saturday afternoon. You reason that if your man's not in your physical presence he must be with another woman. You're exhausting to date and most men will dump you because of your lack of trust.

In reality, the individual represented by the Reversed Five feels overwhelmed by his competitor's superiority. He believes he's at a disadvantage because he doesn't have comparable talents and skills. He might be right.

RELATIONSHIP: The alliance described by the Reversed Five is a freak show of jealousies. This couple can't go to a simple dinner party without heated accusations.

"I saw the way you looked at her!"

"If you like him so much why don't you just go home with him?!"

All relationships described by the Five have competition at their core. The Reversed Five says the core has eroded into jealousy. Both parties to this marriage know which of them earns more money, which is the better looking, or who has more friends. They have a long history of affectionate put-downs. This is the scenario where the woman gave up her own ambitions to support her husband while he went to medical school. Now she lives an idle life in the suburbs, envious of her husband's education and career. She takes potshots at him in public, laughs at his plastic surgery practice, and calls him Dr. Boobs behind his back.

If you pulled the Reversed card to represent a new love interest, don't return his calls anymore. This relationship doesn't have the potential to become a sane, rational, mutually supportive association.

CIRCUMSTANCES: Under these circumstances, you don't just envy your peers; you kind of hate them, obsess over their flaws, and plot against them. Don't think for a moment they haven't noticed. They probably feel the same way about you.

The car, job, or apartment described by the Reversed Five will be too great a challenge to obtain. Twenty other people have applied for it and they're more qualified than you are. Find another one.

NOTE

The Five of Clubs wants us to acknowledge the admiration we feel for those who incite us to compete. The card wants us to recognize that our opponents challenge us and raise our own performance level.

Admiring your competitor is a tough assignment when you're losing your boyfriend to another woman. But metaphysics teaches "What is ours can never be taken from us, and what is not ours can never stay." If your boyfriend took off with a new girl, let him go. The man who's right for you would never leave you or value another woman above you. Be happy for your boyfriend. Let him win the race to the altar. You'll stand there yourself when the time and the man are right.

Jealousy is the most painful of emotions, therefore the Five of Clubs asks you to look into the heart of your competitor and be happy for her.

Be glad she found love or prosperity, because her struggle is no different from your own. The Five warns against pride and preaches that modesty will cement your friendships while arrogance will alienate those you respect.

When the Five of Clubs appears in your spread Upright or Reversed, you'll stand in comparison to another person. In all probability the other gal will win and you'll be obligated to shake her hand in the spirit of good sportsmanship.

UPRIGHT or REVERSED: It's a "No" card either way.

Six of Clubs

Sixes: Faith
Clubs: Social and Spiritual

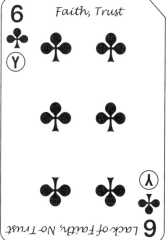

When theology masters religion, religion dies: it becomes a doctrine instead of a life.
—THE URANTIA BOOK

FAITH

The Ace of Clubs represents your religion or personal system of worship. The Six of Clubs stands for the daily application of your spiritual beliefs. People think these two functions overlap, but they don't. Churches and Twelve-Step meetings are venues for gathering together. They attract like-thinking souls who support one another's efforts to cultivate their spirituality and provide a group identity. But, inevitably, the day comes when you're all alone and have to decide if you'll pick up the twenty-dollar bill on the supermarket floor and hand it back to the lady who dropped it or put it in your pocket. Your pastor or your sponsor won't be standing there that day.

The Six of Clubs is the card of the *application* of your faith. It stands for the belief that a loving, benevolent higher power will protect and provide for you. The Six is the card of what you do when no one is looking, which is the true measure of your character.

The ancient Gypsy tradition of card divination suggests a second interpretation. The Gypsies believed the Six was a card of celebration, that it rules dancing, merriment, and intoxication, so it's also the card of alcohol.

UPRIGHT

The Sixes are cards of faith and the Clubs represent our culture and spirituality. These two components combine to describe the faith we place both in mankind and in our higher power. The Six of Clubs is the card of our collective consciousness.

Primarily, the Upright Six of Clubs describes the ability to go with the flow, to "Let go and let God." It's the card of handing over control to the Universe.

In modern times, we rise to the challenge of the Upright Six when we accept a date. Agreeing to see a movie with an unfamiliar person is an act of faith. It says we believe the members of our society are bound by a uniform code of conduct. Our acceptance of the date says we believe our date observes the same codes we do. Therefore, it's safe to entrust our physical bodies to his care.

Let's imagine a friend of ours went to her college roommate's wedding where she met a handsome friend of the groom's. Let's say they shared a glass of champagne, danced, and before she left, she gave him her home phone number. Later that week, the groom's friend called her and made a date to meet downtown for coffee. That went well, he called again, and they made another date for dinner. Now let's suppose on the night of the big dinner date, the guy came to her house with flowers, escorted her to his sports car, and drove away with her.

Reality Check! *Our girl just got into a car with a relative stranger who has complete control of the car and outweighs her by seventy pounds!*

She doesn't know anything about her date other than he's cute, drives a sports car, and his friend married her friend. For all she knows, he could be Ted Bundy or Charlie Manson. *What is she thinking?*

Well, for one thing, she's thinking, We have a mutual friend, we spoke on the phone, he seems normal, and he showed up on time for the coffee date. She knows that at some point she has to put her trust in him and in our culture as a whole. She knows she can place her faith in the rules of social deportment, which dictate how he's supposed to act. We girls should acknowledge that when she gets into his car, she's placing her faith in humanity as a whole, in society in general, and in him in particular.

INDIVIDUAL: The Six of Clubs describes a man who's a lot of fun. This guy loves to dance and party, but he also has a deep and wondrous faith in his maker.

Sometimes the Six of Clubs says you're dating the man just so you can tell your girlfriends you went out on Saturday night. If so, look at him more closely. He's a sleeper and a keeper. As you get to know him, you'll discover he's someone you can trust with your secrets, heart, and body. You'll find he's candid, positive, and faithful. He's the guy described above who stopped the old lady in the supermarket to give her back her twenty.

The man represented by the Six tends to be average looking at first but he'll grow on you. Over time, his wholesome sandy hair and freckles will come to represent character. This one has a hearty laugh, strength of purpose, and a quiet morality. He's stronger than he looks and you can trust him.

RELATIONSHIP: The old married couple described by the Upright Six of Clubs has faith in one another. They believe in their partner more than they believe in any other person in the world. These two are bound together by their spirituality. They may not attend a traditional temple of worship, but they've organized their life around their belief in a just and benevolent God.

The brand-new union described by the Six is in the early dating stage. Pull another card if you want to know how the connection will progress.

CIRCUMSTANCES: Any job, house, or car represented by the Upright Six of Clubs is low-key but solid. This is a corporation, rental management company, or auto dealer you can trust because an honorable soul is calling the shots behind the scenes. As a result, things will only improve with time. Say "Yes." Then sit back and watch. You're going to be pleased.

REVERSED

The Reversed Six of Clubs is the card of a lack of faith. It describes the inability to trust.

INDIVIDUAL: The Reversed Six shows us a man who's unable or unwilling to place his faith in a higher power. This one feels the pressure to release his grip, to let go and surrender, but he can't do it. He hangs on in the vain belief that he can control his life.

The Reversed Six person has realistic, disturbing, prophetic dreams that he pushes aside, but they haunt him anyway. Sometimes he turns to alcohol to numb his psychic nerve endings, but it can take a heap of cocktails to deaden sensory impressions. The Reversed Six stands for the addicts among us. Addictive personalities are actually sensitive, vulnerable, open channels who grow up in homes that don't trust intuition. Very sensitive men can sometimes turn to drugs and alcohol in an attempt to tone down the psychic impressions they pick up twenty-four hours a day like a radio receiving station.

In order to Upright his card, the sensitive, emotional Reversed Six man must allow a sense of God to enter his life. If he were to relax and surrender to the weightlessness of not being in control, synchronicity would guide him.

The Reversed Six personality can trace his current lack of faith to his original mistrust of the powerful parental supreme beings of his infancy. His parents taught him to conceal his feelings and rely instead on superficial charm. Mom and Dad probably fought constantly and violently. And, when their child asked if they were going to get a divorce, they told him no, that they were just having a discussion. Their denial created a huge problem for the child, because his parents didn't validate his perception of reality. The man represented by the Reversed Six couldn't trust his original supreme beings to confirm his intuitive impressions or to be honest with him, so he lives his adult life with an ancient, sort of hysterical mistrust in God.

Another version of the Reversed Six man is someone who has allowed the celebration to go too far. He's one of those loud, collegiate young men who party rough and drunk. Those guys think they're fun, but they're really just loud and obnoxious.

If you drew the Reversed Six to describe your new boyfriend, the card doesn't automatically say he's an alcoholic. It might be a warning not to trust him or that he doesn't trust you. The spread you're using and the cards surrounding the Six will tell you which meaning applies to your situation. You can always pull additional cards if you want more information about the Six.

If the Reversed Six describes you, go back to the top of this section and read it again. Then you might want to buy a copy of *Conversations with God* by Neale Donald Walsch.

RELATIONSHIP: The established couple depicted by the Reversed Six doesn't have much faith in their union, perhaps for good reason.

Additional cards will describe why they don't believe in their marriage or in one another.

You won't trust the new lover represented by the Reversed Six. In fact, some tiny place in your heart already doubts this relationship, or you wouldn't have drawn the card.

CIRCUMSTANCES: Although these circumstances are quite positive, you won't be inclined to surrender to them, so they may not work out. As regards this car, house, dog, or job, plan to hand the decision over to the Universe. If it's meant to be, it will be, and nothing you can do will pull it toward you or push it away.

NOTE

The Upright Six of Clubs is the card of the *application* of our belief system. It stands for the Golden Rule and our spiritual practices. When the card appears Upright in your spread, simply let go and allow the Universe to take over. When the Six falls Reversed, you might want to check your alcohol intake and pay more attention to your dreams.

Whether it's Upright or Reversed, the Six of Clubs says listen to your heart. That edgy feeling and the whispers inside your heart are your Higher Power showing you the way.

UPRIGHT: "Oh, yes!"
REVERSED: "Yeah, because no matter how big a sinner you are, Jesus still loves you."

Seven of Clubs

Sevens: Tension
Clubs: Social and Spiritual

ORDER VERSUS CHAOS

UPRIGHT

The Upright Seven of Clubs describes the ability to take on complicated clerical tasks and see them through to completion.

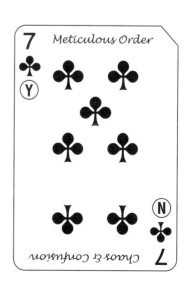

It's the card of tax returns, term papers, and loan documents. The Upright card stands for the ability to set aside exhaustion, exemption, or boredom and buckle down until the project is finished, regardless of what time or what day it is.

INDIVIDUAL: The person represented by the Upright Seven is organized, efficient, and has an enormous capacity for detailed work. These are the folks who alphabetize their canned goods and color code their sock drawer.

As a romantic interest, Seven of Clubs types are fussy. They don't relax into lovemaking until they've folded back the bedspread, brushed their teeth, taken off their watch, and neatly hung up their clothes. They like to regulate their activities into a systematic formula because spontaneity makes them nervous. One-night stands are out of the question.

Once they've completed their bedtime rituals they make interesting lovers. You'd never dream how imaginative and hardworking they are once you get them between the sheets.

RELATIONSHIP: The success or failure of the Seven of Clubs relationship depends upon the couple's ability to sort out the details. This is the wedding that will take place as soon as he finishes college, buys a car, and pays off his credit cards. That is, if she sold the junk in her storage unit, went to court one last time to finalize her divorce, and moved a hundred miles north to live with him.

The long-term relationship described by the Seven works quite well because these two have organized their life into a system. Laundry day is Saturday and grocery day is Sunday. Monday is bill paying, Tuesday is house cleaning, and Wednesday night is sex night. Thursday is mambo class and bowling is on Fridays. These two pay for their vacations six months in advance and their Christmas gifts are wrapped by Halloween.

The new love interest represented by the Upright Seven of Clubs will call a week in advance to schedule a date. When he picks you up, he could very well hand you a copy of your itinerary for the evening. On the positive side, once he decides you're the right girl to fill the empty slot marked "girlfriend," you'll have a date every Saturday night for the rest of your life. On the negative side, should you find his relentless adherence to routines claustrophobic and suggest an unscheduled activity, he may view your need for variety as evidence of your chaotic nature and leave you.

CIRCUMSTANCES: The Upright Seven of Clubs says there's a stack of papers on the corner of your desk that needs attention. The primary message of the Upright card is *Process those papers.* It says, Watch the details and stay on top of the job until you've entered every tiny number into every skinny column because if you don't you'll be sorry.

The response to any question about a car, house, or job depends upon whether the paperwork was filled out correctly and submitted on time.

REVERSED

The Reversed Seven of Clubs is the card of chaos and the premature assumption that all is well. The Reversed card describes a person who brings home his pay, writes out the checks to pay his bills, puts the checks in envelopes, and affixes the stamps. Then he tucks the envelopes into his jacket pocket and forgets to mail them. His failure to drop the envelopes into a mailbox will have far-reaching results. The electric bill won't be paid and neither will the rent, phone, Visa, car payment, insurance, cable TV, cleaning lady, or Internet service. He'll be in danger of eviction, disconnection, and late fees. His premature assumption that all is well will create an amazing amount of chaos.

INDIVIDUAL: The Reversed Seven stands for a person who knows what he's supposed to do, and does most of it. Near the end, he sets the project aside because he can see the light at the end of the tunnel and figures, "Piece of cake, I can finish in no time." Then he forgets something or falls behind so the job isn't completed on schedule. His easy attitude creates chaos and he builds a reputation for unreliability.

The Reversed Seven lover is charming, but vague. He thinks, "Oh, I'll just decide later what I want, or how I feel. It's all good anyway." To him, his looseness reflects his hopefulness. Others see him as ungrounded, airheaded, or as making decisions based on whims. The Reversed Seven of Clubs person thinks his mind-set is buoyant and cheery, but his attitude leaves others feeling disoriented and manipulated. This person needs to tighten up his act and develop stronger principles or rules of conduct. He should learn to make decisions and *keep to them.* Being "casual" or "flexible" are not positive traits when the Seven is involved.

RELATIONSHIP: If you pulled the Reversed Seven to describe a new liaison, don't get your hopes up. The card says your coupling will be disorganized, careless, and, as a result, unreliable. You and your partner won't call each other when you say you will and you won't show up on time either. You won't know where you stand, where he stands, or what's going on with your relationship. The word "flaky" comes up a lot around the Reversed card and it will certainly come to define your connection.

The established couple represented by the Reversed Seven doesn't know what to make of their alliance. Nobody seems to be in charge of it. No one is responsible for the housework or for earning a steady paycheck. Their kids get to school when they get there. These two are wandering through life loosely connected to one another with no particular direction or purpose.

CIRCUMSTANCES: Vague and unreliable, the circumstances ruled by the Seven of Clubs may not even happen. This landlord could accept deposits from three different prospects. This car doesn't always start in the morning and no one at your workplace knows what your job actually is. Don't invest your money or your time in any situation represented by the Reversed Seven of Clubs.

NOTE

Upright, the Seven foretells success because of your ability to pay attention to the details. The Upright card is meticulous and persevering, if a bit anal.

The Reversed card says the details have been neglected and confusion reigns. It says you need to tighten up your act because the people around you are beginning to use the word "flake."

UPRIGHT: "Hmm . . . Okay. I guess so."
REVERSED: "No!"

Eight of Clubs

Eights: Philosophy
Clubs: Social and Spiritual

I'm built for comfort. I ain't built for speed.
—HOWLIN' WOLF

HAPPINESS

UPRIGHT

When I see the Eight of Clubs, I picture a chart or graph like the ones they use for sales meetings. The chart has a bright red line lurching up and down from end to end across evenly spaced horizontal lines. Except, the horizontal line in the center is gone. In its place is a row of Clubs.

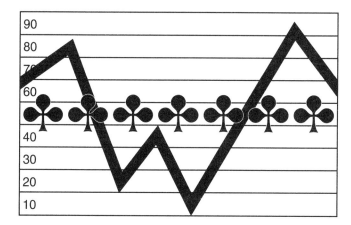

    The Upright Eight represents the string of Clubs in the center of the graph and the bright red line represents life. As the line falls below the band of Clubs, it represents our losses; as it shoots above it shows our gains. The Eight of Clubs has no interest in the line of fate and its fickle ups and downs. Its only concern is with the bar of Clubs in the middle.

    The Eight carries a message about modesty. It says big houses and expensive cars won't make us happy because happiness lies in small daily pleasures. The card believes our gains don't define us any more than our losses do. To the Eight of Clubs, winning the lottery and going bankrupt are not steps up or down at all, they're merely stages in an infinitely shifting universe. Happiness, in Eight of Clubs terms, is the natural by-product of two people who share one blanket, a bowl of popcorn, and a video. Happiness is found walking in the woods, planting tomatoes every spring, and attending your son's football game every fall.

    When you pull the Eight of Clubs, it guarantees you'll be happy, but only if you find your life in the band of clubs. Once you do, outside pressures won't disrupt your harmony. It won't matter whether the red line of fate chooses to propel your life to the heights or to the depths because you'll accept your external circumstances calmly, with grace. This one simple shift in your thinking, the decision to participate in life's small daily pleasures as if money, power, and status were meaningless, will bring you total happiness and complete protection from the whims of fortune.

INDIVIDUAL: The Eight describes a quiet, philosophical soul who is content with his life because he has the key to happiness. This person works at a profession he likes, one he believes is important. He lives beneath his resources, which means he could buy a bigger, fancier house in a nicer neighborhood if he wanted to, but he doesn't need to impress anyone so he doesn't. It means he's a city lawyer five days a week, but a country gardener the other two. He doesn't go to upscale, trendy restaurants on Saturday night. Instead, he gathers his family and friends in his kitchen to sip wine, cook dinner together, and share stories from their busy week. This man enjoys the day-to-day aspect of love. He likes his kids for their individual spirits and talents. He loves his wife because she shares his quiet appreciation of life.

If you've pulled the Upright Eight of Clubs to describe a new romantic prospect, you'll find your connection in small ways. Don't expect champagne and a diamond tennis bracelet for Valentine's Day. Instead, expect roses he grew himself and a dinner he prepared with his own hands. He'll rent your favorite video, pick up your favorite wine, and make love to you for hours. This man is warm and real.

RELATIONSHIP: Do you ever read the personal ads? Not that you need to stoop to the personals, for heaven's sake, but do you read them for fun once in a while? Well, you know how men always submit those ads saying they like to "Walk on the beach at sunset, read poetry, and play with puppy dogs on the floor"? And you know how we girls never believe them because we're not stupid? Well, this couple actually *does that stuff!*

This is the duo whose tastes run toward romantic little moments. They believe their happiness depends on how they interact with one another and not on how they look to the outside world. She tucks love notes in his briefcase. He surprises her with the newest plate from the Franklin Mint. (She has all 350,000 of them displayed on shelves that rim the ceiling of every room in the house.) Locked inside their private world, oblivious to the dramas that most couples engage in, this couple is the happiest, most contented pair you know.

If you pulled the Upright Eight to predict the future of your new romance, you've hit the jackpot. That is, if you can remember not to lust after flashy gestures or a showy lifestyle. When you pull the Eight, you can expect to fall into a quiet little groove with your man. You will jog together, cook together, and hold hands in the grocery store. Yours will be a peaceful and serene connection. You lucky dog.

CIRCUMSTANCES: The Upright Eight stands for contentment and satisfaction. Therefore, any job, home, car, or situation defined by the card will suit you.

REVERSED

INDIVIDUAL: The individual represented by the Reversed Eight doesn't value the modest daily pleasures available all around him. He's guilty of seeking the glamorous life or of dismissing everyday activities as insignificant. He has grandiose ideas about money, prestige, and love. He thinks you need a limo if you're going to the prom and you need to join a country club if you want to play golf. No municipal course for this guy. He's not at peace with himself because he doesn't participate in the small comforts that make up a tranquil existence. He's dissatisfied because he craves the fantasy life he sees on TV and in the movies. He thinks happiness only comes with brand names and it'll arrive just as soon as he buys a yacht and the right aftershave.

RELATIONSHIP: This union is not a pleasant one. Neither party is satisfied with their partner. They both long for someone with more flash, more style, and more oomph. Neither of them value life's small daily pleasures; they think cooking is a drag and so is mowing the lawn. They don't understand that washing the car on a hot Sunday morning, all covered in suds, and squirting each other with the hose is a form of enjoyment. They think it's work and should be hired out.

    The new romance described by the Reversed Eight won't suit you. One of you will be disappointed because his or her goal is to live a modest, humble life and the other will write off the whole arrangement as boring and unglamorous.

CIRCUMSTANCES: The Reversed Eight always leaves a bad taste in your mouth.

    If you pulled the card to describe a new job, car, or home you won't like it. The Reversed card says you'll select your apartment for its glamorous high-rise image but it'll turn out to be too fancy for the real you so you won't be able to relax there. You'll find yourself rattling around the house after dark all alone with a wineglass in one hand and the phone or remote in the other. You ought to ask yourself, "What's the point of an ultramodern apartment with an expensive view, anyway?"

NOTE

The Upright Eight of Clubs is a lovely card of quiet well-being and a blessing to receive because we all seek happiness. If we allow it, the Upright card will guide us to that state of mind. The Reversed Eight struggles to capture the mass media concept of "*HAPPINESS!!*" But satisfaction of that sort only exists for a moment in time, never for the stretch of a life.

UPRIGHT: "Yes."
REVERSED: "No."

Nine of Clubs

Nines: Culmination
Clubs: Social and Spiritual

INTEGRITY

I tend to see this card as the dirt slope we played on when I was a child. It rose up behind the bus stop, in the vacant lot next to our house. The rain carved skinny channels down its face and the wind blew dust into the narrow ravines to fill them up. The summer sun baked the dirt until it was as hard as adobe and then winter storms melted it into mud. We kids played on the slope year-round, regardless of its condition.

A dirt bank is hard to climb, even for a kid. You have to bend over and grasp at rocks and weeds to pull yourself up. You can slide back down on loose pebbles and fall into the crevices cut like scars into the slope. You can crawl up the ravines like a stairway or pull yourself up along the sides the way you use a handrail. But going down is easier because it's faster—a kid can run down the hill. Except, he can build up too much speed and the loose dirt can crumble beneath his feet. He can step into the ravines and twist his ankle or slip and slide down the muddy grade and ruin his clothes. Running down a dirt hill is thrilling, but scary.

The Upright Nine of Clubs represents the climb up the slope. It stands for the creativity of the ascent, for choosing where to put your hands and feet, and the way in which it's an inner game because of the choices a kid makes as he climbs. The Reversed Nine represents the run back down the grade with all the mud and holes and opportunities for disaster.

UPRIGHT

The struggle to climb up the face of the little dirt slope from my childhood illustrates the Upright Nine. It's the labored grasp for a weed, a stone, or a place to put your foot, but progressing nonetheless. It stands for the triumphant moment when you pull yourself on top of the ridge, stand up, look back down the dirt incline, and yell "*Yes!*" while you hop around with both fists in the air.

The Nine of Clubs is a card of general improvement. It represents slow, steady progress in all the major areas of your life. The advancement is the natural by-product of a commitment to your own private ethics and values. Although the Nine says you should be prepared to step off the beaten path and find your own way, to follow your heart at your own speed, it's not a card of isolation. The card only suggests that solitude may be a side effect of the process. The Nine of Clubs says if you're willing to stand up for your convictions, which will take a little fortitude and a lot of backbone, you can expect to see tangible improvements sprinkled throughout your life. Those improvements will manifest as more fulfilling relationships, more money, or better health.

INDIVIDUAL: The Nine of Clubs individual is a man of integrity. He quietly accepts the slow, steady uphill climb. He knows he can undertake it only for himself, by himself, and that his reward will follow.

He moves forward in life in conscientious increments. When he buys a new house, it's the same price as his old one, except the new one is in a better neighborhood. He'll retile the bathroom, varnish the hardwood floors, and turn a profit when he sells it. He knows if he adds twenty extra sit-ups to his morning workout every week he'll firm up and feel more energetic. When he breaks up with his girlfriend he doesn't abandon her. He makes sure she knows that even though she's not the one for him, she's likable and love worthy nonetheless. He's an ethical ex.

The new lover represented by the Upright Nine is a better-quality human being than the guys you usually date. This one will hold you and your new alliance to higher standards than you're accustomed to.

RELATIONSHIP: The old married couple defined by the Upright Nine ascends the dirt slope together and their attachment grows stronger and more intimate as they climb. They're an ethical couple who live by an identical moral code. They would never, ever betray one another. Currently their relationship is building or deepening, which is the result of both parties sticking to their principles.

When you pull the Upright Nine to describe a new connection, you should let your partner take the lead because he's not interested in seducing you. He intends to date you in a polite manner until he ascertains your moral fiber. Then, if you make the cut, he'll move the relationship forward in small but solid increments until he's moved it all the way to the altar. You don't need to defend your honor with the man represented by the Upright Nine because he's more likely to be concerned with the morality of your union than you are.

Please don't make the mistake of thinking this man is a prude just because he doesn't try to make out in the backseat on the first date or because he invited you to church the morning after. Never forget the Nine of Clubs man is a step up. If you want a higher-quality relationship than you've known in the past, let him court you in his own way, at his own speed. You'll be glad you did.

CIRCUMSTANCES: The Nine of Clubs recommends you stick with what you've got. It says you've seen tangible improvements as the natural result of your efforts so you should continue to build on what you have. In regard to a car, house, or job, somewhere in a deep, private part of you, you already know it's a good one and you only drew this card because you wanted your feelings confirmed. They're confirmed. It's good.

REVERSED

The Reversed Nine is the card of running down the dirt slope in the vacant lot next to my parents' house.

When you descend the hill you have to make decisions about where to put your feet, where to sit and slide down, or where to use your shoes like brakes. But sometimes you don't get a chance to make those decisions because the descent has a momentum of its own and you might lose control. If you're running downhill and picking up speed, you might start praying that you don't stumble, or if you do fall, that you land on your butt and not on your face.

Going down the hill is much easier, but it's more dangerous and doesn't teach you about life or your own character. In fact, it may expose your shortcomings. The things we do when we lose control of our lives are revealing.

INDIVIDUAL: This person is naturally attracted to the easiest route down the hill, so much so that his moral fiber is a bit too flexible. He has the capacity to steal, to sleep around, or to sue for whiplash he doesn't have. He's the kind of guy who milks the system. He files phony worker's comp claims, cheats on his taxes, or collects disability when he's in perfect health. His moral fiber is elastic and his philosophy of life is, "If I don't get caught it doesn't count."

The new romantic interest defined by the Reversed Nine has fuzzy, unclear relations with others. His best friend in the entire world is a married woman whose husband feels uneasy around him. The husband can't prove anything is going on between him and his wife, so he doesn't publicly object to their friendship. But in his heart, he doesn't trust either of them. When the Reversed Nine man introduces you to his best friend she'll be sugary sweet so you'll feel guilty when the little voice inside your head murmurs, "Are these two foolin' around on the side, or what?"

Sometimes the life of the man defined by the Reversed Nine is falling apart for reasons beyond his control and he isn't an emotional outlaw. The Reversed Nine also stands for the victim of a deception. But if he's been ripped off, it's because the perpetrator was able to engage that little spark of "get something for nothing" in his soul.

RELATIONSHIP: The Reversed Nine couple is unscrupulous. They're the folks who steal from their employer, get caught in the act, and cry foul. They insist another employee stole the stuff, not them. When they rent a house, the first thing they do is break the plumbing and flood the living room. That way, they can refuse to pay the rent until the flood damage is repaired. By the time the landlord gets them out of his house, they'll owe six months' back rent. When they move, they'll pack up the stove, light fixtures, and switch plates and take them with them. This couple's entire life is sliding downhill and the trend will continue until they can't rent a house or get a job in their community. They'll have to move to another state where they'll begin the whole process over again.

The new lover described by the card will be a step down for you. He's just not up to your standards. He's uglier, dumber, poorer, or lazier than the guys you usually date. You won't be seeing him three months from now.

The established marriage described by the Reversed Nine is on the decline. Neither of these partners is able to resist the natural flow, which is toward an end to their alliance.

CIRCUMSTANCES: The landlord, employer, or car dealer described by the Reversed Nine is unethical. Don't rent, work, or buy from a person represented by the card.

NOTE

When it appears Upright, the Nine of Clubs is a remarkable card. It speaks to a general improvement in your life. The progress comes as a direct result of your values and choices. It's the result of the places you chose to dig in your toe and which weeds you held on to during your solo climb up the face of the slope. The decision to go it alone and follow deeply held private beliefs can be lonely, but the Nine promises if you follow your own ideals, you won't regret it.

The Reversed Nine represents a gradual but steady disintegration due to flexible ethics. The Reversed Nine describes the running and sliding down the hill. It's just a matter of how fast you'll get to the bottom and whether or not you'll land on your face.

UPRIGHT: Yes, absolutely.
REVERSED: No.

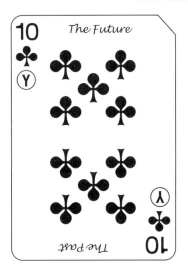

Ten of Clubs

Tens: Doorways
Clubs: Social and Spiritual

PAST AND FUTURE

The Ten of Clubs corresponds to the Wheel of Fortune of the Tarot and has something of a carnival atmosphere about it. The Upright card is exciting and fun. It sweeps you up into the air and spins you high in the sky. It moves you forward into new people, places, and experiences. The Reversed Ten rides the Wheel back down to earth. It returns to people and places from the past.

The Upright Ten is a card of good luck and good fortune, of leaning forward into an unfamiliar future with an open heart and a spark of anticipation in your eye. The Reversed card feels out of control because the Wheel has spun too high, too fast. The Reversed Ten says "No!" to the future and retreats into the past.

UPRIGHT

All Tens are doorways and Clubs are the cards of society. Therefore, the Upright Ten of Clubs opens its door onto a bright new social environment. This is the card of expansion, which includes expansion into new social territories, expansive gestures, or expanding as a person. The Ten broadens and stretches and always has a laugh in the process.

INDIVIDUAL: In the ancient Gypsy fortune-telling tradition, the Ten of Clubs represents a child between the ages of ten and fifteen. The Gypsies believed the card described a person standing with one foot in the past and one foot in the future. They taught that this symbolic figure used one of his hands to reach behind him (backward in time) and one to reach ahead (forward in time), which is the condition of children aged ten to fifteen. Between these ages, children must integrate who they were raised to be (the past) with who they will become on their own (the future).

The child represented by the Four of Hearts is a young, dependent toddler. In contrast, the child represented by the Ten is older and vulnerable to the pressures of his playground society. He's at a stage of life where he will develop preferences in music, sports, and academic subjects and he will adjust his list of friends to accommodate his new interests. Adolescent children have one hand reaching into the past because they're still entirely dependent on Mom and Dad and still attached to their family's values and standards. Their other hand reaches into the future because they're making their first life choices based on their new interests.

The adult represented by the Upright Ten of Clubs is fascinated by new people and new places. He's friendly, outgoing, and spontaneous in a healthy, delightful way. He has an adolescent quality without being immature. He's bright and philosophical with an arsenal of hilarious puns and jokes. This guy has a lot of energy.

The romantic interest described by the Upright Ten of Clubs is a new person in your life. You haven't met him yet. He's about to roll into the picture though, and when he does he'll bring the circus to town with him. This is a positive, extroverted, optimistic, extravagant, and generous soul with a good sense of humor. He's sociable, original, and has a great number of close friends. He likes to look on the sunny side, or at least the funny side of life. He'll be sensitive to your feelings, but he won't be interested in long drawn-out fights, grumpy moods, or rampant negativism. He's not one to wallow in self-pity when he has the blues, and he won't find the wallowing trait very attractive in you either.

RELATIONSHIP: The couple defined by the Upright Ten of Clubs would rather pal around together than make romantic gaga moon faces at one another. It's not that they aren't in love, they love each other plenty. It's just that they would rather go camping, bike riding, hiking, or in-line skating. These two feel like a couple of rollicking, playful kids when they're together, which is the basis of their attachment. Nobody else is as much fun to them as their mate is. Other people think they're a riot because of the way they play practical jokes on one another and take turns telling funny stories. In fact, they're so witty together that if all else fails they could take their act on the road.

If you're single and you pulled the Upright Ten to describe your dating life, this is the perfect time to see a number of people without committing yourself. If the romance department has been dull and dreary lately, all that is about to change. Expect to receive a lot of calls and to date several men at the same time.

CIRCUMSTANCES: The car, boat, house, et cetera described by the Ten of Clubs is spanking clean and shiny new. Any situation described by the card will be fun, stimulating, and a positive influence in your life.

REVERSED

The Reversed Ten is the card of contraction. It's represented by the Ferris wheel's slow rotation back to earth. The Reversed card sits a minute while it shifts gears. Then it slowly grinds backward through time.

INDIVIDUAL: This guy is hung up on the past. He's more attracted to what "was" than to what "is" or what "might be." When he meets a new woman, he compares her to his old girlfriend and the comparison only makes his old one look good. The man represented by the Reversed card is hard to get rid of because he never completely gets over the woman he loves. He doesn't stick around because the relationship was so remarkable, but rather because he finds it difficult to go forward in life.

The new romantic prospect defined by the Reversed Ten is someone from your past. He's your old boyfriend or a guy you once dated. If your love life has been a barren wasteland lately, and you pulled the Ten of Clubs Reversed to describe your next romantic prospect, get out the phone book. It's time to call your old boyfriend to see if there's any juice left in your connection. The chances are good that he's been thinking about you lately, too.

RELATIONSHIP: The established couple described by the Reversed Ten is in a reunion phase. These two have a long history of breakups and reconciliations.

The truth is that they're more attracted to going backward in time than to going forward. They actually get along pretty well, but this one tiny handicap causes them to choke when they have to make a change, so their transitions don't go smoothly. Every time they change jobs, cars, or apartments, the disruption is a threat to their union. Suddenly one or both of them starts looking backward in time, falls head over heels in love with the past, and becomes resistant to the future. A shiny new car makes the old car seem soulful and a treasured lifelong friend. Suddenly she doesn't see the rust anymore. The fresh-coat-of-paint smell in the new apartment makes him miss the fragrance of the orange tree that grew outside his bedroom window at the old apartment.

The Reversed Ten couple can seem overly sentimental at times. For fun, they revisit their old neighborhood, drive by the park where he proposed, or go to eat where they ate on their first date. They maintain their old friendships from high school so they can get together once a year and recall the details of every football game, Christmas formal, and history class they ever shared. These little forays into the past nurture and energize the Reversed Ten couple. The excursions make them feel young again.

The brand-new romance described by the Reversed Ten is a reunion between two people who were lovers a long time ago. This is the middle-age couple who dated in college and bumped into each other at the DMV, shared a cup of coffee, started dating, and wound up getting married.

Their long acquaintance and the manner in which they reconnected are the primary features of their marriage.

CIRCUMSTANCES: The house, truck, or job represented by the Reversed Ten is one from your past. The card says go back to your old apartment building, buy another car like the one you used to have, or call your old boss to see if he has any positions open. The Reversed Ten says you could move into the exact same unit you used to live in, you could buy back your own truck, or return to your old cubicle. The card also says that to do so would be a smart move right now.

NOTE

The Ten of Clubs contains a youthful, exuberant message about looking forward and backward in time. The Upright card counsels new faces or new places and the Reversed card says if you look to the past, you'll be glad you did.

UPRIGHT or REVERSED: This is a "Yes" card.

Jack of Clubs

Jacks: Young People
Clubs: Social and Spiritual

THE BEST FRIEND

UPRIGHT

INDIVIDUAL: The Jack of Clubs describes a person who is in your life right now, but he's probably not the one you would automatically think of if someone asked who your best friend was. The individual represented by the Jack is content to remain in the background while you go on blind dates, Internet dates, or one of those desperate dinners with a man from your past whom you swore you would never go out with again.

The Jack is the neighbor who pops in for coffee the morning after and listens to your war stories from the dating trenches. He laughs at your jokes, asks what you wore, and gives you advice on how to handle men. This is the guy who shares your cynical perspective and swears if you two ever hooked up it would be a disaster. But this is also the one who won't abandon you, abuse you, or try to change you. He likes you the way you are.

Your Jack of Clubs will always be there for you in times of pain and loneliness. He'll offer you a loan when you're broke and invite you to a movie when he thinks you've been lying on the couch, eating ice cream, and channel surfing long enough.

The Jack of Clubs is a wallflower in many ways. You might take him for granted because you don't think he's glamorous or exciting enough to be considered a viable romantic prospect. You'll dismiss him as a candidate because he isn't rich or gorgeous enough for you. The Jack knows what you think of him and he's okay with it because he wants to be your friend more than he wants to be your lover.

If the Jack in your spread describes a child, it says when this one grows up he or she will develop into a King or Queen of Clubs. This youngster is the one who likes hanging around with you. He sits next to you on the couch and watches your TV shows. He's the one who trails behind you chattering knock-knock jokes as you make your way from the laundry, through the kitchen, and into the bedroom where he helps you fold the clean clothes. He likes your company.

If you pulled the Upright Jack to describe your kid and you're not experiencing him as this cool little sidekick, look to yourself. This child waits patiently for you to notice him. I recommend you pay more attention to the little one represented by the Jack because he has a real talent for generosity, devotion, and companionship. This kid has a loving nature and friendship is his strong suit.

Jacks usually represent young people between fifteen and twenty-five years of age, but the Jack could be any age. If you want to recognize him, look for the quiet person with the smiling eyes. He'll be standing near you and he'll be laughing along with you.

RELATIONSHIP: There's no romance between the two described by the Upright Jack of Clubs. They're "just friends."

The married couple represented by the Jack is in a platonic phase. Long-term relationships go through many stages. Those times when they feel more like brother and sister than husband and wife aren't very sexy, but they contribute to the union. Friendship is stronger than romance. A platonic patch of time serves the relationship by strengthening its foundation. A basis of friendship will get a couple through a crisis better than any quantity of Valentines will. Every therapist recommends that people "become friends first."

If you pulled the Upright Jack to describe your new boyfriend, expect the connection to begin as a friendship. If you don't become lovers, you'll always be friends.

If you pass your weekends alone, hoping and praying your future holds a new alliance; if you believe one is building up on the horizon like a tidal wave gathering strength; if you just know that someday the wave will crash and flood your life with love, you should examine your friends for their romantic potential. The Jack says your heart's desire is right beside you. Perhaps you're preoccupied with "finding Mr. Right" or some other ambitious romantic notion. The Jack is telling you that your best friend in the entire world has been quietly in love with you all along. His feelings are so real and unassuming that you haven't even noticed him. It says, "What you seek is at your elbow."

CIRCUMSTANCES: The Jack of Clubs describes very companionable circumstances. If you're looking to purchase a car, buy it from a friend. If you seek a new home, your friends will move and you'll inherit their place, which is how the best ones always change hands. The working environment defined by the Upright Jack is friendly. These folks are good to one another, are supportive and cooperative, and function as a team. You're going to like it there.

REVERSED

INDIVIDUAL: Reversing the card seems to deepen the association and add another dimension to the friendship. It's the best friend who's actually your lover, spouse, child, sibling, parent, or boss. When the Jack of Clubs falls Reversed, the "best friend" becomes the "special friend." The card says there's another aspect to an existing relationship that serves to deepen it.

If you pulled the Reversed Jack, you already know what I'm talking about and you're probably nodding your head right now. You already know that your best friend is your little kid, your mother, or your husband.

The new romantic prospect represented by the card is a friend of yours. By deciding to date, you're adding another dimension to your friendship.

RELATIONSHIP: This is one of the best unions in the deck. These two play together. They have compatible inner children.

I know of a couple that breaks into song. They'll be driving in the car and he'll say to her, "Hey, did you ever realize the theme to *The Brady Bunch* is a cha-cha?" Her face will light up and they'll sing out, *"Here's the story, cha-cha-cha. Of a lovely lady, cha-cha-cha."* Their kids will groan and pretend to faint in the backseat while they belt out, *"That's the way they all became the Brady Bunch, cha-cha-cha!"*

The Reversed Jack of Clubs couple spends huge amounts of time together because they like all the same things, and they're never petty. They don't criticize, contradict, compete, or interfere with one another.

When the Jack is drawn to describe a new romantic prospect, the union has tremendous potential. This person is already a close friend and your decision to date will turn your existing connection into a "special friendship."

Any romance defined by the Reversed Jack of Clubs is on the buddy system and so companionable that it's hard to imagine these two with anyone else.

CIRCUMSTANCES: The home described by the Reversed Jack was chosen because of the neighborhood. The folks in this subdivision have block parties and ten-house garage sales. The kids are safe playing in the street, everyone carpools, and each residence participates in the neighborhood watch program.

The car defined by the Reversed Jack is a member of the family and has a name. Right out of college, I bought a '65 Volkswagen Bug. I named her Gloria. When my friends would call, they'd ask about the car. They'd say, "How's Gloria?" I'd answer, "Good! She made it to Los Angeles and back this week."

NOTE

I want you to cultivate the Jack of Clubs when he appears. If you give him a chance, he'll develop into a devoted friend or lover. Whenever you see the card, try to remember that the Jack is a sleeper and never underestimate him.

UPRIGHT or REVERSED: Your loyal friend is a "Yes."

The Pretty Woman

Q ♣ Y

Socially Incorrect Woman

Queen of Clubs

Queens: Women
Clubs: Social and Spiritual

THE PRETTY WOMAN

UPRIGHT

INDIVIDUAL: The Queen of Clubs is the Queen of Society. She has more phone numbers in her Rolodex than you and I put together because she makes friends everywhere she goes. She chats up the waitress and her employer with equal charm. She calls the grocery boy by his name and has him carry her bags to the car so she can ask about his college plans or how his baseball team is doing.

The Queen will strike up a conversation with the man seated next to her at the Vegas slot machines. In ten minutes she'll know his wife died of cancer, that his daughter took it so hard she dropped out of school for an entire year, and how lonely he is rattling around the house by himself. If he's cute (and she's single), she'll date him. If she's married, she'll fix him up with her manicurist.

The Queen of Clubs is the Queen of fashion, beauty, and home decoration. She's also the best-looking woman in the deck. But she fears that her pretty face is the only reason for her popularity, which means she fears that if she were to lose her looks she'd lose her social life. Therefore, she works to create a valuable, permanent place for herself in her community, primarily by giving parties.

Even the simplest occasion is a major event in her home because her style is opulent and abundant. She favors voluptuous art, richly textured fabrics, and armloads of fresh flowers. She hosts parties because she likes the way they smell. She loves the fragrance of lilies and roses, of wine left to breathe, and of chicken cooked in lemon. She loves the way her guests smell of fresh laundry, aftershave, and hair spray. Theirs is the scent of preparation for her party. She hugs each one as they arrive so she can inhale their aroma. She knows they primped for her.

Her wardrobe reflects the times in which she lives. She leans toward the newest, hippest fashions, but her closet holds everything from designer originals to thrift store treasures. She has the right outfit whether she's going to the midnight Bowl-a-Rama or the Academy Awards. When she's young, she takes every fashion risk in the book, like short short microskirts with leopard print nylons, Cleopatra makeup, rhinestone tattoos, and two-tone hair. She starts out as a fashion victim, but as she matures she develops an eye and invents a personal style. By thirty-five she knows how to be wholly contemporary without appearing foolish or girlish; she discovers beauty, subtlety, and taste. The Queen of Clubs remains a fashion pioneer and a fearless trendsetter all her life.

The Queen knows she has a superficial side. She was raised in a household that valued dressing well and saying "Hi!" in a super-cheery voice above most other virtues. Some of these gals were too moody and artistic to be the perky cheerleader type so their mom allowed them to pursue a life in the arts. The Queen of Clubs is melancholy, complicated by nature, and a bit spoiled by circumstance so she often fails to live up to the jaunty social image she was raised to project. The knowledge that social relations are mostly contrived and empty can frighten her and leave her wondering if people recognize who she really is.

The average Queen keeps a man at her side because she needs an escort to feel socially secure. Her challenge is to find a partner who attempts to understand her, but she doesn't actually require that he succeed. She knows she's complex and difficult to fathom, so her lover's efforts will touch her heart. She'll find her truest happiness with a man who can match her boundless sensuality and share her love of textures and smells. The Queen is an expensive partner, but she'll add glamour and style to the life of the man who understands she's a brand-new Porsche and not a reliable station wagon.

The Queen of Clubs is usually a Fire sign woman (Leo, Aries, or Sagittarius).

RELATIONSHIP: This is the union between the captain of the football team and the homecoming queen. Beautiful, athletic, and affluent, they're the envy of their entire school.

The adult relationship represented by the card is still a movie star romance. These two are gorgeous, sexy, and famous. Or at least they're very popular and, as a result, their alliance is lived out in public places or in the social columns.

If you pulled the Upright Queen to describe a brand-new romance, your girlfriends will love the union. They'll pull you into the bathroom and ask, "How's it going?" They'll tell you he's a dreamboat and you're the perfect couple. The only problem with a Queen of Clubs relationship is how tempting it will be to say too much and feed the gossip mill or to avoid sharing at all by saying, "Great! It's going great!"

The Queen represents a sensual connection between two well-suited people who will attract a lot of attention. Don't get caught up in how you look to strangers. If you concentrate on one another and forget the outside world, you should be very happy together because you're very much alike.

CIRCUMSTANCES: The Queen of Clubs is a card of self-confidence. It foretells a period of time during which you will feel sexy and attractive. It's the card of how we feel when we've lost weight, changed our hairstyle, or our social life has improved in some way. The Queen represents social advancement. Therefore, the job, car, or house represented by the card will reflect well on you.

REVERSED

INDIVIDUAL: When she falls Reversed, the Queen has lost her shine. Either she's gained weight, accidentally dyed her hair green, or has spotted the ominous signs of aging. The Reversed Queen feels left out of her normally active social life or is overwhelmed by its relentlessness.

If you pulled the Reversed Queen of Society to describe yourself, in some way you're not socially perfect for your man. Search for the imperfection. Is there a significant age difference between you? Are you Catholic and he Jewish? Are you different races or from different backgrounds? Were you raised rich and he poor? The Reversed Queen says you're not the most socially correct choice he could make, but if so, she also says he thinks you're so gorgeous and glamorous that he doesn't care a bit.

Another interpretation of the Reversed Queen is the woman who may be avoiding sex or postponing it until she's married. Or perhaps the *unthinkable* has happened; the Queen's husband no longer desires her. Our Lady of Beauty and Sensuality will be heartbroken and deeply shamed by her inability to attract her own mate. This woman needs romance the way she needs air to breathe. Under these conditions the Queen of Clubs will shift her focus and devote her life to worthy social causes, charity events, and fund-raisers. But good works are small compensation for the loss of her special gift, which is her remarkable sensuality.

RELATIONSHIP: The established connection described by the Reversed Queen is in a celibate phase or the issues described above, the ones that separate this couple socially, are interfering with their attachment right now.

Regardless of whether the Queen represents a well-established relationship or a new one, there is an undeniable attraction between this pair that isn't being acted upon. Sometimes the choice to postpone sex is temporary, or appropriate. As when the couple is too young, or very religious, or so old that their equipment doesn't work anymore. The partnership defined by the Queen is loving and strong, nonetheless, and these two have no intention of splitting.

If you pulled the Reversed card to describe a new alliance, it will endure a chaste phase before the physical connection develops. There will be something so foreign about the partner represented by the Reversed card that you'll naturally slow the pace until you get to know him. If loving, supportive cards surround the Queen, she'll eventually turn Upright, and you'll discover you're involved in one of the best relationships in the deck. But, if she's surrounded by negative cards, you'll be glad you held back.

CIRCUMSTANCES: These circumstances are difficult, but good nonetheless.

This apartment has too many female roommates. The environment is memorable for all the candlelight dinners, the smell of dying flowers, the clashing floral upholsteries, and the line outside the bathroom door. It has too much estrogen for the average man, but that's okay, because with all the good-looking female roommates the place is a guy magnet. If the extreme femininity of this living condition drives your boyfriend away, don't worry. Another romantic prospect will knock on the door in ten minutes.

The car represented by the Reversed Queen is nice, but it's unlike any you ever thought you'd own. It's the red pickup truck you inherited from your brother that turned out to be fun and handy. It's the last thing on earth you'd buy for yourself, but it's a lifesaver when a friend needs to move.

NOTE

The Queen of Clubs stands for the day we're sharp and sexy, and all eyes are on us. We've all had those days when we look good and know it, when we enter a room and we own it. The Queen corresponds to the day we *rule the school!*

UPRIGHT or REVERSED: This Lady is always a "Yes."

King of Clubs

Kings: Men
Clubs: Social and Spiritual

MR. RIGHT

UPRIGHT

This guy is handsome, charming, well educated, lives in a lovely home in a nice neighborhood, has a great job, is in love with his wife, and adores his children. He's Mr. Perfect.

INDIVIDUAL: The Upright King of Clubs is the best-looking, most popular, and most socially appropriate man you could hope to meet. He's the dream lover in the sports car with the *GQ* good looks, the high school football star, or president of his class. He's the attractive intern, the rugged fireman, or the beefcake auto mechanic with the megawatt smile who decides to throw in a free oil filter because he likes the way you look in a sundress.

The King's respect for society drives him to be the perfect member of his community. He sells insurance so he can be the hero with the check when the flood hits. He sits on the board of his condo association because he wants to be responsible for the growth and prosperity of his neighborhood. He's a social worker because he wants to save those less fortunate.

In his personal life, he goes to church, exercises, and dances with his wife. He coaches Little League and helps his kids with their homework. He vacations with his family and alone with his wife because he wants to be the ideal father and husband, and he understands "father" and "husband" are separate jobs.

The King of Clubs often becomes so deeply involved in creating the American Dream that he forgets to stop and think about who he is or how he feels. He just crosses his fingers and leaps in. Then he loses sleep thinking about his new mortgage, or his Rotary Club presidency, or how the heck he's gonna coach soccer *and* Little League on Wednesday nights. Once in a while, the struggle to keep up appearances overwhelms him. He would disappoint so many people if his house went into foreclosure, or one of his teams came in last, or if he couldn't flip pancakes at the Rotary breakfast.

Which brings us to the King's other side. Deep down, he craves understanding. Too often he selects his wife for superficial, social reasons and she's incapable of going to his dark place with him, which is a terrible loss for the King. He needs an attentive listener, someone who can dispel his fears, cheer him up, and support his vision of the perfect life. He needs an emotionally warm woman who believes in him and trusts him, one who understands his moods.

The King of Clubs works hard to live right and he needs a wife who knows how much effort it takes. He'll desert the princess who believes marriage is easy and life is great because she's a precious winner who *deserves* to be married to the best-looking, most socially acceptable man in town. The wife who assumes it's her birthright to live in a lovely home, married to a hard-working pillar of the community, could be in for a rude awakening. If she isn't careful, the King of Clubs will run off with the waitress who "gets it." Be prepared to step down off the pedestal if you want to wed this complicated man.

RELATIONSHIP: The union described by the Upright King is the kind of high-powered coupling that's good for the community. Charitable organizations, churches, and synagogues in particular benefit from their time, ideology, and generosity.

The husband and wife defined by the Upright King are "right" for each other. They have the same philosophy of life, are equally beautiful to look at, and share the same brand of relaxed elegance. They're a JFK and Jackie couple.

This courtship was conducted within a tight social set. These two met at the yacht club or a charity ball. Throughout their married years this very popular couple will live at the center of a tight, glittering clique. They're stylish, attractive, and a perfect match. Their chemistry together radiates a kind of warmth that neither may possess on his or her own.

When the Upright King describes a new romantic interest, he's quite possibly the man of your dreams. He'll travel in the same social circles you do and like the same kinds of food and music you like. The King of Clubs twosome has matching styles: they favor vintage clothes and Mercedes coupes from the sixties or they're conservative professionals who wear gray his-and-her sport coats, carry matching briefcases, and work out together on the weekends.

When you pull the King to describe your new romance, the card says you think he's perfect and he makes you feel like you are too. But don't forget, this man needs a girl who listens to him. He needs someone who likes him just the way he is; one who will support his efforts to be the Most Wonderful Man Alive. You may have to pawn the silver to get through some of his adventures, but if you have faith in the King of Clubs he'll stay with you. Deep in his heart, all he's ever wanted is to be your hero.

CIRCUMSTANCES: The workplace described by the King is sunny, progressive, and employee oriented. They have a softball team and hold an annual company picnic. They post a photo of their employee of the month and hire graduates from the local colleges. This is a community-oriented corporate environment that will call upon you to participate as a classic corporate wife, unless you're the employee. In which case your husband has to play softball at the picnics.

The primary feature of this house is that it's located in a neighborhood known more for its style than its average income. It's an artist's loft, beach cottage, or farmhouse in the south of France. This residence sits in the romantic, exotic spot where you always dreamed of living someday.

REVERSED

INDIVIDUAL: When he falls reversed, the King isn't 100 percent perfect for you. He's either a wonderful guy but too old, or terribly attractive but too young. Sometimes the King is a different race or religion and sometimes he comes from a background so dissimilar to your own that the contrast is a bit of a problem. Perhaps he was raised dirt poor and you were raised upper middle class. Maybe you're an astrologer and he's the son of a Baptist minister. Perhaps he's a macho guy from Latin America and you were raised by a gay couple in San Francisco. This one can still be your Mr. Right, but only if you both work to accept the cultural differences between you.

The Reversed King of Society can turn against his community when he fails to achieve his vision of the perfect life. Should he give up, he'll withdraw and grow cynical or paranoid. The Reversed King is the neighborhood crazy man. He's the hermit neighbor with signs all over his front yard warning the public about police conspiracies and government plots. He's the guy who hasn't shaved in ten years who paints biblical quotes all over his van.

The Reversed King of Clubs is an outlaw, but he's not the scary kind. He's more like that guy who hacked into the computer systems of the top companies in the world. He didn't steal anything, but the companies had to restructure their security systems, which cost them millions. The guy said he wasn't trying to get any money, he just wanted to prove that he was beyond the rules of society. They sent him to jail anyway.

The final interpretation of the Reversed King of Clubs is a man in a celibate phase. The Reversed King is doing the socially correct thing of waiting until he's married to bed the girl. If he's married, he's either lost interest in his wife or the wife cut him off.

RELATIONSHIP: On the surface, the marriage defined by the Reversed King doesn't look like it would work, but in reality the alliance works very well. It's the union of two people from different races, religions, ages, or income brackets. These two are crazy about each other so they'll stay together.

The new alliance described by the Reversed King just needs a little more time. These two are so dissimilar, yet so attracted to one another, that it may take a while for each to find their footing in the relationship. This is the romance between a very tall woman and a very short man, or of a female Harvard graduate and her truck driver boyfriend. The alliance will work as long as they realize it's the quality of their connection that matters and not the opinion of the society in which they live.

CIRCUMSTANCES: The environment described by the Reversed King is pleasant, charming, and sociable, but not your usual arena.

NOTE

The King of Clubs is a great guy. He's responsible, sexy, wholesome, and a complement to any life. If you're approaching the oracle to inquire about your new boyfriend, he's right for you. If Reversed, he's close, maybe even close enough. The King of Clubs is usually a Fire sign (Leo, Aries, or Sagittarius), but not necessarily. All men have the four Kings buried in their psyche, so they all have it in them to be a King of Clubs kind of a guy.

UPRIGHT or REVERSED: The King is a "Yes" in either direction.

```
A ♥   Permanent Love
♥
(Y)


      ♥


              (Y)
              ♥
ǝʌo˥           A
|ɐuo!ʇuǝʌuoɔu∩
```

Ace of Hearts

Aces: Achievement
Hearts: Emotions

*I've learned that the things I'm afraid of are temporary,
of greater endurance is the love I feel. I've come to understand
that love outlasts fear.*
—MARY CATHERINE BLIZZARD

PERMANENT LOVE

. . . As opposed to "romantic love" or "passionate love" or the tenuous, spiritual "soul mate connection."

The Ace of Hearts is the card of the permanent emotional attachments we form with others. It represents hearty, enduring alliances like those we are born into or the ones we develop with our lifelong partners and friends. The Ace has a practical component, too, because permanent relationships aren't just built on "love." Permanent relationships contain other elements like money, children, property, social traditions, and extended families.

Once we have the peak experience of finding and marrying our life partners, our attention shifts to other things. It turns to our careers, or to reseeding the lawn, or to learning to play the guitar. In reality, our marriages become nothing more than the passage of time. That time is marked by all the goofy, stupid things we get ourselves into and then get ourselves out of. Our kids, money, spirituality, and community are the support beams beneath the journey we call wedlock but those beams must be set in concrete if they're to be sturdy enough to hold up our lives. The concrete is the timeless love we feel for our mates.

UPRIGHT

INDIVIDUAL: The individual identified by the Upright Ace is true-blue and stable. He loves his baseball team, his kids, and his friends. He's not a saccharine phony; he's genuine and his style is to connect for the long, long haul. This person knows how to love and *wants* to love. He has no fears, doubts, or reservations about forming permanent emotional attachments.

The man represented by the Upright Ace of Hearts pays attention to other people and to the way they conduct their marriages. When he takes the dog out for his evening walk, he notices that the neighbors on the left tiptoe across the lawn to mix martinis and marital beds with the neighbors on the right. The neighbor ladies may wink and flirt with him when his wife isn't around, but he would no more go next door on a Saturday night than he would leave his wallet on a bench at the mall. This man got married because he believes in love, home, and family. The last thing on earth he would do is commit a foolish, self-destructive act that might destroy his marriage.

The Ace represents the husband who sticks with his wife through her weight problem or her mastectomy. His wife is always beautiful to him. He never looks into her eyes and sees her crow's feet. He sees the coed with the ponytail he fell in love with ten years ago. He thinks she's warm, loving, and comfortable, which is all he ever wanted in a woman. The man represented by the Ace of Hearts is content and happily married.

If you pulled the Upright Ace to describe a new love interest, you're probably looking at your ultimate life partner.

RELATIONSHIP: Every person who comes to me for a reading eventually says they love someone and they often say this after telling me how evil, rude, cheap, or cruel that person has been. I ask them to define love and they give me answers something like these:

"It's when you can't live without him."

"It's just a feeling. You know it when you're in it."

"It sweeps you off your feet."

To me these answers sound more like our connection to chocolate than to a good man. To tell my clients how love works, I have to explain how anger works: Anger is a strong and powerful feeling, but it's not an emotion. Anger is felt *in response* to primary emotions. That's why we ask people what they're angry about. Their explanation describes the emotions behind their anger. Their real emotions are betrayal, humiliation, disappointment, neglect, disrespect, et cetera.

We feel love in response to primary emotions too. Except, in the case of love, the list of primary emotions adds up to exactly two: respect and admiration.

Here's an exercise: Make a list of the qualities you most respect and admire in another person, then ask yourself who in your life has those traits. The folks who possess the traits on your list are the people you love the most. The list will show that your favorite person in the world is someone who struggled with difficult circumstances and emerged with her values and principles intact.

Think of your aunt whose husband died and left her with three small children and a failing public relations firm. She's the widow who went to college and learned the public relations business so she could provide for the family. While you watched, she struggled and prevailed. Today you look up to her as a role model of perseverance and integrity. You love her (respect and admire her) because you have hard evidence that she's reliable, loyal, consistent, and loving even under the most difficult conditions.

Now, ask yourself what you admire in a good man. Does he keep his promises? Is he nice to children? Does he pay his bills on time? Is he polite and respectful? Employed? Faithful? Do you trust him with your heart, your kids, and your money?

If your man doesn't speak to you in a loving way, follow through on his promises, hold down a job, or avoid other women, then logic dictates that you don't respect him and you can't love him in a permanent, fulfilling way.

If you aspire to be married to a man who will stay with you until the day you die, you've got to find one you believe to be the finest, most sincere, hardest working guy you have ever known. You're going to sit across the breakfast table from that man for the rest of your life—and your life is going to have a lot of ups and downs. You can get through any number of disasters as a couple if you believe in the deepest part of you that this is the finest, most honorable, most well-intentioned man God ever placed on this earth. Your faith in him is all you're going to have when times get tough.

You may lust after the guy you're dating now and you may long to possess your old boyfriend, body and soul, one more time. But don't tell yourself you love the man if you don't admire how he lives his life.

The Upright Ace of Hearts represents your marital partner. When drawn to describe a new relationship, it promises an enduring, lifelong connection built on mutual love and respect.

CIRCUMSTANCES: These circumstances are connected to your family of origin. If your question is about a car, home, or job, you will find your next one through your family. Mom will sell you her car, you'll move back home, or they'll put you to work in the family business.

REVERSED

INDIVIDUAL: The individual represented by the Reversed Ace of Hearts doesn't have a family and feels adrift because he needs one. He's a family man without a family.

The Reversed Ace man will create a new clan from the scraps of his assorted friendships. He won't embrace every newcomer with a hearty smile and a slap on the back. Instead, he'll form specific, meaningful, long-term connections. He'll spend every Christmas Eve with his business partner, his birthday with his golf buddies, and go to St. Thomas every spring with his old neighbor. He finds his psychic family.

RELATIONSHIP: The established couple represented by the Reversed Ace has a lifelong romantic connection that doesn't require an actual trip to the altar. This relationship is unconventional but permanent.

The new romantic prospect described by the Reversed Ace of Hearts has deep, emotionally fulfilling relationships, but they're unorthodox. He's the guy who's lived with his woman for eighteen years without the benefit of marriage. He introduces her as his wife, bought a house with her, and had a child with her, but he won't legally marry her. He has a rebellious streak. He refuses to allow "a piece of paper" to legitimize his relationship. The affection he feels for his mate makes their union plenty legit to him.

CIRCUMSTANCES: The Reversed card defines other collectives we find emotionally nourishing, like a job or club that functions as a second family. In my own life the Reversed Ace represents a closely knit group of swing dancers. We dance every Friday and Sunday evening. These are the friends I call when I'm moving or when I need a ride to the airport. They throw my birthday party every year and feed me martinis when my heart is broken.

NOTE

The single, long-stemmed, bloodred Ace of Hearts is symbolic of permanent love and represents your ultimate life partner regardless of whether your connection is traditional or nonconformist.

UPRIGHT or REVERSED: It's a "Yes" card in any direction.

2 ♥ ♥
(Y) ♥

The Soul Mate Connection

♠

(N)
♠
2

Not a Match

Two of Hearts

Twos: Union
Hearts: Emotions

THE SOUL MATE CONNECTION

The primary thesis of this book is that there is no one, perfect soul mate wandering the planet searching for you. I don't believe there's a mysterious twin soul from a parallel universe who will recognize you one day in a flash of light.

Although I believe it's possible to make a connection at the soul level, I think you're as likely to connect with a pet, child, or parent in this way as with a lover. Sometimes a new acquaintance will strike a chord so deep that it feels as if you knew them in another lifetime. Certainly you know couples who have such similar spirits and are such genuine friends that it seems they were meant for one another. It's hard not to envy their union and brush off your jealousy by saying, "Well, they're soul mates." It's encouraging to think "It" could happen to you, too, but there's no magic to it.

My friend June says we connect with people who share our wounds. She believes we fall in love with the person who understands abandonment and betrayal the same way we do. She says our experience of pain, loss, and the workings of the culture combine to create our soul and what we seek in another is someone whose experience of life is similar to our own. When we find the precious twin spirit the recognition of our sameness washes over us like a revelation, and we say we have found our soul mate.

UPRIGHT

INDIVIDUAL: When you pull this card to describe a new romantic prospect you're looking at your next boyfriend.

The character defined by the Two of Hearts is a sweet, sincere person. This one loves you and you'll love him. The card always describes someone easy to get along with. Even when you pull the Two to describe your boss or landlord, it says you have a relationship so harmonious that it's practically a romance.

RELATIONSHIP: The Two of Hearts represents *the process* of plugging two compatible spirits together. An attachment begins with a phone call, builds to intimate conversations, and when you're very lucky and the timing is right, the talks advance all the way to soul communion. It takes a certain amount of time and a handful of dates to realize how much your essence resonates with another's.

The first date described by the Two of Hearts is one of those shiny, sparkly experiences, the kind where you're self-conscious but thrilled, nervous but confident. It's the kind of date you wouldn't miss unless both your legs were in plaster casts.

Phase two of the process will find you seated at a nice table in a good restaurant. He'll talk about marriage, kids, his education, or parents. You'll share how disappointed you felt when you didn't get the promotion, and how sad it was last week when you had to put the dog down. He'll counter with the story about putting his cat to sleep and you discover you feel the same way about such things. They break both your hearts.

The relationship will grow over time and the connection will deepen. The Two of Hearts isn't a card of passion. It's a card of liking, which is so different and so much more rare. The Upright card describes an affinity between two whole, independent people who are able to accept one another just as they are, eccentricities and all.

By the end of the process, the Two of Hearts stands for the realization that you are two halves of a whole, that this person shares your depth and purpose and you are soul mates.

The established partnership defined by the Two is a real love match. These two probably found each other in high school and, as a result, their relationship has a charming puppy dog quality. The married couple defined by the Upright Two of Hearts will never grow cynical and bitter about love. They believe there is someone for everyone because their own love story worked out. They believe yours will too.

CIRCUMSTANCES: This situation is a joy. If the Two describes your job, you'll feel you belong there from day one. If it describes a car, it's the model you always wanted. It's the perfect color, make, style, and year. The seat fits, the price was right, and the stereo is bigger, better, and louder than you had hoped it would be. If the Two describes your new apartment, you'll adore the landlord, your roommate, and the neighbors. Regardless of where it lands in a spread, the Upright Two is the perfect pairing of any two components.

REVERSED

INDIVIDUAL: This man either can't seem to meet anyone significant or he's recently broken off a meaningful relationship. If so, the parting has come without adequate explanation and he may feel bitter or resentful. Although his understanding of love has deepened as a result of this breakup, the Reversed Two man isn't really interested in an alliance with you because his recent separation is still consuming him. Once he has the closure he needs he'll be a wonderful prospect for the right woman.

RELATIONSHIP: This is the relationship that never took off. Your failure to connect didn't result in emotional turmoil because the union didn't build up through the steps. You spoke on the phone a few times, maybe went on a date or two, but the spark wasn't be there so you politely decided not to see each other again. You told your friends, "It just wasn't a match."

The established couple represented by the Reversed Two is drifting apart. They no longer engage in long, open conversations about their dreams and fears. Lately, they have new, separate interests and they're beginning to think their partner is holding them back. This couple used to be deeply in love, but these days they think their mate is a ball and chain; just a ton of dead weight they have to haul around behind them. Normally, a couple doesn't make it through a phase represented by the Reversed card. Maybe you ought to draw additional cards to help you Upright the Two.

CIRCUMSTANCES: This is just flat out the wrong situation. It's a complete mismatch. It's as if the ringmaster hired a seventy-year-old grandmother to perform a high-wire act in a rhinestone bikini. "Improbable" is the word. Just the last two elements we would want to see plugged together.

NOTE

The Two of Hearts is a beautiful card with a gentle message about the melding of two personalities into a harmonious whole. The individual looking for romance who finds the Upright Two in his spread is a lucky person. He will be well and truly loved.

The Reversed card describes the spark that never ignited into a flame. When Reversed, the Two is a no-harm/no-foul card. It represents two lovely people who just aren't meant to be a couple.

UPRIGHT: "Oh, yes."
REVERSED: "No, I'm afraid not."

Three of Hearts

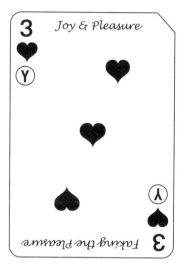

Threes: Expansion
Hearts: Emotions

JOY

The Three of Hearts is the card of the pleasure we take in the company of our same-sex friends. This is the group of women whose children are growing up with yours, the gals so dear to you that they've taken the place of your sisters. They're your children's unofficial, but closest, aunties. I do mean to say this in the plural too. The Three of Hearts doesn't represent one special person. Instead, it describes a group of friends who have loyally stuck together since they first met at the Laundromat, college, or Weight Watchers.

My father went to high school in the tiny beach town north of San Diego, where I still live. These days our little town is a sophisticated village on the California Riviera, but back then the region was rural, agricultural, and isolated.

After World War II ended, my father's high school friends came home and started a poker club. They called their club the Jolly Boys and met on the first Friday of the month. Their club is still going strong today, although there aren't many Jolly Boys left.

The JB's, as they were called by their families, stood as best man for one another and played godfather for each other's children. They sought consolation among their airtight ranks during times of death and divorce while they continued to meet every first Friday. We, the JB children, called the other members Uncle Jerry, Uncle Red, Uncle Lyle, et cetera. We called their wives Aunt Dottie and Auntie 'Ree.

These days, we grown JB kids bump into one another in the grocery store and try to explain to our own children how we're cousins, but not really, how we grew up in each other's households, although we weren't technically related. We second-generation poker-club kids feel a rich connection to our community that we wouldn't feel if our fathers hadn't had the capacity to love their same-sex friends with such permanence and devotion.

UPRIGHT

The Three of Hearts is a merry little card about people coming together in celebration. It's a reunion or a night on the town with your girlfriends. The Three describes a carbonated atmosphere charged with loyal affection and big cheesy smiles. It stands for the delightful, amusing connections that warm us and entertain us. The Three inspires us to dance, eat, drink, laugh, hug, and smile. When we pull this card, we feel released from polite constraints and we open up to more joyful contact with those around us.

INDIVIDUAL: The individual defined by the Three of Hearts looks back fondly upon his past, recalling the pleasure he felt in the presence of old friends. He wishes his friends well and seeks them out to enjoy their company again. A Three of Hearts person is not necessarily a party person, although he may socialize a lot. The Three represents the *emotions* of pleasure. This person wants to enjoy his relationships, but not necessarily to drink or close the clubs every weekend. He wants to be with the people whom he loves because he likes them. This is a fun, warmhearted individual who's friendly and well intentioned.

The new romantic prospect described by the Upright Three is a treasure. This man has heart and grace. From the very first date your connection will be amusing, delightful, and highly satisfying.

RELATIONSHIP: The most prominent aspect of the marriage represented by the Upright Three is this couple's identification with a particular clique or group of friends. These are the folks who have been hanging out with the identical cast of characters from their yacht club for the past fifteen years. Their group meets at the same place, at the same time year-round, where they bake in the sun, or play gin rummy, and drink margaritas together. Tight little knots of like-thinking friends are often envied by more solitary couples, and for good reason. These too-tan, middle-aged yachties are a bottomless resource of love and support for one another.

The brand-new romance described by the card will develop into a society of two. They'll have more fun together than they could possibly have with anyone else. This is a match between two warm, fun-loving, sunny souls who belong together.

If you're presently alone and long to meet someone new, the Upright Three will be an important card. It advises you to seek out your same-sex friends and suggests the possibility of a reunion.

The cards surrounding the Three will describe a number of circumstances under which a romance might begin. Coupled with the Joker it says a new relationship will develop while you're out with friends. When pulled with the Ten of Clubs Reversed, it promises a reunion with a lover from the past. If found among the Diamonds, cocktails after work will create fertile ground for romance.

CIRCUMSTANCES: By all means, rent, buy, or accept anything represented by the Three of Hearts. You and your house, car, boat, or computer will bond into a cheery little unit that will make you feel loved and appreciated. You belong together.

REVERSED

The Reversed Three of Hearts says you'll have to force the good feelings. It says you should *make* yourself go out with your girlfriends because you need to, even though you aren't in the mood. The Reversed card nags you to have a good time, doctor's orders.

Let's face it, Mr. Perfect isn't going to walk between the couch and the TV. Go get some new clothes! Pretend you're having fun! The *real* fun will come later, but you have to start somewhere and you can't get comfortable with the process until you begin it. Fortunately, the effects of the Reversed Three don't last very long. This is a temporary condition, so get started. I want you to go out every weekend until you wake up one day to realize you're a regular at Sunday salsa night.

INDIVIDUAL: When musicians climb onstage, they act as if they're having a blast, but they usually aren't. They're at work and it's their job to show the audience a good time. The lead vocalist may have a headache or have just gotten into a dispute with the club owner in the alley. But when the band hits that first note, the party begins and his problems "disappear." No rational thinker could imagine that the average American musician is a freewheeling soul who can party seven nights a week for twenty years with no particular side effect other than pasty skin. If a musician's a pro, he knows how to fake the fun. He knows how to convince the audience there's no place in the world he'd rather be than right there, and that the good times are rollin' tonight.

The new romantic interest represented by the Reversed Card of Joy is a lot like the musician described above. He's an effervescent, witty, hand holding, look-sincere-while-she-tells-her-sad-story-but-don't-bother-to-remember-much-of-it kind of guy. He's not a complete phony though. He's probably just nervous or convinced it's up to him to show you a good time, so he acts "Fabulous!" to amuse you. That's okay. Everybody fakes it once in a while, right?

RELATIONSHIP: I wouldn't want to predict the outcome of a new relationship while it's still being represented by the Reversed Three of Hearts. This is a pretty good card with which to begin the dating process, but you should pay attention to your date's emotional undercurrents and to the way the relationship develops.

Sometimes a girl accepts a date just to get out of the house, or to make her parents happy, or because she would be crazy to turn down such a ripe prospect. Shortly after my divorce, I was feeling painfully single and staying home most Saturday nights. Then I met a man who looked exactly like Tom Selleck. I was so flattered that such a beautiful specimen wanted to date me that I saw him exclusively for six months. But we never grew close or fell in love because we only dated out of boredom. We weren't seeing one another out of respect and admiration. We were going out so we would have something to do on Saturday night. We were faking it. My experience with the Tom Selleck guy taught me a few dating skills though. He tooled me up for the courting game and when we parted, we parted as friends.

Later on, another card will represent your connection to the man defined by the Reversed Three of Hearts. Until you see that card, expect your polished Barbie doll veneer to spend Saturday nights with his polished Ken doll veneer.

The established couple represented by the Reversed Three is in an odd phase. For some reason they're putting on a show for one another. They're making themselves come to the breakfast table all chipper and ready to take on the world when in reality, that's not how they feel. This phase won't last very long, so in some respects faking it is the most loving thing they can do. Over time, another card will represent their union. Until then, the Reversed Three couple is determined to smile and be pleasant.

CIRCUMSTANCES: Any situation represented by the Reversed Three will start out saccharine sweet and soon segue to another condition.

Therefore, I recommend you accept the job, rent the apartment, or buy the car because the Reversed Three might spin Upright on its own. If it does, you'll be delighted.

NOTE

I say "lucky you" when you find the Three of Hearts in your spread regardless of whether it's Upright or Reversed. Eventually, charming, amusing people who feel a great deal of affection for you will surround you. There's a serious possibility of finding love here too. You just have to go out and make it happen!

P.S. The Gypsies believe the Three is the card of fertility, that it indicates pregnancy and covers the birthing process. So be careful, somebody's ovulating!

UPRIGHT or REVERSED: It's a "Yes" card every time.

Four of Hearts

Fours: Effort
Hearts: Emotions

CAREGIVING

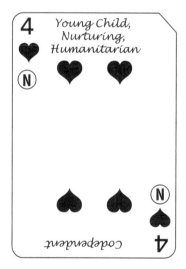

The Four of Hearts wants to know, "Who do you depend on?" and "Who depends on you?" The Four is the card of nurturing in its most generous, idealistic form and in its sickest, most smothering form.

The Four describes a child beneath the age of ten who is entirely dependent on the adults in his life to provide for him. It also describes his caregiver. Good parents watch over their children, guide them, and allow them to try their wings when they're ready.

The Upright card stands for both the child and his early nurturers. The Reversed card stands for the parents who overdo when it comes to their children. If Sonny Boy is forty years old and still living in his old bedroom, eating for free, and his mom is doing his laundry, he's a loser. He's not the problem, though; Mom is. The mom represented by the Reversed Four of Hearts uses her son to give purpose to her life. She doesn't see how he could love her unless he needed her. So she does everything for him, which makes her feel loved.

Now, don't write me a letter and tell me you think caring for the family is a noble enterprise because I already agree with you. That's not what we're talking about here. We aren't talking about the young mother who has two babies and a hardworking husband, who set aside her own ambitions for a few years to raise her youngsters. That's the Upright card and the admirable way to work the energy.

The Reversed Four talks about the woman who meekly or angrily calls her husband's office with a lame excuse when he's too hungover to go in to work. We're talking about the father who does his son's college term paper because he's afraid his son won't do it and he desperately wants a lawyer in the family.

The Four of Hearts asks you to examine the idea of nurturing and wants you to find your place on the learning curve between its healthy and unhealthy forms.

UPRIGHT

INDIVIDUAL: The Upright Four of Hearts describes an individual with a destiny path of setting aside his own interests in favor of what is best for society as a whole. This is a healthy, idealistic person with a sincere universal love of humanity. He will protect and nurture any of God's children who fall into his sphere of responsibility.

Our society thrives because of people who possess noble ideals and the energy to assert them. The Four of Hearts represents our doctors, honest politicians, and Peace Corps volunteers. It stands for our nurses, teen drug counselors, and police officers.

The Upright Four rarely represents a new romantic prospect. When it does, this person will act the same with everybody. He'll treat his daughter the same way he treats the supermarket checkout lady. He'll be equally polite and equally distant with them both. As his lover, you'll be subject to his uniform manner too. You won't feel singled out or special. The Four of Hearts man is a wonderful person with a big heart and noble ideals, but he isn't close to his intimate partners. Most women can't handle his impersonal manner. Should you grow to love the man represented by the Upright Four, you must accept him as he is and allow him his distance because the universal brotherhood routine is actually the healthiest style of relating he has at his disposal.

RELATIONSHIP: The marriage described by the Upright Four is reliable because these two are comrades in arms. They're actively devoted to the same causes and united in their efforts to uplift the unfortunate or oppressed among us. This couple is politically correct and politically involved.

The new liaison described by the Upright Four will begin in a public place or through a group affiliation. This man won't ask you out on a date right off the bat, because he isn't thinking of you in a sexy, flirty way. That's not to say he never will, it's just that he's more likely to invite you to a seminar than to ask you out for a drink. He'll be quite passionate about the seminar though. What he's looking for is a woman who shares his political opinions and his concern for the environment. He wants a partner who's as worked up over oil rigs in the Arctic Refuge as he is. He's looking for a girl who'll boycott grapes until the migrant workers get a decent health plan or at least help him hand out flyers at the "Save the Harp Seals" rally.

CIRCUMSTANCES: The environment defined by the Four is a clique, a neighborhood, or a committee assembled for a worthy cause. The Four represents a group of like-thinking people whose ideals bond them together.

The car, house, or job depicted by the Upright Four of Hearts will be community oriented or owned by a collective. This is the car you went thirds on with your two roommates. It's government housing or a job working for Greenpeace.

REVERSED

INDIVIDUAL: The Reversed Four person resents setting aside his own interests for the sake of others. He prefers to live a life of juvenile pursuits in search of a caregiver to enable those pursuits. He sees *himself* as the one in need and he expects others to nurture and care for him. He's dependent at any age.

The individual represented by the Reversed Four has a significant destiny. His life's task is to make the transition from child to parent. I'll repeat that: *He must mature sufficiently to make the shift from being the child to being the parent.*

Eventually he'll learn to set aside his own egocentric needs for the sake of humankind. In order to accomplish his assignment, he must learn to take care of himself. Once he's completely independent, he'll develop a reservoir of surplus time, money, and energy he can donate to others.

The new romantic prospect represented by the Reversed Four is hungry for love. He's the needy type who can't survive for another twenty minutes unless you swear on a stack of Bibles that you adore him above everyone and everything else on earth and will never leave him. He's completely codependent. So much so that after a mere three months of dating he would quit his job, sell his house, and move to another state if he thought you'd love him for doing so. Until he works a Twelve-Step program for his dependency issues, he's not a stable marital prospect.

RELATIONSHIP: If you accept a date with a guy represented by the Reversed Four he's going to hook your dependency issues. He'll have a subtle way of getting you to do things for him without making a clear request. He'll sort of gently mention in passing that he has a mountain of receipts he needs to organize before the accountant can do his taxes, but he just can't bring himself to organize the receipts. He'll say, "Tiny piles of paper just don't get along with me," as he runs his hands through his hair and exhales a sigh of resignation. Any girl who ever took a high school bookkeeping class would chirp, "I'll sort them out for you." Especially if he's good looking. Within six months you'll be doing all the office work for his construction company, free of charge, on the weekends. Within a year, he'll assign you his brother's bookkeeping system too.

If you pull the Reversed Four of Hearts to describe a new man, resist the urge to say, "Sure, anything you like," and decline his invitations to dinner. This relationship is like a tar baby. You'll get one hand stuck, push with another to pull out the first, and wind up wrapped in a suffocating black ball of goo. The Reversed Four is a trap. Stay away.

The established relationship represented by the Reversed Four of Hearts is so classically codependent that one half of this duo has no idea how he really feels or what he wants for himself. He only knows what his partner feels and wants. This is the classic marriage between a Giver and a Taker. The weepy, self-abnegating, overwhelmed Giver has the power to stop the cycle of unhealthy relating, but he or she is the least likely to do so.

CIRCUMSTANCES: There's a third side to the Four of Hearts, which lies between the Upright and Reversed positions. It's a transition zone. When we enter the zone we turn and gaze back across our shoulder to another time, person, or event and allow our heart to fill with a deep longing for what might have been. When we feel like this, we're caught between our twin needs for freedom and safety, which is part of the journey from youth to maturity. Therefore, you will long to possess the car, job, or apartment represented by the Reversed card, but you won't be able to.

NOTE

When the Four appears in your spread, it comes as a reminder that assuming the role of caretaker is an insolent act of vanity. The Four believes we only succeed in hobbling those who depend on us because our "help" doesn't allow them to develop living and coping skills on their own. In Four of Hearts terms, it's an arrogance to assume our loved ones are incompetent and unable to function without our superior intervention.

The Upright Four says you must care for yourself before you can provide for another. The Upright card compliments those who pour their hearts into the well-being of children and it says you're a bona fide saint if you donate your time to the volunteer police force.

The Reversed card scolds you. It's the card of the Parasite and the Host. It says you've taken on too much, more than is reasonable. It says you've thrown yourself away in the hopes that a man, child, or parent will love you. Or perhaps you've allowed someone to set their life aside in order to cater to yours. Read the Ace of Hearts if you want to know what real love is like. Upright or Reversed, the Four of Hearts doesn't come close to the warm, empathetic connection you seek.

UPRIGHT: "You wish!" Throw this card away and pull another.
REVERSED: "Absolutely not," even though you long for it!

Five of Hearts

Fives: Conflict
Hearts: Emotions

GRIEF

When my father died, my uncle Archie called the house at 6 A.M. He said, "I'm sorry, honey. Your dad passed away this morning." I still had the phone in my hand when I stumbled backward into my husband's arms.

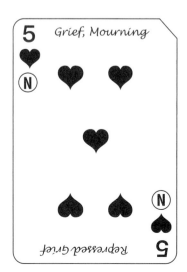

I still miss my dad every day of my life. I can't drive past our rural community airport without a twinge in my stomach. My father used Granddad's tractor to plow the first runway into an unused tomato field right after World War II. He and his buddies used the level ribbon of dirt to fly their wives to Vegas in Uncle Jerry's Piper Cub. I picture the guys young and handsome in dark trousers, neckties loosened, sport coats tossed over their shoulders, hanging off a thumb. Their wives are excited, with matching handbags and pumps, white gloves clutched in their fists as they tiptoe-run across the tomato rows, trying to save their new shoes. I can see the mothers of my playmates demurely crawling into the cockpit of the tiny new plane. I idle at the light by the airport entrance and my heart swells with pain and pride. I become a girl again and my grief for my lost father is as fresh as it was ten years ago on the morning my uncle called to say he was gone forever.

The Five of Hearts is the card of the loss I feel even now, so many years later.

UPRIGHT

The Five of Hearts depicts the tears we shed over real injuries. It stands as a reminder that when we suffer a great loss, extreme feelings are normal, healthy, and appropriate.

They say there are specific stages to the grieving process: shock, denial, anger, and resolution. A few sources include bargaining and others substitute the word "acceptance" for "resolution." They say some people move through the stages quickly and others work through them very slowly.

INDIVIDUAL: The individual described by the Upright Five of Hearts is in mourning. He needs love and support because his loss is deep and significant.

The new romantic prospect represented by the Five is despondent. This man is in tears over a breakup, a death, or a betrayal so startling that it's fractured his fundamental beliefs about life and love. You can't expect him to begin a flirtatious romance with you right now, but he sure could use a friend.

RELATIONSHIP: When the Five appears in response to a relationship question, it speaks to heart-wrenching disappointment.

The married couple represented by the card is in mourning. They've lost a family member, a child, or one another.

If the Card of Tears represents your bright new union, it will make you sadder than you can imagine. It will break your heart.

CIRCUMSTANCES: Any car, job, or house represented by the Five will disappoint you. The car will die, the company will downsize, and the apartment will slip through your fingers. For some reason, this loss will be an emotional setback for you and you won't get over it quickly.

REVERSED

When the bruised and delicate Five falls Reversed it stands for the repression or intellectualization of heartache:

"I never loved him/her anyway."

"Everyone has to die sometime."

INDIVIDUAL: The Reversed Five describes a person who's made a conscious decision to set aside his anguish in order to feel "okay." He's disappointed, but he shrugs off his broken heart in an attempt to postpone his grief or to avoid it altogether.

Let's imagine a friend of ours took his girlfriend to his company Christmas party where she drank a whole bottle of wine, flirted outrageously with his manager, and completely ignored her date. Perhaps she even went so far as to give the manager her home phone number, sit on his lap, or ask him to drive her home. When our guy called her up the morning after, she told him she didn't remember a thing because she was drunk.

Now, picture our friend telling his coworkers, "I should never allow my girlfriend to drink. Boy, I won't make that mistake at next year's party!"

Translation: "I'm going to pretend this doesn't hurt so I won't have to leave her, lose at love, or put in any grief time."

It's better for our guy to be disappointed and move on. Turning a blind eye to the obvious to avoid the pain of failure is just a Band-Aid flapping in the breeze. His attitude is a temporary solution to a serious problem.

A second version of the individual defined by the Reversed Five is someone who puts pressure on himself to "get over it." It may have been a year since he broke up with that girl from the Christmas party and he's still sad and disheartened. Now he thinks it's been long enough and he ought to be improved emotionally, but he's still sad. He says, "Great, I'm doing great!" But he's not. He's still hurt, and slightly ashamed that he continues to mourn the loss of such a person.

Our Reversed Five guy ought to turn on his emotional faucets and let his tears run out. Open sadness will appear more honest to his friends and family. Our Five of Hearts friend doesn't know it's okay to weep and grieve, even to rage at God, and to grant himself the time he needs to complete the mourning process, no matter how long it takes. If he were "over it" the card wouldn't be in his spread Upright or Reversed. The Five will disappear from his readings when he has no more tears to shed, when his loss has been absorbed and he's healed, but not before.

RELATIONSHIP: The established couple represented by the Reversed card is no longer together. They tell their friends their breakup didn't hurt that much, but the truth is that it did and sometimes it still does.

The new romance represented by the card has already disappointed you and by now you're aware of the problems that will terminate it.

CIRCUMSTANCES: This situation is falling apart and is already a sore spot. You don't want to talk about it or investigate it any further. Whatever this is, it hasn't worked out and you're more upset about it than you let on.

NOTE

The Five of Hearts is a card of sadness and disappointment. When Upright, it says you're in mourning now or aware your grief is inevitable. When the Five is Reversed, you're trying to dismiss your sorrow as insignificant. But your friends know the truth—that beneath the scab is a vicious wound. Until the abrasion disappears altogether, be kind to yourself. Take your time and try to own your feelings.

UPRIGHT or REVERSED: The Five of Hearts is one of the great "NOs" in the deck.

Six of Hearts

Sixes: Faith
Hearts: Emotions

FOREVER AND EVER, 'TIL DEATH DO US PART

UPRIGHT

The Six stands for the faith we have that our partner will stay with us all our life. The card represents our belief that one connection can last forever, that the capacity to love one person for thirty or forty years is hardwired into our DNA. The Six of Hearts corresponds to the part of us that persists, perseveres, and prevails over a long period of time.

INDIVIDUAL: The Upright Six of Hearts describes a person of vision who instinctively sets his sights far into the future. He's not the capricious, casual type who dances merrily along with an unabashed conviction that the Universe has him covered. The Six of Hearts guy *constructs* his life. He builds it by planning, saving, sacrificing, and by knowing who he is, where he's going, and why. He has always looked ahead and he always will.

If you pulled the Upright Six of Hearts to describe your new love interest, the card says he seeks a person he can live with for the rest of his life. He wants a woman who's easy to be around. She must have goals similar to his, be a team player, and appreciate a man who knows how to hang in there.

A Six of Hearts person understands that when he marries you, he marries your wounds, your baggage, and your family. He also understands that once you marry him you will live forever with his Oreo addiction and his baseball cap collection. It is in his nature to size up the girl he's dating. He asks himself, "Does she realize what she's getting herself into if she falls in love with me? Can this girl handle my schizophrenic brother who lives in the home? Is she a good enough sport to visit Tommy every Sunday for the rest of her life? Does she recognize what our existence will be like when Mom and Dad are gone and we're all the family Tommy has left?"

He'll sit with you in a delightful downtown bistro and charm you with witty stories from his Navy days. He'll share a bottle of Sauvignon Blanc and the goat cheese crostini. Meanwhile, in the back of his mind he'll be picturing his family and wondering if you're the kind of girl who would help him take care of Tommy.

The man described by the Upright Six of Hearts knows he defines himself by his choices. He understands that *who* he chooses and *what* he chooses will design his fate. Therefore, he carefully crafts his life by making long-term plans and careful decisions. The Six of Hearts man takes responsibility for his time on earth.

RELATIONSHIP: If you pulled this card to describe an established connection, it says the relationship will go on forever, just as it is. This person has always been there and they always will be.

When the Six of Hearts describes a new relationship it says the romance has long-term potential, that it will endure for the rest of your life in one form or another. If you meet his criteria (and apparently you do because you pulled this card) you can expect to build a life together.

The Six of Hearts describes the relationship that lasts a lifetime. Even if you don't remain lovers, you will remain friends.

CIRCUMSTANCES: The Upright Six is about mapping out an overview. It's an important card because at some point we have to ask ourselves what kind of life we want to live. The card stands for writing down where you intend to be in ten years and how you plan to get there.

The Six also corresponds to the child-rearing process, because your kids never totally leave you. They stay connected until one of them wheels you into Shady Acres.

The car, house, or job represented by the Upright Six has been around forever. This car is at least twelve years old and you've owned it for ten. You've been living in this house for an eternity and you've been at this job for years and years. If you pulled the card to describe a *brand-new* job, house, or car, you'll stay there until they have to dynamite you out.

REVERSED

INDIVIDUAL: The person represented by the Reversed Six *needs* a ten-year plan.

This guy doesn't think much beyond his next paycheck, next month's rent, or next Saturday night. He doesn't have a blueprint for life. He's made no provision for retirement, and he doesn't even have a savings account. He drives a leased vehicle and rents a small apartment. He's guilty of neglect. He simply hasn't thought to make plans for himself in any long-term way.

It's easy for him to meet a great girl, but he stays in the relationship only until she starts planning a future together. He can't (or won't) look that far down the road, so they part.

His jobs don't last either. Sometimes they're temporary by design, like when he's in construction and the work is seasonal or he finishes one house and moves on to the next one, but most often he quits or gets fired after a while. Everything in his life is temporary because he doesn't have an overview. Should he make a plan and adhere to it, the card will turn Upright automatically.

The Reversed Six man has great potential for longevity, but not until he learns the value of regular deposits into a mutual fund.

If you pulled the Reversed Six to describe yourself, you'd better make a list right now. Ask yourself, what kind of man do you need and what kind of relationship do you want? Do you want to get married, play the field, or find a good, solid union that isn't legally binding? What kind of career do you see in your future? Have you put any money aside for your retirement or your children's education? Are you running up your credit cards without any thoughts about how you'll pay the money back? What have you been doing with your life and what are you going to do with it from now on?

The Reversed Six says you're living in the present and it's not working for you. You need to focus on the big picture. The time has come to design a life you would like to live and to figure out how to make it happen.

RELATIONSHIP: This new romance will be temporary but quite positive. The Reversed card represents an important step. It's a rung on the ladder to your romantic destiny. This relationship will teach you how to be a good life partner for Mr. Right.

The established couple defined by the Reversed Six is either in a temporary situation that will end soon, or they're thinking the whole connection won't last much longer. Additional cards will predict the outcome of their current phase.

CIRCUMSTANCES: These circumstances won't last, which is great news if you're in college and dying to graduate, but bad news if you just found the roommate of your dreams.

The job described by the Reversed Six is temporary or literally a temp job. You'll learn new skills while you work there, and those skills will be valuable as you go forward to the next job. The car represented by the Six won't stay with you very long, but you'll upgrade to a better car when it goes.

NOTE

If you approached the oracle to ask the question "What will my new lover be like?" the answer is, "Like they have all been."

To the question "Will our love endure?" the Upright Six says, "Yes, forever." Reversed? "No. It's temporary."

UPRIGHT or REVERSED: It's a "Yes" card either way.

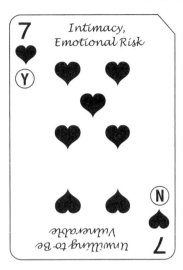

Seven of Hearts

Sevens: Tension and Self-Interest
Hearts: Emotions

After 50 years of treating sexual dysfunction, Masters & Johnson have a humble definition of good communication in a relationship: It's the privilege of exchanging vulnerabilities.
—People MAGAZINE

INTIMACY AND EMOTIONAL RISK

This is the card of communicating at a depth many people find uncomfortable. In the Two of Clubs we have a superficial style of talking used to exchange everyday pleasantries and common information. The Seven of Hearts speaks at another level—one that reveals the soul.

The Seven knows how difficult it is to expose your hopes, dreams, fears, and doubts to another person. It knows that looking into the deep recesses of your heart and searching for the shaky, gelatinous lump we call personal truth is a delicate, frightening process. The Seven understands the deep trust you place in the one who listens because sharing at this level can expose you to ridicule, disapproval, or rejection.

We call sharing the softest, most tender part of ourselves intimacy. People speak about "being intimate" but they often mistake sexual intercourse for closeness. They say, "Oh yes, we've been intimate for months." But any two people of any age and any gender, whether they know each other or not, can get naked and roll around in the dark together. That's not intimacy. You're intimate when you're vulnerable and honest.

We all enjoy the company of accessible people, so when you pull the Seven of Hearts Upright or Reversed, go ahead and make messy with your feelings. No one can really love you unless you expose the wacky carnival whirling inside your head.

UPRIGHT

INDIVIDUAL: The person represented by the Upright Seven of Hearts is open and unprotected by nature. He shares his inner world easily. You can trust him to listen without judging. This man will pay attention to you with his heart. Although he may not agree with you, he'll respect your right to feel the way you do. You can tell him anything.

The new lover portrayed by the Upright Seven is a natural-born Father Confessor so you'll be tempted to spill your guts on the first date. Later that night, after you kiss him good-bye, you'll lean the full weight of your body against the inside of the front door, exhale a huge sigh, and shake your head to clear the fog. You'll have had an intensely intimate experience and it will have left you breathless. You're going to fall in love with the new man represented by the Upright Seven of Hearts because he's just about the coolest guy you'll ever meet.

RELATIONSHIP: The Seven describes a deep, familiar connection based on the freedom to speak without censorship. There are no conversational taboos between these two. Theirs is an alliance that not only permits the full range of emotion but encourages it. Every great relationship has the Seven at its core because honesty is one of the primary components of a long-lasting, successful union.

The married couple defined by the Upright Seven permits one another to roam the world and come back with experiences and opinions to share. They've long since exposed every facet of their complex personalities to one another, everyone from their naughty inner child to their lame inner jerk.

As they get to know one another, the new twosome described by the Seven will discover it's okay to get real, bare their souls, and act like themselves.

The following quote by Maria Muldaur Craik sums up the Seven of Hearts relationship:

Oh, the comfort, the inexpressible comfort of feeling safe with a person, having neither to weigh thoughts nor measure words, but pouring them all right out, just as they are, chaff and grain together; certain that a faithful hand will take and sift them, keep what is worth keeping, and then with the breath of kindness blow the rest away.

CIRCUMSTANCES: Under these circumstances, you'll walk in circles as you wonder if you should speak, and once you decide you must speak, you'll wonder how to form the words. You'll tell yourself to get it together, find your courage, face your fears, and share the plain, honest truth. When you finally say what's on your mind you'll receive a positive response because people reward the truth no matter what it is. It's liberating to witness someone share their heart; it grants us permission to do the same. And the truth usually verifies what the other person was beginning to suspect, anyway.

If you want the apartment/job/car, just tell the landlord/boss/car dealer the truth. If you're totally honest, it'll be yours.

REVERSED

The Reversed card shows a reluctance to get close, to be exposed, and to share your feelings.

INDIVIDUAL: This one has many unspoken hopes, dreams, and anxieties, but he's incapable of expressing them for fear of being vulnerable, being known, and being rejected. This is a man with intimacy issues. The Reversed Seven husband feels intimidated by the demands of soul communion. He takes a job as a traveling salesman or as a tuna fisherman, so he can go on the road or out to sea for three months at a time. He's the guy who picks a fight when you run out of milk, just so he can stomp out the door and escape the relentlessness of day-to-day intimacy.

Men who fear vulnerability make jokes in moments of extreme honesty. A sense of humor is charming, but ask yourself, "Does the humor push me away or draw me in?" If the jokes don't pull you in, they're being used to lure you away from a topic that frightens the Reversed Seven man and makes him feel exposed.

If you pulled the Reversed card to describe your new boyfriend, he'll be reluctant to share his inner life because he's afraid to look needy or foolish. Perhaps you can create an emotionally open environment by sharing some of your own fears, ambitions, or anxieties. Someone has to go first, so why not you?

RELATIONSHIP: The established couple represented by the upside-down Seven of Hearts isn't close. They may be married and walk through life shoulder to shoulder, but each one feels separate and alone. Their conversations are about scheduling, finances, and children. They don't turn to one another in times of crisis because neither is willing to be open with the other. Besides, they have intimate relationships built up elsewhere. He tells his troubles to his minister, his golf buddies, or his mother. She tells her problems to her sister. They can't find the friendship and under-standing they need within the confines of their marriage so they find it elsewhere. This man and wife may sleep together, but they're more inti-mate with their children, their friends, or their parents.

The new couple depicted by the card doesn't aspire to share at a level that will hold them together for a lifetime. Neither is willing to expose his tender underside so even if they find their way to the altar they won't connect emotionally. They're unwilling to risk the exposure.

CIRCUMSTANCES: If you pulled the Reversed Seven to describe a car, job, or apartment, it says don't tell the car dealer/boss/landlord anything. Keep your feelings to yourself.

NOTE

The individual defined by the Upright Seven of Hearts is a warm, open, vulnerable soul who seeks closeness and honesty in all his dealings. This is a rich, mature card with a message of trust and love.

The person defined by the Reversed card should try exposing his most private hopes and fears. The experience of speaking up won't destroy him. In fact, he'll find greater love and understanding if he shares his inner life.

UPRIGHT: "Yes!"
REVERSED: "No," but only because you're chicken.

Eight of Hearts

Eights: Philosophy
Hearts: Emotions

GENEROSITY

In the ancient Gypsy fortune-telling tradition the Eight of Hearts describes a monetary gift or bribe. In modern times it is more likely to represent the gift of love.

The Eight of Hearts describes the need to accept love as it exists in the moment. It doesn't address sex or romance, but depicts the warmth and affection that sustain relationships on a

day-to-day basis. The card says the gift of another's affection only has as much value as you place on it, and recommends that you be grateful for the daily love in your life.

UPRIGHT

Often the Upright Eight says your romantic goals are eclipsing the essence of your union. Just because you've been dating for twelve months it doesn't logically conclude the relationship should progress to an engagement, and then a wedding, next a newborn, and ultimately to a house in the suburbs. To hold the union to a specific, linear timetable is to place destructive, ambitious pressures on it.

The Eight of Hearts says relax. High regard is a gift unto itself and an end in itself. Other logical manifestations of adoration, or symbolic "steps forward," have no value at this time. A strong and enduring love is without demands. It exists in the moment, and is fueled by a tenacious belief that mutual generosity is the best basis for attachment.

INDIVIDUAL: This is the middle-age love card because the individual represented by the Eight has already fulfilled his childhood dream. He had the fantasy wedding to his high school sweetheart, had the firstborn child, and bought his starter home. This person no longer seeks emotional milestones in his life. At this stage of the game he wants to pass his time in pleasant company without the ardent romantic ambitions of his youth. He's probably divorced. Therefore, he seeks the *affection* of relationships and not the symbolic manifestations of Great Love. To this one, Great Love didn't pan out; now he needs a friend.

The person represented by the Upright Eight of Hearts is a philosophical, benevolent soul who will never surrender his belief in the basic goodness of mankind. When he's single he trusts in the whims of fate. He knows one day he could turn a busy street corner, bump into the newspaper vendor, and find true love. He believes in hope as a way of life.

The new prospect defined by the Upright Eight will respond to you with generosity and kindness. You will long to stand next to him because he'll radiate a personal warmth that appeals to something primitive in you. The Eight of Hearts man represents your second chance at love. If you've been married before, he'll slowly develop into your second husband.

RELATIONSHIP: The established union described by the Upright Eight exists between two people who agree that respect, kindness, and generosity create the only successful basis for a relationship. This is the second marriage that turns out to be an enormous improvement over the first one. The Upright Eight represents the kind of union you always dreamed of creating with the right person.

The new alliance depicted by the card will develop into the friendly romance described above. This man won't care if the public approves of his significant other. He'll care how much she loves him just the way he is. He'll allow the relationship to develop at a leisurely pace because he'll want to make sure you're nothing like his ex. When the Eight represents your relationship, he'll find the right woman in you.

CIRCUMSTANCES: These circumstances are some of the best in the deck. The job represented by the Upright Eight will offer you more money than you ever thought you could earn. This car will be karmic payback. It'll be compensation for the good deeds you've done all your life. This apartment will be a lovely dwelling in a divine setting and the landlord will throw in a new washer and dryer just because he likes you.

REVERSED

When the Eight of Hearts falls Reversed it dries up, and its boundless generosity turns into scorekeeping and penny pinching.

INDIVIDUAL: The individual defined by the Reversed Eight is a hit-and-run lover with drive-thru romance on his mind. He won't offer you more because he doesn't have anything more to give. Cynical and selfish, he places no value on tender affection. He's just looking for a one-night stand. At his best, he's hyper-aware of "what *he* did for you" versus "what *you* did for him." Scorekeeping never works out, either. If you want to tally up all the dinners, back rubs, and phone calls you both made, it's not hard to find an imbalance. Don't extend your heart to the miserly soul represented by the Reversed Eight. He won't perceive your attempts at love for what they are.

RELATIONSHIP: When the Reversed Eight describes an actual relationship, which it rarely does, the union isn't reliable. Both parties have doubts about finding fulfillment here because neither has much to offer or shows up on a regular basis. These two are ships that pass in the night. Theirs is a pit-stop romance. They bump into one another briefly and continue on their separate ways, living their separate lives.

The married couple represented by the card will interact with love and generosity one day and then turn stingy and emotionally unavailable the next. This relationship is blocked and, for now, these two are caught in a stalemate.

CIRCUMSTANCES: The environment described by the Reversed Eight isn't fulfilling because there is no budget for unnecessary extras. This corporation wouldn't dream of throwing money away on employee benefits like paid vacations, health insurance, or maternity leave. The house defined by the Reversed Eight has no mirror over the bathroom sink and no curtains on the windows. There are no flowers on the table and no pictures on the walls. This car lies in the driveway bleeding oil all day. It only runs when it's in the mood to.

If you pulled the Reversed Eight to describe yourself you aren't valuing simple love, aren't participating fully in the moment, and you might be guilty of keeping score. It's easy to turn the Eight around. Just pledge never to measure your efforts against his again. Don't attempt to move this relationship forward either. There's nowhere for it to go, it just *is*. In your moments of doubt, look into the eyes of your best friend/lover and smile at him from way down inside. This card is what Life and Love are all about.

NOTE

Upright, the Eight of Hearts refers to the precious but intangible gift of love. Reversed, the gift is minor, if it exists at all.

UPRIGHT: A gracious, grown-up "Yes."
REVERSED: A whiny, pinched "No."

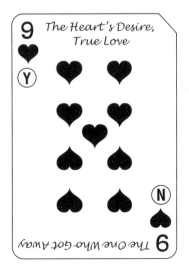

Nine of Hearts

Nines: Culmination
Hearts: Emotions

THE HEART'S DESIRE

The Nine of Hearts is the card you were hoping to pull when you bought this book. It represents True Love and promises the fulfillment of your romantic hopes and dreams beyond your most inflated expectations. The Nine stands for the person, relationship, or circumstance you most desire in the deepest part of your soul. I don't think the mind is capable of absorbing the depth of this card. You can only feel it with your heart. Even then, your joy will be so great that you may not be able to express it.

UPRIGHT

INDIVIDUAL: The Upright Nine of Hearts stands for "the One." This man is a gift from heaven. He's exactly the person you've been praying for all your life. He has the precise character traits you put on the wish list that you taped to the refrigerator door the night you decided to manifest Mr. Right.

The man represented by the Nine of Hearts will recognize who you really are and will love that person more than any other in the world. He won't pick you because you were a cheerleader, or have a gorgeous figure, or drive a nice car. He'll pick you because he genuinely knows who you are and desires to be with you. The Nine of Hearts represents your match. He's the one who's been in training all his life to be right for you.

RELATIONSHIP: Nines are cards of culmination, so the Nine of Hearts doesn't ordinarily appear at the beginning of a romance. It tends to show up after you've dated awhile and made love. You pull it when your union already has a solid foundation and you're examining the connection for its long-term potential. But if it does define a new relationship, it describes a smooth courtship that evolves easily and rapidly into a very special alliance.

The married couple represented by the Upright Nine is fully satisfied with their partnership. Neither believes they could find a better mate than the one they married. These two are so connected, so in tune, that there's no person or problem that could pull them apart for a fraction of a nanosecond.

Another description of the Upright Nine relationship is the one where you loved the guy with your whole heart, but it didn't work out and you had to give up on him. He was the "Great Love of Your Life" who got away. Luckily, he came to his senses and came back. The time apart showed him you're the best he can ever hope to do. It showed him how empty his world is without you.

The Nine of Hearts romance has a Cinderella quality. It glitters and sparkles. It inspires and uplifts those of us who watch it from the bleachers with our hands folded over our hearts and sighs of wonder and fascination on our lips.

CIRCUMSTANCES: The Upright Nine describes your dream job, your dream house, your dream car, or your dream vacation. Any undertaking represented by the card will be more successful than you ever thought possible and more suited to you than you dared to hope. Congratulations! You may have just won the lottery.

REVERSED

INDIVIDUAL: This person has the whole list: a great personality, a decent job, and a nice home. He goes to church, is a sweet lover, is physically attractive, likes kids, and is good to your parents.

Now subtract one or two traits. He's not perfect, but he's close. Real close.

A young woman might be "settling" if she married this guy. But, if you're middle-age and you pulled the Reversed Nine to describe your boyfriend, he'll suffice.

By midlife a woman has a greater understanding of human nature. At forty she knows no one is perfect, especially her. She knows that anyone she believes to be ideal isn't. She knows the Ideal Man is either a phony or that she's so blinded by lust that she isn't capable of evaluating his character. If you're over forty and you pulled this card to describe your boyfriend, leave him alone. Allow him to do his thing while you go do yours and you'll be fine together. If you're under forty you won't be happy married to the Reversed Nine man because he won't fulfill your romantic notion of how a Knight in Shining Armor would look, act, or think.

RELATIONSHIP: When this most coveted of cards falls Reversed, it talks about the relationship that looks superior and enduring, but isn't. You will love this person and he will love you, but the timing will be wrong, external circumstances will interfere, or some tiny piece of his character won't work for you.

Your objection to the new prospect represented by the Reversed Nine may be so petty that you'll be too embarrassed to mention it. The minor irritation will terminate the union nonetheless.

The established couple represented by the Reversed card is pruning the list of traits their ideal mate ought to have. This is the phase during which they must either accept that their partner has a few more flaws than they originally noticed or terminate the union because of those flaws. When the Reversed Nine represents an existing alliance, both parties are in the process of adjusting their perception of their mate. Only time will tell if they survive the adjustment or if it causes them to part for good.

For a single woman, the Reversed Nine represents the perfect match she couldn't hold on to. This is the one she will always remember, the one whose letters she will keep all her life, the one whose name will stick in her throat when she has to say it out loud. She will go on to marry and bear children with another, equally wonderful man who will possess 90 percent of her heart. The other 10 percent will always belong to the Reversed Nine lover. It's just a fact of life she will live with because she'll never completely get over the man represented by the Reversed card. She may not say a word, but every year on his birthday, she'll stop for a bittersweet moment to remember how much she loved him and how sad it is that they were unable to stay together.

CIRCUMSTANCES: The Reversed Nine of Hearts says the situation won't be ideal, but if you're willing to work with what you have, it might turn out okay.

This is the car you always wanted at the price you needed, but unfortunately, it's the wrong color. This is the apartment in the building across the street from the beach, but the only available unit doesn't have an ocean view.

If you pulled the Nine of Hearts Reversed, rent the two-bedroom with the city view and put your name on the waiting list for an ocean view. Eventually you'll get the better apartment, but it will take time. Go ahead and buy the tangerine-colored car because you can always paint it. You'll have to save up for the paint job, so the car won't be perfect right away. If you're patient, you'll get the money and the paint job will turn the car into a reasonable facsimile of your dream vehicle.

NOTE

When Upright, the Nine of Hearts describes your heart's desire. It stands for your dream lover, your White Knight, and your True Love.

When Reversed, you'll have no choice in the matter. Your fingers will slowly untie and you'll float apart. You two were not meant to be together despite the depth of feeling between you.

UPRIGHT: The card is a blessing to receive.
   "Yes" does not begin to say it.
REVERSED: It's sad to be so close and to lose.
   But the answer is, "No, I'm afraid not."

Ten of Hearts

Tens: Doorways
Hearts: Emotions

HOME

All Tens are doorways. The Ten of Hearts opens its door onto a more satisfying emotional environment. This is the emotional climate-control card and represents an adjustment on your emotional thermostat. The card will manifest as a new home or a new relationship.

UPRIGHT

When I pull the Ten, I feel wrapped in my gold chenille afghan with the long fringe. I shrug deeper into the arms of my favorite chair and reach for my coffee cup while the cat purrs at my side. I see piles of books, smell the lavender growing in the field behind my house, and the slow Delta blues float on the air around me.

INDIVIDUAL: Whether male or female, the person described by the Ten of Hearts is a regular down-home Earth Mother. He or she is just a great big cozy lap we can crawl onto when we need a hug. These folks are the absolute heart and soul of their families. Tubs of homemade spaghetti sauce, gallons of ice cream, chickens, turkeys, sides of salmon, and pork chops are crammed into their freezer. There's always room for one more at their table. This one keeps extra slippers, toothbrushes, and pillows on hand just in case someone needs to sleep over.

   If you pulled the Ten of Hearts to describe a new romantic prospect the card says he's the domestic type. He likes to cook, knows how to iron, and is not allergic to washing dishes. This guy likes to spend his weekends at home in a T-shirt and sweatpants. He stirs the stew with one hand and runs the vacuum with the other while he explains to the neighbor kid how to assemble his Styrofoam airplane. He's most comfortable sleeping in his own bed and prefers to eat at his own table or in front of his own TV. His dog even has his own chair in the living room.

The Ten of Hearts man seeks a relationship with a person like himself. He's in favor of blended families and extended families, so he'll make real friends with your mother. Expect him to be very attached to his own mother, but not in the cloying way that makes a girl feel like the other woman. He just thinks his mother is a nice person, respects her, and enjoys her company.

RELATIONSHIP: The Ten of Hearts describes the process of movin' on down the road to the next relationship. There are three stages to the process:

1. The decision to move away from an old alliance.
2. The angst of the process, including the healing phase.
3. The decision to open another door and meet somebody new.

The Upright card covers positions one and three.
The Reversed card covers position two.
The Ten of Hearts speaks to the first few dates in a new relationship. This is when couples talk about their backgrounds, their jobs, and their exes. It's when he takes her out for dinner or buys tickets to a concert. It's the first time she cooks her chicken pesto for him.

The Ten bestows a quiet domesticity to an established relationship. This couple lives together. They pass their early mornings in comfortable silence while they read the morning papers. Children and pets fall naturally into their household.

CIRCUMSTANCES: On a mundane level, the Upright Ten of Hearts is a physical move to a new home. The process has the same three parts:

1. The decision to move.
2. The turmoil of the process.
3. The settling-in phase.

Once again, the Upright card represents positions one and three of the process and the Reversed card represents position two.

Stage one is the decision to relocate. It includes listing the old place with a Realtor, searching the classifieds, and making an appointment to view a new place.

Stage three is the settling-in phase when the unpacking is finished and you're free to explore the new neighborhood.

When the Ten describes a dwelling, it has a sunny kitchen, a cozy fireplace, and a pleasant little garden. This house has Grandma's furniture in the living room and the kids' height marks on the kitchen doorjamb.

The job defined by the Ten of Hearts employs such a closely knit group of people that they function as a kind of family. The group will stay in touch long after they move on to new jobs.

REVERSED

INDIVIDUAL: The new romantic prospect represented by the Reversed Ten is in the process of movin' on. He's struggling for closure on his last relationship. Eventually he'll be a good catch, but he isn't right now. He has unfinished business to take care of and, until he puts the past behind him, he's not completely available for you. In fact, he might be dating you in the hope you'll help bury the memory of his last girlfriend.

The mother of the Reversed Ten man clings to him. He makes sincere efforts to disengage from her, but she pulls him back. She needs him and he needs a home. Before you invest your emotions here, you should know that part of his package is a difficult, needy mother.

The Reversed Ten of Hearts man is involved in a major life shift. Proceed slowly and wait until after his life is settled to pin your hopes on him.

RELATIONSHIP: In the section on the Upright Card, I listed the three stages of leaving an established relationship and starting a new one. The Reversed Ten governs step two, which is the turmoil of closing the door on an emotional environment that no longer satisfies. The Reversed card governs "Dear John" letters and those horrible "Let's Just Be Friends" speeches. It covers the decision to join a dating service, to subscribe to an online matchmaker site, or to accept a blind date with your roommate's cousin.

We all feel displaced when we attempt to make a new romantic connection. We know a new person is going to evaluate us, so we feel a degree of discomfort. It makes most of us want to stay home and curl up with a blanket and a good book. It makes us want a safe, familiar person or place. But we can't get to the relaxed stage of the dating process until we have endured this edgy, transitional one.

CIRCUMSTANCES: The Reversed Ten represents step two of the moving process, which is the hustle of packing, labeling, truck loading, and the drive across town with your mattress and bicycle tied on top of the car.

When pulled to describe your job, the Reversed Ten says you want out of there. In fact, it describes the steps you're taking to leave, like sending out your résumé, scanning the "Help Wanted" section, or listing yourself with a headhunter.

NOTE

The Ten always predicts a move. It stands for the process of finding a better place to hang your hat or your heart. The card stands for a new home or new arms to hold you gently, warmly, safely.

UPRIGHT or REVERSED: The Ten is always a "Yes."

Jack of Hearts

Jacks: Young People
Hearts: Emotions

PASSION AND DESIRE

The Jack of Hearts is the primary indicator of sexual attraction and stands for high achievement in the sensuality department. The card's erotic energy settles over a couple like a fog. Lovers lose themselves under its influence because the Jack's romantic haze softens the harder, more practical aspects of their union. The card adds nothing to a relationship but a flirtatious sensuality. Other cards describe tenderness of emotion (Two of Hearts), intellectual intimacy (Seven of Hearts), or commitment (Four of Clubs). The Jack of Hearts only represents the seductive allure of pheromones, the scent cues animals use to find and identify their mates.

UPRIGHT

The couple represented by the Upright Jack is definitely sleeping together and the sex is gourmet caliber.

INDIVIDUAL: The Jack depicts a lover who's dazzling in the early stages of a relationship, but has no real staying power. This is an emotionally dwarfed individual who enjoys the pursuit, the wooing, and the first few sexual encounters. He's not interested in a long-term alliance with its expectations and obligations. He seeks to be adorable, romantic, and worshipped. He's watching for that look of lust/trust/love in your eyes. He'll produce an endless stream of flattering, romantic gestures until he spots that look on your face. Once he sees it, he'll have his conquest and he'll move on. One day he'll wave cheerily to you from across a crowded dance floor where he'll sit perched over cocktails with his newest flame—poor girl. He'll wink at you, like you were in on the fun of the game all along. Jacks don't correspond to gender, so it could be a male or female who's the player.

My friend Jill told me a story about meeting a handsome Jack of Hearts in a nightclub. He was the lead singer in the band. As his group began a slow ballad he spotted Jill in the audience and locked eyes with her. He held her gaze as he hopped gracefully off the stage and navigated the crowd crooning the romantic words. She claims the spotlight stayed with him as he moved toward her across the dark dance floor. She said a white light glowed behind his perfect silhouette like a halo. He finished his song just as he reached her. He was moist eyed and obviously moved by her beauty and her soulful demeanor. The audience went wild with applause when he folded her into his arms at the end of the song. Then he bounced back onstage, broke into another number, and wandered off to the next girl. After melting her knees in front of all her friends, he never noticed Jill again.

RELATIONSHIP: The new relationship defined by the Jack is a sexy cocktail of tenderness and lust. This card describes the high we feel in the beginning stages of a passionate courtship. When you pull the Jack to describe your new liaison, try to keep your wits about you. Don't make any permanent decisions until you sober up. The card signals a Club Med kind of union and there may be no real basis for a full relationship. Wait and see.

The Jack of Hearts romance is described here, as the card stands alone. Additional cards will show other aspects of the connection. Richer, more permanent cards will supply the anchor the Jack needs to be a positive influence for a prolonged period of time. The card's a special addition to a well-established union. Any more earthbound couple would envy the twenty-year marriage represented by the Jack.

CIRCUMSTANCES: These circumstances are romantic, flirtatious, and openly sexual. In response to the question, "What will our new home be like?" the Jack says it will have a Jacuzzi in the garden, a minibar in the bedroom, and a deep cushy love seat on the balcony. Your new home will be a romantic haven.

The working environment described by the Jack is the one with the racy jokes taped to the microwave. It has the Christmas party that ends with the traffic manager and the receptionist emerging from the supply room together, he with lipstick on his collar and she with her sweater on backwards. A place like this would be fun if you were single and open minded, but threatening if you were married or conservative.

The car represented by the Jack is a sexy Corvette, Porsche, or bright red Mustang convertible.

REVERSED

The "Not Doing It" card.

INDIVIDUAL: The new romantic prospect described by the Reversed Card of Passion has sex on the brain but he's not taking action on his desire. He isn't holding back because of his religious or social convictions. The sensual Hearts don't moralize; the Clubs do. It's more likely that he has performance anxiety, doesn't want to make his move until he's sure you have feelings for him, or thinks his attraction to you is inappropriate in some way. But, make no mistake; he's definitely infatuated.

A second interpretation for the Reversed Jack is the beloved, over-protected, emotionally indulged child of any age. This is a True Romance between parent and offspring. It's the ultimate nonsexual, chaste attachment.

When I see this card I want to caution the parents. I know they love their baby, but their love may be holding him back. As the Favorite, he's at risk of maturing into a flirtatious Jack of Hearts because he believes his adorability is his primary attribute. Early responsibilities, restrictions, and disappointments are crucial to his long-term development. Without them, he could spend his life floating high above the real world, searching for his dream of unconditional admiration like Mom and Dad gave him, even at forty.

RELATIONSHIP: The Reversed Jack describes a brand-new, very romantic connection between two people so turned on by one another that even total strangers are tempted to hose 'em down. Their relationship hasn't built up to sexual contact yet, but they're both filled with an overwhelming anticipation of the big event. Let's hope they don't explode in the meantime.

The established couple represented by the card isn't sleeping together. Maybe they're separated or physically unable to participate. Perhaps they've drifted apart or one member refuses to cooperate with the other. Throw additional cards on the Jack to find the cause of the sexual drought. Perhaps it's because of ill health, guilt, or feelings of inadequacy. Sometimes one partner likes to control the alliance by withholding sex. Or maybe one isn't physically attracted to the other. Additional cards will describe the source of the problem.

CIRCUMSTANCES: The corporate environment represented by the Reversed Card of Physical Pleasure is so circumspect that no woman would dare to wear a skirt above the knee. Dating a coworker is discouraged or prohibited, the office parties are so wholesome that they leave a sugary aftertaste in your mouth, and management has a long history of favoritism. Any environment represented by the Jack of Hearts contains a great deal of sexual tension, but no one is taking action on the energy.

This home accommodates the children rather than the parents. The patio is a roller rink, the garden is a soccer field, and the wet bar has been converted to a soda fountain. The adults in this household claim all their children as their favorites.

This car is a beige Buick with clear plastic seat covers, a window shade on the passenger's side, and a Kleenex dispenser between the seats. Soccer balls and Pampers fill the trunk and AAA decals cover the windows. It's the least sexy car on the road.

NOTE

The Jack of Hearts sets the passion meter on high. It describes the sexual tension found at the beginning of a brand-new encounter and is the most clear indicator of whether or not a couple is doin' the deed. Romantic and stimulating, the Jack of Hearts is the hubba-hubba card.

UPRIGHT or REVERSED: "Yeah, baby."

Queen of Hearts

Queens: Women
Hearts: Emotions

MOM

The Queen of Hearts is sensitive, emotionally available, family oriented, and aware she has a domesticated nature from an early age. She's your mother, grandmother, wife, or sister. The Queen is the nurturing woman who kissed away your owies and baked your birthday cakes when you were little. To this day she still knows how you feel or what you need because she's still completely tuned in to you.

The Queen of Hearts is usually a Water sign woman: Pisces, Cancer, or Scorpio.

UPRIGHT

INDIVIDUAL: The Queen of Hearts has a highly developed intuition. In the middle of the night she'll sit bolt upright in bed to say, "Little Johnny needs me!" And she'll be right, even when Johnny is forty and living on the other side of the continent.

I have a Queen of Hearts girlfriend who always volunteers to drive despite the fact that she never has the directions. She shrugs and says, "Oh, I'll just know it when we get there." I've learned over time to sit back and enjoy the view. She never gets lost. Not ever.

The Queen's home is her sanctuary. It's the one place where she can be herself and feel comfortable. She likes to fill up her refrigerator with her favorite foods and cover her walls with the soothing colors and prints that appeal to her romantic sensibilities. She meditates on her curtains and fusses with her linens. She wants to get the *feeling* of her environment just right. When she invites you into her home for tea or spaghetti she's acknowledging the special place you hold in her heart. She's inviting you to witness her at her core. This puts you on another level, on the inside.

The Queen's favorite colors reflect her moods and her watery nature. She loves all the colors of the sea, from the palest celadon to the deep bloody burgundies of the ocean's depth. Teal or mossy green velvet makes her sigh. Tiny luminescent threads running through fabrics remind her of an abalone. Harsh whites don't appeal to her; the pale blushes found in the creams and pinks of seashells do.

The Queen's days revolve around her emotional connections and her sensual nature. Therefore, her sex life is all Gothic domesticity. She never gets bored making love to her man because he's the lord and protector of her world, but her children will outrank even him.

The Queen of Hearts is the Queen of Sentimentality. Drawings, souvenirs, and snapshots cover her refrigerator door. She keeps Junior's homemade Mother's Day cards well into his middle age and she keeps the final torn fragment of his blankie in her jewelry box forever.

Your Queen of Hearts friend never drops by empty-handed. She brings a fruit basket, homemade cookies, a new CD, or the latest novel she read. She brings something that will nourish you at some level. Mine brings beer, which reminds me to mention the Alcohol Factor. These girls love a tall, frosty one on a summer afternoon, a bit of the bubbly after work, and a small brandy at bedtime. The Queen of Hearts has been known to overdo the alcohol.

If you pulled the Queen to describe your new boyfriend, she will describe a man who's responsible for young children. The appearance of the Queen tells you he seeks a wife, that he's shopping for a woman who's emotionally available, family oriented, sensual, and affectionate. It wouldn't hurt if she could cook too.

RELATIONSHIP: You'll find the Queen of Hearts alliance to be deeply satisfying. Within this union you'll be free to express your feelings, your sensuality, and your intuition.

The marriage represented by the Queen is a loving connection between two people who value home, family, and children above all else. Fertility will never be a problem for this couple.

The new romance depicted by the card will fill your heart with hope and unleash your tender, sentimental side. You will come to feel you belong with this partner, and someday he'll fold you into his loving arms and propose.

CIRCUMSTANCES: When the Queen describes your job, a maternal woman will own the company and it will be mom-friendly. You'll get time off for your kid's recital, for parent-teacher conferences, and when your baby has a fever, which will be a blessing if you're a single parent.

The home represented by the Queen is your mother's house, your sister's house, your hometown, or the family farm in West Virginia.

When the Upright Queen describes a car it's the most reliable thing on the road, which reminds me of a car a friend of mine used to own. He called it the Lizard and claimed it could grow a new tail if it needed to. He said if he just parked it in the shade for a while it would heal itself, and grow a new carburetor.

REVERSED

When the Queen's Upright she's in touch with her feelings. But, when she's drawn Reversed she doesn't know how she feels.

INDIVIDUAL: This girl is sick of her husband and can't wait for the kids to grow up. She hates to cook, won't grocery shop, and her intuition and sensuality have shut down. She's demanding, needy, and whiny, yet she longs to receive the love and support she's unwilling to give.

The Reversed Queen is ambivalent. She knows she's from the Heart family and wishes she felt more emotionally engaged, but she's either unwilling or unable to plug in to her household. So there you have it. She doesn't know what to do so she coasts along. She goes through the motions dreaming of another life. She's hoping to meet someone else, someone more sensitive, maybe someone who won't make so many emotional demands on her, maybe someone who will finally take care of *her* for a change.

She doesn't want to parent her children either. She's a burned-out mom and the Queen of the Microwave. She'll be extremely put out if the PTA asks her to work a booth for an hour at the Halloween carnival.

The Queen of Hearts Reversed represents an aspect of all us women. She's the part that throws up our hands and declares we don't want to do anything for anybody. It's the part of us that wants the freedom to be selfish.

The new boyfriend represented by the Reversed Queen won't be interesting to you and won't engage you emotionally. In fact, you might string him along out of boredom. You could give him a hard time if you aren't careful, and you could hurt him badly.

RELATIONSHIP: The established relationship described by the upside-down Queen is falling apart because the feminine half of this couple has one foot out the door. At best, she'll sit on the fence about the marriage while she debates its pros and cons. At worst, she's actively shopping for a replacement.

When the Reversed Queen predicts the future prospects for a new romance, it foretells a suspicious attitude on your part. You won't be entirely convinced that this man can satisfy your needs so you'll hold back. You won't cherish your lover because you'll suspect he can't give you what you want. The problem isn't the man. It's you. You aren't emotionally available, don't know what you want, or are unable to make a commitment.

I wouldn't recommend the Reversed Queen to any man.

CIRCUMSTANCES: Whatever these circumstances may be, you won't want to participate.

You'll turn up your nose at the car represented by the Reversed Queen. You won't like its vibe and the upholstery will be too scratchy. A job? You'll be turned off by the way your cubicle smells and you won't feel appreciated by your manager. When she describes a house the Reversed Queen says you won't line your kitchen shelves, buy flowers for the dining table, or plug in the vacuum. This is the card of domestic neglect.

NOTE

The Upright Queen of Hearts is a touchstone for the people in her life. She's a bottomless wellspring of support and affection for those she loves. I tend to select my dearest girlfriends from the Queen of Hearts category. That's how much I appreciate her tenderness, her devotion, and her well-stocked refrigerator.

UPRIGHT: The Queen is a hearty "Yes!"
REVERSED: Still a "Yes" because she'll always be your mother.

King of Hearts

Kings: Men
Hearts: Emotions

THE FAMILY MAN

The King of Hearts is the King of Permanent Emotional Connections. The card stands for your father, brother, or adult son, but mainly it represents your husband.

The King is a very important card when you're searching for your soul mate. He represents any man with whom you become emotionally involved, regardless of how that man treats you, feels about you, or responds to you. He can be the creep who stands you up or the prince who showers you with diamonds. He represents both your most probable marital prospect and the one who will break your heart. The King of Hearts can be delicate and unsteady or strong and sure. Because of his broad emotional range, I recommend that you familiarize yourself with his types. I've taken care to describe this man in excruciating detail so you can Xerox these pages and carry them in your purse.

Foremost, you need to know that the King of Hearts is highly emotional, and his emotional condition depends upon his marital status. As a result, he comes in four varieties. The *married* King has two versions and the *single* King has two versions.

The King of Hearts is usually a Water sign man: Pisces, Cancer, or Scorpio.

UPRIGHT

THE MARRIED INDIVIDUAL: This man is your basic, middle-class family man. He works hard at a decent job, but he's not on a hot career track because he prefers to be home at a reasonable hour to participate in his family life. I don't want to devalue the hard work this man puts in all day, but I want to emphasize that he's not working fifty hours a week, taking classes all night, and attending seminars on weekends. This guy's at home at night helping his kids with their homework.

The Upright married King of Hearts attends his children's school functions and baseball games. After he puts the kids to bed, he sits up with his wife and talks over the events of their day. He washes dishes, mows his own lawn, and relies on his wife's paycheck.

The married King is emotionally strong, committed, and *available* to his family and friends. He's sensitive, tactile, sensual, and his emotions run deep. He would never fool around on his wife because his primary interest is in the maintenance of a happy, healthy, homey existence.

THE SINGLE INDIVIDUAL: When the Upright King of Hearts is single (which is rarely) he's a walking Relationship Waiting to Happen. He doesn't function well when all alone. He needs companionship. He needs the purpose a relationship gives to his life. He's the marrying kind and he's looking for love.

If you find the Upright King in your spread and he's a single guy, he's a very good match for you. He's probably exactly what you've been looking for. The Upright King is in touch with his feelings and he's not a player. He takes his emotional connections seriously and is proud to be loyal and steadfast once a woman gets under his skin. When he offers you his heart, it will be with confidence that you're the one for him.

If you pulled this card to describe your boyfriend or husband, it says he adores you and he wants to take care of you. He wants to hold on to you, protect you, and live the rest of his life with you. He loves you.

RELATIONSHIP: When a relationship is defined by a Court card, the individual represented by the card is always the force behind the union. In this case, the King will be the glue that holds you together.

The union defined by the King of Marriage is legally binding and solid. If you haven't walked down the aisle with this man there will be something old and established about your connection nonetheless. Either you've been together forever or your natures blend so naturally that your wedding is pure inevitability.

CIRCUMSTANCES: A benevolent patriarch controls this situation. If your question is about your job, the boss will do what's best for the whole team, including you. If you're asking about a car, a man who loves you will either take you to test-drive it or loan you the money to purchase it. Under these conditions, you won't have much control over the outcome, but the compassionate soul who does will protect you.

REVERSED

THE MARRIED INDIVIDUAL: The Reversed married King of Hearts is a Warrior Earner who believes that a good husband and father is, above all, a good provider. He works hard and uses his money to buy the perfect house and marry the perfect wife. Then he produces two lovely children to complete his facsimile of the ideal family.

This King is rarely present to parent his children or be a friend to his woman. He's a competitive, plush provider who spends his days working hard to sustain his romantic family ideal. He's the King of the killer vacations and lovely new cars. His wife has a beautiful home, an extensive wardrobe, and an idle lifestyle. This man believes that the creation of a warm family *image* is equal to real family warmth. He believes in a flawless framed portrait of a robust, athletic, affluent family of winners. He spends his energy subsidizing his dream and, as a result, is proud of his household.

On the downside, the Reversed married King is not very comfortable with the touchy-feely side of life. He provides materially what he cannot provide emotionally.

THE SINGLE INDIVIDUAL: When the single King of Hearts falls Reversed, we see his darkest side. He's emotionally delicate and will author a "push-pull" style of relating, which means he'll only want you when you *don't* want him.

The Reversed single King overreacts to the fluctuations in feeling normal to any relationship. When he's in a reunion phase you'll be "the most astonishing woman ever to walk on the planet." He'll fill every pore of his being with his amazement of you until you hog the remote one night, at which point your callousness and emptiness will destroy his love for you. As he squeezes into a corner of the couch he'll completely reexamine the relationship (quietly, on his own, without your input). He'll scrutinize you as you channel surf in your sweats covered in wrinkle-cream. (He said he *liked* you casual!) He'll conclude it's not a match because you're not sensitive enough. He may even get up and go home.

You'll never know what happened. He'll tell you he "just doesn't see it working out."

You never know where you stand with the Reversed single King of Hearts. But, I can guarantee that wherever you stand today you won't stand next week . . . which is when he'll begin to miss you, and decide to forgive you, and will begin to say or do whatever will pull you back to him. Push-pull, push-pull. The longer this goes on, the less likely he is to settle down with you. His ambivalence will build rather than diminish.

The Reversed single King can make a life out of this stuff. These are your loners who find it easier not to participate in relationships. For them, love is a roller-coaster ride and they become exhausted by the ups and downs of their own creation, so they opt out. They can be lifelong bachelors.

When you pull the Reversed single King, it's important to realize that he's not emotionally available. He may act like he is, but he isn't. Don't place your hopes for the future on him because he doesn't know how he feels and he doesn't know what he wants. He'll waffle on you.

RELATIONSHIP: If you drew the Reversed single King of Hearts to describe the soul responsible for holding your marriage together, you're in trouble. Your alliance will be vulnerable to the push-pull dynamics that are the trademark of an emotionally unstable, emotionally unavailable man. Read the section about the Single Reversed King for details on what to expect.

The new prospect represented by the card isn't as enamored of you as he may have led you to think. There's nothing you can do to engage his affections, so you would be better off avoiding him or declining his invitations, which ought to engage his push-pull tendencies. This man is a messy romantic prospect for any woman.

CIRCUMSTANCES: The Reversed King will agree to come over and help you paint, but he may not show up. He said, "Sure" when you asked him to bring his roller and drop cloth on Saturday, but he'll resent that you asked for a favor so he may not put in an appearance.

This boss will rub shoulders with his employees because he thinks it's good for business, but he doesn't want to participate in their *lives*, for goodness' sake.

This landlord doesn't want to hear from you, ever, under any circumstances. He doesn't want to fix anything or listen to your complaints about the Overeaters Anonymous meeting they hold upstairs every Sunday morning at 7:30, which is the only opportunity you have to sleep in. You're on your own if this guy owns the building.

NOTE

Once a man marries, he has to make a choice about what kind of family man he will be and how he will distribute his energy. A woman can't expect to have both versions of the married King rolled up into one package. The odds of a man being both types at the same time are so rare as to be unrealistic. I recommend women appreciate their guy no matter which breed he is. If he's a worker beast and not around much, she needs to acknowledge how comfortable and secure she feels wrapped in his strong, provider arms. If she wishes her snuggle bunny were more of a go-getter financially, she should remember that she chose him for his availability to the family.

The Reversed King of Hearts is too squeamish to be a reliable emotional investment for any girl. At best he'll marry you and create a pretty portrait of a perfect family. He'll put on a good show for your parents and the community but the experience of being his wife might be an empty one for you. At best, he'll be overtly adoring one day, shut down or withdrawn the next, and bounce back into your arms on the third.

The Upright King represents the men who are born into our families or those who marry into them. In particular, the card stands for that army of devoted males who struggle to maintain a solid emotional foundation for us year after year. We women and children are lucky when we find the loving Upright King of Hearts in our spreads.

UPRIGHT: "Bingo!"
REVERSED: "I don't know. Maybe not."

Ace of Spades

Aces: Achievement
Spades: Attitudes and Problems

POWER

The Ace of Spades is a card of extremes. The best way to understand its message is to picture a surgeon's knife. When a surgeon cuts into the human body he has the power to heal his patient or to mutilate him. The Ace of Spades is the scalpel.

UPRIGHT

The Upright Ace is the card of empowerment.

INDIVIDUAL: The man defined by the Upright Ace of Spades is clear and direct. Should he doubt your capacity to be faithful to him, he'll make a statement of intent. He'll sit you down and say, "I want to be in a relationship free from the threat of infidelity. You have a 100 percent capacity to provide that security for me. What do you choose to do?" He's not going to get involved in what Sally said to Joe and how that made you feel. He's not interested in how you create the emotional safety for him either. He's a core-intention kind of guy who's in touch with his basic needs. He addresses the bottom line and leaves the details to be sorted out along the way. He needs a responsible, emotionally mature partner who isn't threatened by straight talk.

The new romantic interest defined by the Ace is strong and direct. He's open-minded, independent, positive, and assertive. You needn't worry if he'll call because when he's smitten, he's the initiator. He *likes* to make calls and plan dates.

RELATIONSHIP: Mutual respect, consideration, and cooperation are the foundation of the alliance described by the Upright Ace of Spades.

This is the union of two doctors or lawyers who met in school, got married, and went on to practice their chosen professions. At home, they kick in the same amount of money and do a parallel number of chores because they believe in equality in the relationship. The Ace of Spades couple is open, honest, and fair. Their disputes are resolved quickly and easily because neither is afraid to speak up. They know they're fifty-fifty shareholders in their marriage, which means they aren't living in a hierarchy. The husband's opinion doesn't automatically become the tiebreaker when they can't make a decision and the wife doesn't have the final word either. These two continue to discuss their options until they draw a mutual conclusion.

The union represented by the Ace of Spades isn't a pact between two cold fish. It's quite the contrary. This pair is warm and affectionate. They plan scuba diving trips to Tahiti, attend each other's lectures, and jog together. They host contemporary parties with themes, costumes, belly dancers, and fortune-tellers. This creative, hearty couple is an inspiration and the role model for a modern, empowered connection between equals.

The budding romance defined by the Ace will evolve into an equal partnership. These two will be drawn to the competence and maturity they recognize in one another.

CIRCUMSTANCES: The home defined by the Ace of Spades will be well constructed, nicely landscaped, and traditional but modern. The job represented by the card is a dynamic position with a generous salary and room for advancement. If you pulled the Ace to describe your chances with a new company, you're definitely their best candidate.

REVERSED

When the Ace of Spades falls Reversed, it's quite another story.

INDIVIDUAL: Any person represented by the Reversed Ace is suffering. The surgeon's knife has carved him into a million pieces. Battered, bruised, and bleeding, this person is sore to the touch.

The Reversed Ace lover is an absolute dictator. I like to call this guy the Pain Machine because he has a talent for knowing where to stick the knife to do the most damage. Of course, he's cruel because of the horrible things that were done to him a long time ago, which means he comes by his sadistic nature honestly. But so what? You should know he isn't going to surrender his mean streak without years and years of therapy. Please, do not, I repeat *do not*, tell me, "He doesn't mean it. He had a rough childhood." No woman looking for a loving relationship with an equal partner will find her dream with the personality defined by the Reversed Ace of Spades.

RELATIONSHIP: The Reversed Ace wrestles with issues of dominance and submission. It describes a union that exists despite a total lack of cooperation and power struggles for control.

As a professional Reader, I often hear clients describe a lifetime of "giving":

"I gave and gave! My whole life has been nothing but giving! For thirty years I never wanted anything for myself, it was all for him or the kids! And they are so ungrateful!"

I listen to her cry and wonder, Why is this woman complaining about thirty years of giving? She's not complaining about the necktie she gave him for his birthday ten years ago that he never wore. Why would a generous person resent giving?

The answer is, she hasn't been "giving" at all. Long ago she adopted a passive stance in the hopes of winning his approval or to avoid being abandoned by him. But one day she woke up burned-out on surrender, which was the day she had the temper tantrum. By turning into a screaming she-devil in the kitchen she forced him to listen to her. On that day *she* dominated and *she* won, but not without a price. Her husband recoiled as a result of her outburst. The next day she had to double her efforts at passivity so the cycle could continue.

What's required here is an adjustment to the patterns of dominance and submission in the relationship. The only way to make the adjustment is to learn how to speak with more truth and love.

First, the wife needs to understand the tremendous role she played in setting up the dynamic. She is NOT the sweet little victim she thinks she is. The first time she said, "Oh, I don't know, honey, I just want whatever you want to do," was the day the pattern began. She can't blame her man. He simply took full responsibility for the relationship when she didn't hold up her half. Our girl needs to face her fear of abandonment, disapproval, rejection, or ridicule. She needs to understand that her efforts to repress her feelings, her efforts to be a really, really, really good little girl and earn Big Daddy's love is a mistake. She has to override her fear and shame in the face of abandonment or rejection and start telling the truth. In this way she will Upright the Ace and create the adult relationship described in the Upright section, which is one of the best unions in the deck.

Here's how to turn the card around: When your man wakes up on Saturday morning, tears open the curtains, and throws his arms out to say, "What a beautiful day! Let's go to the swap meet!" (just like he has every beautiful Saturday for the past five years), instead of sighing, "Okay," this time tell the truth.

Lovingly and confidently say, "Honey, I want to go to the movies today, but I see you want to go to the swap meet. I've decided to go to the swap meet with you because I love you and want to make you happy. In return, I would like you to take me to the movies tonight." This ought to inspire a hearty "Of course!" in your mate.

If it doesn't, go to the swap meet as planned and to the movies by yourself in the evening. Then try again next week, or next week you can politely decline his offer of the swap meet and tell him you have other plans. Stay on course, don't apologize, explain, defend, blame, or accuse. Don't be a wimpy, blaming, whiny girl and remind him he let you down last Saturday when he didn't take you to the movies. Be patient and take your time. Remember, *you're changing the rules*. It may take a few beats for him to get in step.

Over time he's going to learn that when you go to the swap meet with him you aren't being passive, frightened, and resentful. He'll come to see that you go because you like his company, that you *chose* to go because you want to be with him, which will make him feel special and loved. Accepting that you are equals in your relationship will create a climate of cooperation and openness for you both.

P.S. Either gender can be the passive one.

♠ ♦ ♣ ♥

Being true to ourselves is the only basis of loyalty to another. We have a responsibility in life to be honest about our feelings. The person who is true to himself is unwilling to do things that will cause a loss of his integrity, or compromise his dignity merely to respond to his partner's expectations.

CIRCUMSTANCES: The situation described by the Reversed Ace of Spades is one of the worst in the deck. When the Reversed card gets involved, you could lose your money, your reputation, or your self-respect. Avoid this environment altogether or it will destroy you.

NOTE

The Ace of Spades is a handful. When we acknowledge its extremes and integrate its power, we become confident, emotionally independent, and self-reliant. But when we fail to own our strength, we sentence ourselves to a lifetime of subordination and suffering.

UPRIGHT: A strong, sure "Yes."
REVERSED: A wounded, bleeding "No!"

Two of Spades

Twos: Union
Spades: Attitudes and Problems

PATIENCE

The Twos are the least assertive of the numbers in the deck and the Spades describe our attitudes, problems, and solutions. The passive Two and the mental Spades combine to create the concept of waiting, which is the simplest solution to any problem.

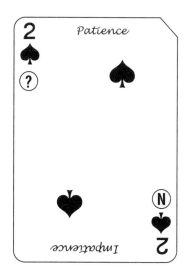

Patience is a great virtue and most of us devote a portion of our lives to developing some. Serenity comes with maturity because as we age, we discover that time heals wounds, promotes understanding, or reveals the truth. Therefore, the Two of Spades is a card of timing.

When Upright, the Two asks that before you take any action, you wait to see if the problem will resolve itself or if new information will come to light. The Reversed Two says you're either unwilling to wait or you shouldn't wait.

UPRIGHT

INDIVIDUAL: Two of Spades men are stoic, unruffled, serene, and composed. They're also hopeful, watchful, quiet, and slow moving. They understand that patience allows a deep "letting their partner be" so she can develop in her own way. These men are good parents who patiently teach their children new skills while watching over them from a respectful distance.

The Two of Spades personality works to preserve the status quo and allows nothing to upset or interfere with his innate tranquillity. He often makes the mistake of believing that by being conciliatory and subordinating himself to others, he can maintain his relationships and, subsequently, his own emotional peace. But by accommodating too much, he can put himself in danger of becoming too passive and neglectful of his own needs.

The primary flaw in the unattached Two of Spades man is his attraction to cheerful, upbeat, exciting women. He likes the way an excitable mate stimulates his quiet life. But over time her temperamental, edgy qualities will get on his nerves. In response, he'll slow down his movements to control the pace of their life together. This slowing down can manifest as six hours a night in an easy chair, a failure to come home after work, indirect responses to direct questions, or the refusal to participate in his partner's social life. Eventually she'll come to view him as a slug and he'll tell his friends she's crazy. The woman interested in a man described by the Upright Two of Spades should ask herself if she's built for a slow-paced life with a gentle giant.

RELATIONSHIP: The brand-new relationship represented by the Upright Two will take forever to unfold. If you want to put in the time, you can make it to the altar, but you have to ask yourself how long you're willing to wait. If you're young and healthy and believe you've found your perfect match, patience will be the key to your happiness. But, if your biological clock is ticking and the pickings are getting slimmer, the wait might be excruciating.

The old married couple represented by the Upright Two is in limbo. They're waiting to see what the other will do—or not do. Theirs is an excellent strategy because neither wants to disrupt their life if they don't have to. Eventually the Two of Spades couple will break through this period of suspended animation. But, until they do, they should take a deep breath and be patient.

CIRCUMSTANCES: If you pulled the Two of Spades, you're probably waiting to hear if you will get the house, car, or job. Don't expect to find out right away because they're going to take their own sweet time contacting you. If you simply *have* to know *right now* whether you're destined to be the new tenant/owner/employee or not, pull another card.

REVERSED

The Reversed Two of Spades is the card of impatience. In this position, the Two is cranky, in a hurry, irritated, easily frustrated, and annoyed.

INDIVIDUAL: The Reversed Two of Spades person dashes through life short-tempered and exasperated with others. He begins new projects with big ideas and a gallon of enthusiasm, but then he gets bored, drops out, and turns to the next idea. His love life follows a similar pattern. His problem is that he's afraid of being complacent. He's convinced that if he rests on his previous success or slackens his pace he'll lose his girl, his job, or his position in the community. He argues that time is money, the early bird catches the worm, or some other dreadful cliché designed to justify his hurry-up attitude.

His destiny is to develop the virtue of a leisurely pace. He must learn to drive slowly, make decisions gradually, and wait for opportunities to float within range. He must allow others to take their time, too. He will discover that life's prime treasures and finest delights come to him piecemeal, over a long period of time. It could take the first fifty years of his life to realize that something as simple as calm perseverance will solve all his problems.

The new romantic prospect described by the Reversed Two is the kind of guy who parks at Make Out Point on the first date and then becomes outraged when you drag your feet about putting out in the backseat. "I'm already in love with you!" he'll cry. "Don't you love me, too?" It's his style to slam out of your apartment in a huff at least once a month.

RELATIONSHIP: Your new Reversed Two boyfriend will make you feel like a pledge during Rush Week. He'll send dozens of flowers, call six times a day, claim to have fallen deeply in love with you on sight, and smother you in compliments. If you like him, reciprocate immediately with equal ardor because the Reversed Two man has a short attention span. If you don't respond instantly, he'll lose patience and disappear. This man wants sex yesterday and will start making plans for a future on the second date.

The Reversed Two lover is flattering and exciting, but he isn't stable. Don't open your heart to him until he's shown you he can hang around for at least six months.

The established couple represented by the Reversed card has been together for years but is losing patience with one another. Both of them have thrown their hands into the air in exasperation. They're tired of trying to make it work; they're sick of their differences. One of them wants to move slowly and wait to see what the other will do. That other wants some action and wishes they had a partner with more energy. The slow-moving half of this pair craves a sane, steady spouse. These two have had it.

CIRCUMSTANCES: The house, job, or car represented by the Reversed Two of Spades has already passed you by. The owner didn't wait for you. He sold the car, rented the unit, or filled the position yesterday.

NOTE

When Upright, the Two of Spades counsels patience and respect for the slow, calm ways of the universal flow. But when the Two falls Reversed, it's tired of waiting around and wants outta here. It's the "See ya!" card.

UPRIGHT: Maybe later.
REVERSED: No.

Three of Spades

Threes: Expansion
Spades: Attitudes and Problems

INTERFERENCE

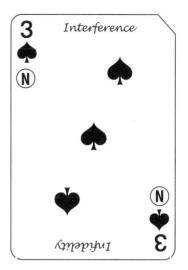

UPRIGHT

The Three of Spades invites a third person to wedge him- or herself between two people.

When the Three is Upright the interfering person is either benign or their intrusion is small and annoying. The Upright position describes any number of wedges, like Aunt Stella's irritating annual visit. The card represents your husband's bass-fishing buddies who come over to drink beer and compare fish stories in your garage on Sunday afternoons, which gets in the way of your laundry chores. It also stands for the anonymous Samaritan who stopped in the rain to change your flat tire the night you were stranded alongside the freeway. The black-hearted little Three is rarely malicious when it's drawn Upright and sometimes it's even helpful.

The Reversed card takes on a sinister aspect and has but one very specific meaning. It stands for the Eternal Triangle. It describes the married man with a honey on the side, or the wife who's having an affair. There is no other definition. Either another woman has entered the arena and she is there to claim your man, or you yourself are fooling around.

INDIVIDUAL: The Upright Three of Spades represents a style of interaction therapists call "triangling."

Triangling works like this: Mother and Father have children, but the children rarely speak directly to their father because Mother speaks on their behalf. The kids channel information and requests through Mom, who presents their case to Dad, and returns to the children with his response. Therapists say triangling is very common, but very destructive because Father and the kids never develop a full relationship. Mother believes she's trying to help or keeping the peace, but in reality she has control of all the communication in the family. Anyone who wants access to the other side has to go through her. As a result, everyone in the household lives with some level of frustration all the time.

The Three recommends direct communication between all parties. It asks Mother to back off and let the others relate independently because she's not really helpful. Besides, she probably sees herself as always in the middle and could use a break from the constant relaying of information.

The Three of Spades individual is attracted to triangulated relationships. He likes married women or women who are wedded to their job and he likes to use go-betweens to initiate his romances. He'll ask your girlfriend if you would be willing to go out with him rather than approach you directly. He grew up in the family described above so he's more comfortable triangling information through others.

If you pulled the Upright Three to describe a new romantic prospect, he will use a third person or element to approach you. He'll send his friend over to your table to say, "My buddy thinks you're very attractive and would like to buy you a drink." You'll look over the messenger's shoulder to see a man smiling and waving and holding his beer glass in the air as if to toast the wonderful occasion of your chance encounter. In the office, the Three of Spades man will tell your girlfriend from accounting how attractive you are in the hope that she'll pass the information on to you.

This man's whole style has a sixth-grade ring to it, but if you're interested in him, tell his friend. A third-party hint is just the encouragement he needs.

RELATIONSHIP: The Upright Three describes a marriage punctuated with tiny squabbles. These two bicker rather than talk. They don't seem to have a common vocabulary. They can't just sit down and discuss things. They need another person to step in and translate for them, like a therapist. Sometimes they use their children as go-betweens, which is a common tactic for couples who can hardly stand to be in the same room with one another.

Any relationship described by the Upright Three of Spades has a third person or element lurking at its edges. That person could be your boyfriend's ex who still calls him, or his children who don't want a new mommy. It could be his ancient dog who has slept on the foot of his bed for fifteen years (so you can't kick him out now) or your new mother-in-law who drops off lasagna for her precious son twice a week as if you didn't exist. This third element won't terminate your union, but it'll be completely annoying. It may even require a *fourth* party to step in and remove it: a new husband for the ex-wife, a counselor for the kids, or a father-in-law who can order his wife to leave their son alone.

The new romance represented by the Upright card will be plagued with a laundry list of annoying obstructions, possibly too many.

CIRCUMSTANCES: The apartment represented by the Upright Three is the one on the cliff overlooking the canyon with the river rock fireplace. It's the biggest two-bedroom unit in America and your best friend's fiancé rents it for $500 a month. Once he marries your friend and moves into her condo, this remarkable apartment will be available. But the landlord is ninety years old and the fiancé/tenant is his grandson. The only way you'll get this place is if the fiancé takes you by the hand and introduces you to his grandfather as the nicest, most wholesome girl who ever wrote a rent check.

A car? Someone will turn you on to it.

A job? Your friend will help you get one where she works.

REVERSED

INDIVIDUAL: There are two versions of the Reversed Three individual. The first one is having an affair. The second is a home wrecker.

If this man is unmarried, he's only attracted to married women. When the card describes the cute new guy who moved in next door, it says he's a predator. He'll pick up on how bored you are with your husband and begin doing his laundry at the same time you do yours. In no time at all you'll find yourself in your car, driving to a discreet location in another part of town to meet him for a drink.

If you're single and available, and you pulled the Reversed card to inquire about a new romantic prospect, it says he has a wife or girlfriend and you're just a little something on the side.

RELATIONSHIP: The established couple represented by the Reversed Three has a big problem. Someone has a romantic interest in one of them. Never dismiss the Reversed card when it appears in the spread of a married person. It says an interloper is standing at the edge of their union and they've already made their first move. It says the married person is already returning calls and slipping off to motels.

A second description of the married couple represented by the Reversed Three are the swingers who live a normal, happily married life in the suburbs until Saturday night when they hit the Wife Swapper's Club for a little action. If both parties agree to this way of living and loving, their marriage will continue, but if one of them is capitulating to make the other happy or to keep them from leaving, the Reversed Three foretells marital disaster.

The new romance represented by the Reversed Three of Spades shows one or both parties fooling around on their steady.

CIRCUMSTANCES: The job represented by the Reversed card is notable for its tacky office romances. Everyone knows the boss takes little business trips with his secretary to Barbados behind his wife's back and writes off the airfare. His wife is a sweet woman and you get a nervous rush when she walks past your desk and into his office at lunch, *unannounced.* Expect to keep your mouth shut and your guard up at this place.

NOTE

When you pull the Three of Spades, try to bear in mind that it's only a Three. It's a small number, not the Nine or Ten after all, and its effects are always temporary. Did you hear that? *Always temporary.* The Upright Three is manageable and you can work through it or use its energy. The Reversed Three is a terrible little problem, but solvable. How you choose to solve it, though, is up to you.

UPRIGHT or REVERSED: The Three is a "No."

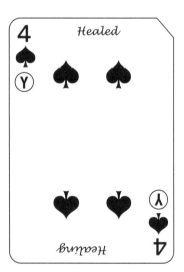

Four of Spades

Fours: Effort
Spades: Attitudes and Problems

HEALING

The Four of Spades represents the need to lie down and rest. It's the card of recuperation. You may feel as if lying low would be a waste of time, but when you pull the card, it says you need to recharge your batteries and renew your strength. The Four of Spades stands for a period of convalescence that will restore you to your usual, robust self.

UPRIGHT

INDIVIDUAL: This person has a destiny path as a healer. When he places his hand on the small of your back it feels like a heating pad and relaxes your whole body. The warmth of his touch makes you want to lean into him and stay there because the Four of Spades man radiates comfort. These folks are your counselors, massage therapists, and nurses. They bring serenity and relief to others.

If he isn't a shaman, this individual has a history of recovery. He attends a Twelve-Step program and knows he's powerless over alcohol, food, drugs, or people. When the Four is Upright, he's been working his program for a long time and his recovery is well established.

The Upright Four of Spades describes a life transformed by the healing process. The card stands for the guy who was hit by a car while riding his bike. He broke his back and spent five years shifting between physical therapy, the chiropractor's office, the YMCA swimming pool, and the massage table. When the Four is Upright his recovery is complete, his back has healed, and he's finally able to walk, run, and ride a bike again. The experience of healing his back will always be the line of demarcation between the life he lived *before* the accident and the life he lives *after* it. The recovery described by the Four can manifest on a physical, spiritual, material, or emotional plane. The Four of Spades individual is an advocate for children's rights, which is the natural outcropping of his own abusive childhood; or, watching his mother die of cancer inspired him to become a doctor.

Because of his unique perspective, this person is uncomfortable in social situations. At a party, he's highly aware of where they put the beer and wine and he counts how many cocktails the host drinks. He recognizes another guest's stiff gait as the sign of a bad back and notices how he rejects the deep, comfy barrel chair for the straight-backed kitchen chair. Socializing is difficult for the Four of Spades man because he listens to the young mother moan about her two-year-old and recoils when she makes cryptic jokes about locking her toddler in a closet. His awareness isolates him. Were he to reach out, it would be to counsel the young mother, caution the designated driver, or discuss healing techniques with the bad-back guy.

If the Four represents your new boyfriend, he'll be a healing presence in your life. Either you'll date him to get over someone else, or his style of loving will heal the wounds you sustained dating all the jerks in your past.

RELATIONSHIP: The alliance defined by the Upright Four of Spades will teach both parties something new about human relations. If she has a history of verbally abusive men just like her father, then her Four of Spades partner will have a gentle voice and exhibit extraordinary kindness under duress. She'll begin the relationship frightened and certain that harsh treatment is inevitable once the honeymoon is over. But, when the Four represents her man, the nasty comments never arrive. Over time, she'll learn to relax and expect the other men in her life to behave more gentlemanly, like her new husband. This marriage will heal her.

The Four of Spades describes the couple who met in a Twelve-Step program. They share a language and value system unique to people in recovery. Or perhaps they met in massage therapy school and together opened a center for the healing arts.

The established union described by the Four has healed both partners.

The new romance will teach both parties that the opposite sex can be loving and sincere. It will restore their ability to love and trust.

CIRCUMSTANCES: Any situation represented by the Upright Four will be fine once you invest a little time and money. The car will be reliable if you repair it. A coat of paint and new carpet will restore the house to its original charm.

REVERSED

When the Four of Spades is drawn Reversed, it stands for time literally spent in the hospital, attending a Twelve-Step study group, or lying in bed on Saturday night with a miserable head cold.

INDIVIDUAL: This person is trying to heal. If he broke his arm, it's still in a cast. If he's decided to quit smoking, he's still wearing the patch. If he's recently divorced, he sees his therapist once a week and has started ballroom dance lessons in preparation for his first foray back into the dating marketplace.

The new romantic prospect defined by the Four is dating you in the hopes you'll heal his broken heart.

Sometimes the man represented by the Reversed Four is chronically attracted to women who just broke up with someone else. This guy has an inner sensor that tells him when a woman needs his particular brand of tenderness. He'll pass just enough time with you to paste you back together again. Then he'll drift to the next girl. It's his destiny to move among the wounded like a surgeon on a battlefield. He wonders why his own love life never works out and why every woman he dates marries another guy. Nonetheless, he keeps moving until he finds the next one and holds her hand through her mending process too.

RELATIONSHIP: The established union described by the Reversed card is in a healing phase. These two may have quarreled and separated in the past, but now they're reunited and in forgiveness mode.

The new romance defined by the Reversed Four is healing you. This guy listens to your office problems and brings you flowers for no reason. He even rents chick flicks. He thinks you're sexy and interesting, and he's restoring your feminine ego or wilted self-esteem. He makes you feel like your old cocky self.

You may not stay with the man defined by the Reversed Four, but you'll always remember him with affection and gratitude because he's the one who put Humpty back together again.

CIRCUMSTANCES: When you pull the Reversed Four, the car is in the shop getting a new transmission, the plumbers are under the sink, or you're sitting at your desk paying off the balance on your credit cards. Regardless of your situation, it's under repair right now.

NOTE

In my practice, I tell my clients there are 200 million people living in America and 100 million of them are the opposite gender. Probably 40 million of those people are age appropriate and maybe one million live within driving distance. So if all your lessons in love and loss have been learned through a handful of partners, maybe the problem is the partners and your criteria for choosing them.

One of my clients said, "Maybe I need a broader random sampling." I laughed, but in reality, that's exactly what he needs. He needs to discover different types of women, types he would never have considered before. If you pulled the Four of Spades, maybe you need to discover a new kind of man.

UPRIGHT or REVERSED: Either way, this card is a "Yes."

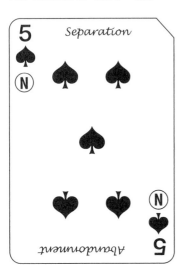

Five of Spades

Fives: Conflict
Spades: Attitudes and Problems

SEPARATION

The Upright Five of Spades stands for blocks of time spent apart from a person or place. These are manageable, painless separations scheduled in advance.

The Reversed card represents final, irreversible partings like death and divorce. When the Five turns upside down, the separations are unplanned, occur despite our best efforts to stay connected, and a great deal of pain accompanies the card. The Reversed Five is the card of abandonment.

UPRIGHT

Throughout our lives we leave lovers, lose jobs, and move away from homes. Separations are inevitable. The Upright Five of Spades represents logical separations, such as when your child leaves for college or your relatives finally go home. The card stands for putting your elderly dog down because you don't want to see him suffer. The loss of a family pet is tragic, but if he's fifteen years old, arthritic, and has cancer, you know letting go is unavoidable and speeding it along can be an act of love.

INDIVIDUAL: The individual described by the Upright Five has left some part of his heart in another place. Perhaps he's an immigrant who grew up on the opposite side of the planet, or perhaps he's a farm boy who went to college in the city and chose to stay. No matter how sophisticated he becomes, he'll never completely shake the hayseed out of his hair. The Five of Spades man will always feel a loyalty to his roots, his ethnicity, or his culture of origin. Therefore, he'll exaggerate his down-home country boy accent or wear a suede cowboy jacket and drive a pickup truck to his Chicago law office. He's the guy whose twang gets thicker and whose anecdotes get cornier when he's angry. This man's life is separated into two halves: the half he lived in his youth and the half he lives now. The dividing line is the day he got on the plane and left home.

The Upright Five of Spades person rarely remains in his place of birth. He seldom attends the same school for long or stays in one profession for a lifetime. And he's rarely suited for marriage. In his heart, he aches to feel love, to connect with a significant other in a permanent way. So much so, that sometimes he'll risk an experiment with matrimony in the hope a wife will fill the empty, lonely place in his heart. But his efforts at marriage rarely succeed because he has a compulsion to disconnect once he's connected.

The new romantic interest represented by the Upright card isn't much of a prospect. He seldom enters into full relationships and when he does, his intellectual, distant manner stalls the romance pretty quickly. If you pulled the Upright Five to describe the blond Adonis who just moved in next door, *forgetaboutit.* He doesn't have what it takes to develop an adequate connection with another person.

The long-term lover represented by the Upright card is either out of town right now or out of your life permanently. When the Five represents your boyfriend, he's your ex now. The fire of love went out some time ago and there's nothing left to rekindle.

RELATIONSHIP: In a relationship spread, the Five says the couple is no longer in close proximity to one another. This could be a controlled, temporary phase in a long and loving union, or the final, mutual decision to stop seeing each other. If you've decided to separate from your partner and you pulled the Five of Spades Upright, you feel no pain about the breakup because you know he's not the man with whom you want to spend your life.

The brand-new alliance described by the Five is already finished. Your new lover already stopped calling and you won't see him again.

CIRCUMSTANCES: Any situation represented by the Five of Spades either won't happen, or you don't want it to happen. When the card describes a job, house, or car, you've already checked out of the idea. You don't want to work there, rent it, or buy it.

REVERSED

When the Five turns upside down it becomes the card of abandonment and the feelings get involved in a big way. Abandonment and our fear of it motivates us girls to do some pretty embarrassing things, like weeping and begging or wrapping our entire bodies around our man's leg when he tries to walk out the door. Abandonment is the issue underlying most addictions, and its impact on our lives can be devastating.

INDIVIDUAL: The man defined by the Reversed Five grew up as a latchkey kid. His mom was the gal whose husband took off and left her with four children and no visible means of support. Once she started working, her son was always the last one to be picked up after school. By the time he was an adolescent, she left him at home alone all day and then went out dancing at night. If he called her boyfriend's house at one in the morning she told him she'd be back to drive him to school. She said he was a big boy and could take care of himself.

Another version of the Reversed Five of Spades man is the one whose father died when he was a little boy. His mom had to go to work and, as much as she loved him, tried to care for him, nurture him, and help him with his homework, he still wound up at the Boys and Girls Club every day after school. Through no fault of her own, she became a remote, unapproachable mother.

This man's abandonment issues color every aspect of his adult life. He's a loner who doesn't expect anyone to be there for him, and he tends to marry women like his mother. He often winds up the classic abandoned spouse whose ex takes the kids and runs off with the gardener. If so, he'll feel the loss every waking moment of his life and he'll allow this new abandonment to define him. He'll replace his childhood rejection with the new adult version. He'll pin all his problems in life, all his ancient grief, rage, and bitterness, on his wife's decision to replace him with another man—a man with less money and less standing in the community. Abandonment has burned a scar into the spirit of the man described by the Reversed Five of Spades and it may never go away. A lifetime of desertion has branded him.

The new prospect represented by the Reversed Five can't get involved right now. Someone he loves left him and he isn't over the loss. Not yet. You don't have a chance with him. Even though he's single, he's not available for any kind of relationship, not even a friendship.

RELATIONSHIP: The married couple defined by the Reversed Five is breaking up and both parties feel resentful and abandoned. These two have no choice but to work through their anguish separately. They will never reconcile.

If you're lucky, the new romance represented by the Reversed card won't get off the ground.

If you're unlucky, you two will fall in tender, delicate love and then he'll move permanently to the opposite side of the planet, leaving you embittered. Nothing will come of this connection except another rotten abandonment.

CIRCUMSTANCES: When the Reversed Five describes your home, car, or job it says you'll be evicted, carjacked, or fired. You're out of luck under these conditions.

NOTE

A shrug of the shoulders and a relaxed, philosophical "Well, that one's over" describe the Upright Five. But when it falls Reversed, the card depicts a devastating abandonment, one that will leave a bruise on your heart for a long time—possibly forever.

UPRIGHT or REVERSED: This is never a good card. It's always a "No."

Six of Spades

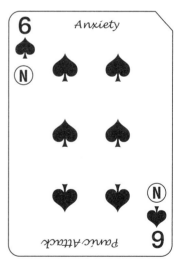

Sixes: Faith
Spades: Attitudes and Problems

ANXIETY

This is a nervous, tiny, little panic attack of a card and I feel tense just looking at it. The Six of Spades is best illustrated with worried hand wringing. It's an "Ohmigod, what's going to happen?!" card.

UPRIGHT

INDIVIDUAL: If you've pulled the Six of Spades to describe your lover, the card will outline a nervous, anxious individual. Since this is a personality type and a lifetime condition, he usually has his outward appearance under control. Often casual and easygoing on the surface, it's what's underneath that you need to examine. Beneath the calm veneer lurks the voice of an overprotective, frightened parent. People who are oriented to life in this way are brought up with a string of nervous messages from Mom and Dad like, "Don't drive without flares in the trunk! You never know what could happen!" Or, "Stop! Put that down! You'll poke your eye out!" This style of parenting creates apprehensive, jumpy people who compulsively scan the horizon in search of threats to their well-being.

These folks survive best in stable, long-term jobs with big organizations because they can't relax without assurances. They need to know that they'll have a paycheck next week, the car will always work, their bodies are healthy, and their spouse will remain faithful to them. They take actions designed to keep their demon-wolves at bay. They work for the post office, change their oil every 3,000 miles, see their dentist twice a year, and get married when they fall in love. These are nice, conservative people who are nervous and vulnerable.

As a romantic interest a Six of Spades person is precarious but stable. These folks worry a lot. In particular, they worry if the two of you possess the capacity to make each other happy for all eternity. They wonder if you have what it takes to remain faithful for decades, if you possess a mature respect for stability and routine. They want a rock solid mate who rarely surprises them, one who can shoulder a hefty portion of their anxieties. Marriage is their natural state because of its boundaries and traditions. A person knows where they stand from day to day when they share the same bed and eat at the same table with an upstanding pillar of the community.

What Six of Spades people need most is a strong belief in a benevolent God. Once they surrender to the notion that they have no real power over their lives, that they are being led by a hand greater than their own, they can relax and permit their destiny to unfold naturally.

The brand-new boyfriend represented by the Upright Six may seem nervous and talk a lot, but you'll sense a fundamental solidity to him nonetheless. Don't be put off by his jumpy ways: by the way he twists his napkin in his hands or by the way he lines up the sugar, salt, and hot sauce on the coffee shop table while he talks. Instead, engage him in a conversation about your anxieties for the future and watch him settle down. You'll discover that, despite how rattled he looks, he's very grounded and has a thousand ideas about how to install a stable lifestyle.

RELATIONSHIP: The established Six of Spades couple sits huddled together on the couch going over their tax return and rechecking each item on the form. Every decision they make and action they take is designed to shield them from random chaos. Overinsured and debt free, they drive five miles an hour under the speed limit in the far right lane with their headlights on. To understand their relationship, picture them standing shoulder to shoulder at the living room window. See them peeking through the vertical blinds with binoculars to watch the neighbors across the street sunbathe on the lawn while their dog and kids run unleashed through the sprinkler. Imagine the Six of Spades couple as fussy, nervous sparrows, tsk-tsking and shaking their heads in unison. These two aren't much fun.

The new romance depicted by the Upright Six isn't anybody's idea of a frisky weekend fling. It ought to bog down in a series of nervous, self-conscious dinner dates. As a couple, you'll fuss if your table is near a drafty window, or if the wine seems too acidic. Should the ketchup bleed across your plate and touch your hamburger bun, you'll send your dinners back to the kitchen. If you decide to stay with the Six of Spades romantic prospect, your connection will develop into the marriage described above. You might wind up wishing you were the gal across the street with the dog and the sprinkler.

CIRCUMSTANCES: For those of us who are civilians in the war against anxiety, for we whose parents allowed us to run free through vacant lots after dark, the effects of the Six are temporary. The card represents a period of time when we wait nervously by the phone or step outside to check the mail every ten minutes.

The Six counsels you to stay on track, push forward, do the best you are capable of, and surrender the outcome to the grace of God.

REVERSED

The Reversed Six describes a full-blown panic attack, including shortness of breath, a racing heart, and bursting into tears inexplicably. The Reversed card is serious and dangerous.

INDIVIDUAL: Regardless of whether the Reversed Six describes your new boyfriend or a longtime life partner, he's losing it. People filled with panic need reassurance, a comforting listener, hot tea, and encouragement. They need a safe place to pour out their hearts, to describe their fears, and to find their solutions.

You must tell your sweetie you believe in him and will stick by him no matter what happens. There are no words more magical to him than these. They are the best medicine you can give him.

The brand-new lover described by the Reversed card is on the verge of freaking out. Something has him in hysterics. Throw more cards on the table to describe his problem. If a minor nervous breakdown appears to be his usual response to problems, dump him. But if his response seems appropriate or the situation looks temporary, be patient because another card will represent him later.

RELATIONSHIP: The permanent alliance described by the Reversed Six endures one emergency after another. Under these conditions, neither party feels safe, stable, or secure. Both sides have serious reservations about the long-term prospects for their marriage. Therefore, they've backed off in fear. Should they stay together, the Reversed Six foretells a match lived out on pins and needles.

The bright new romance represented by the Reversed card shows both parties paranoid and suspicious. Neither feels they can let their guard down or is able to relax and feel comfortable when together. This connection is too nerve wracking to endure.

CIRCUMSTANCES: Any car, house, or job represented by the Reversed Six of Spades will cause you to sit up at night and worry about it. Pass on this one. You can find something more tranquil.

NOTE

We all pull this card at one time or another and half the problem is the simplicity of the solution. The Six asks us to stay calm and remember it's a lack of faith in our own judgment that leads to anxiety. The card asks us to live with the uncertainty of not knowing how things will work out. It wants us to have courage, be strong, do our best, leave the outcome to the mercy of God, and move on to the next task.

UPRIGHT or REVERSED: The Six of Spades is always a "No."

Seven of Spades

Sevens: Tension and Self-Interest
Spades: Attitudes and Problems

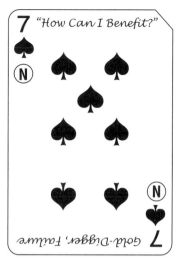

FAILURE

The Sevens are about the self. They're the me, me, me cards. When you combine the angst of the Spades with the tunnel vision of the Seven, the outcome is an extraordinary degree of self-interest, which inevitably leads to failure. To write off the Seven of Spades as a tough, negative card is too easy because it's also a card of nuance, fine lines, and gray areas.

In the Gypsy fortune-telling tradition the Seven of Spades is the card of defeat because it's the card of skipping steps. I'll explain: If a person wants a good position with a successful company, he can obtain it in one of two ways. The first way would be to get an education, earn a degree in the field, get some experience, and approach a top company as a highly qualified candidate. The Seven of Spades person would never adhere to such a traditional formula for career advancement. He'd pursue the job in a second way: he'd schmooze his way into it.

He'd start by introducing himself to the female head of production at a cocktail party. Then he'd ask her personal questions, compliment her on her appearance, and bat his eyes at her until she agreed to meet him for coffee. His plan would be for her to develop a huge crush on him so he could ask her for an introduction to the head of human resources. Then, he'd focus his charms on the director of HR until he was hired.

Because the Seven of Spades person gets the job through his family connections, his sex appeal, or something else (college friends, neighbors, sexual orientation, or ethnicity), he's in trouble. He may possess a superficial knowledge or have short-term experience in the field, but he's in no way authentically qualified for the position. Therefore, once he's hired, he spends his time looking over his shoulder. He barely knows what he's doing, his coworkers are on to him, and he's an embarrassment to the head of human resources who gave him the job. The only solution will be to fire him.

The Seven of Spades person fails because he skips steps.

UPRIGHT

INDIVIDUAL: The man represented by the Upright Seven is prone to the peculiar brand of larceny outlined above. People who know him consider him untrustworthy or irresponsible.

His life task is to adopt a deeper set of rules by which to live and to slow down his relationships. Until he does, those who have dealings with him should view him with a healthy skepticism.

If you pulled the Upright Seven to describe a new love interest, he'll be a selfish person. He has quick sex to "scratch the itch." He's not the type to make love all afternoon or to call the next day. He's only going out with you for what he can get. If you're an affluent woman, and you pulled the card to describe your charming, attentive new boyfriend, you're in big trouble.

RELATIONSHIP: In regard to a new romantic prospect, the Upright Seven says you probably already slept with him. It says you just plain *wanted* him so much that you set your usual code of conduct aside and got involved too quickly. You hoped the sex would show him how wonderful you are, but you were wrong. There's a lesson in this about slowing down and getting to know a man's mind and heart before you try to catch him with your body. The lesson is about the importance of putting in the time to walk through the stages of the dating process.

If you're single, and you haven't jumped into bed with him yet, the Upright Seven of Spades can be a very appropriate card. Sometimes the smartest move is to stand back and ask, "What's in it for me? Why would I want to go out with *this* guy?" If you have a history of giving too much too fast, the decision to hold back until he proves his worth is a smart one.

The marriage represented by the Upright Seven exists between two very selfish, self-centered people. Each expects the other to earn more and be more faithful. Each accuses his or her partner of every sort of chicanery, while they themselves develop relationships on the side and stash money in secret bank accounts. These two will argue, blame, and spend too much on appearances right up until the day they drive their BMWs to divorce court.

CIRCUMSTANCES: The car represented by the Upright Seven of Spades is a lemon. Its current owner is hoping to sell it to you without ever mentioning it needs a valve job.

When they sold you this house they told you the city bought the twenty acres of panoramic view next door and would never build on the land. What the previous owner failed to mention is the acreage is the site of the new city dump.

You found this job off one of those flyers promising $500 to $5,000 a week for part-time work in your home. The flyer doesn't mention that you have to run up $1,000 in phone bills and buy a factory-authorized kit for $1,500 in order to get started.

Don't get involved with any car, house, or job represented by the Upright Seven of Spades. It'll be a better deal for the other guy than it will be for you.

REVERSED

INDIVIDUAL: The Reversed Seven is the card of the gold digger. This man has an invisible ticker tape running across his forehead that spells out "For Sale" in little white lights. His vibes broadcast on the same radio frequency as a hooker's.

A person with the Reversed Seven of Spades governing their soul is capable of amazing acts of selfishness. They believe their primary assets are their looks and their "sexual ability." They think life comes down to having the right package plus the ambition to sell it to the highest bidder. They don't see anything wrong with using their body to snag a rich husband or wife. They think anybody else who had the package would, so why shouldn't they?

People defined by the Seven of Spades "marry up" because they're looking for a shortcut to shopping on Rodeo Drive and weekending at the Four Seasons. But, when a zaftig sex bomb uses his or her physical assets to seduce an affluent prospect, he or she takes a risk. If their partner figures out that he or she was used, they have no choice but to leave. The Reversed Seven personality won't mind if the divorce settlement is generous.

If you pulled the card to describe your brand-new boyfriend, ask yourself how you met him. Was he lounging poolside in a leopard bikini? Were his well-oiled body and pretty blond curls the first things you noticed about him? And do you have more money than he does? If he's coming on strong you'd better slow him down. Otherwise, you may be used.

RELATIONSHIP: The Reversed Seven represents the marriage between the bimbo trophy wife and the eighty-year-old millionaire in a wheelchair. She's the woman who used her body to broker the best marital deal she could get, except her husband's family, friends, and attorney don't trust her. She's allowed to go shopping, play tennis, and decorate the yacht, but she doesn't know how her husband earns his money or where he keeps it. Should he go broke, she'll have to leave him for another rich man. Should he die, her stepchildren will spend every dime of their inheritance contesting the will. Under no circumstances will they permit *her* to control their family fortune. They'll offer to buy her out or pay her off. If she refuses to cooperate, they'll get rid of her another way.

A Reversed Seven of Spades girl always winds up alone in the end because she doesn't connect with her man in a way that would inspire him to stick with her through a mastectomy.

When the card describes what appears to be a fresh, new romance, it doesn't exist at all. Either you're out to seduce this guy, or he's seducing you. In any event, nothing soulful and loving will come of the alliance.

CIRCUMSTANCES: It doesn't get any worse than this. The Reversed Seven says you were fired from this job and you feel like a failure. There is no circumstance under which the card foretells a positive outcome.

NOTE

The Seven of Spades always asks, "What's in it for me?"

Now, I'm of two minds about all this greedy, selfish stuff. On the one hand (Upright), it can be wise to protect yourself and look out for your interests. There's a certain amount of personal power in choosing to put your own concerns above the concerns of others. But on the other hand (Reversed), selfishness, lack of discipline, and avarice go too far. The Reversed card is never okay, but the Upright card is all right if your motives are self-protection and a commitment to getting what you want, *at no one's expense.*

The Seven of Spades is a card of degrees, of nuance, subtlety, and shading. What matters is where you draw the line. What matters is at which point you say, "That would be unethical." If you draw the line out in the back forty your standards are too flexible and you need to tighten them up, but if that line is close in, you're a sensible woman. It's only practical to make sure there's something in it for you.

UPRIGHT or REVERSED: It's an absolute "No" either way.

Eight of Spades

Eights: Philosophy
Spades: Attitudes and Problems

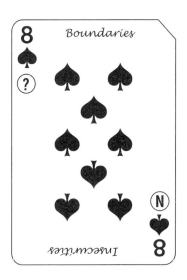

BOUNDARIES

Eights are cards of philosophy and Spades are cards of the mind. One would assume the combination of philosophy and brainpower would create a brilliant study of truth, but it doesn't. Put together, the two implode. They cave in, grow conservative, and become preoccupied with self-protection.

UPRIGHT

I once attended a lecture about boundaries. The speaker said they were fundamental to good mental health. She wasn't saying they were a cure for mental illness, just that people would enjoy more peace of mind if they understood what boundaries were and how important it is to set them. She said the key to recognizing a boundary violation is to recognize your feelings of resentment. She said resentment was our friend, that resentful feelings crop up when our boundaries aren't respected.

If your boyfriend asks for a favor and you resent the request, ask yourself why. Does he want you to baby-sit his kids so he can go to a ball game? Is this the third weekend in a row he's asked? Does this guy have season tickets? You have to set a boundary. Tell him you love him but you're not spending another of your Saturdays with his kids instead of him.

INDIVIDUAL: The Upright Eight sets appropriate limits and describes the perimeters we establish to feel safe and secure. But it also stands for the boundaries that harden and wall people out.

Men and women represented by the Eight of Spades don't participate in life the way other people do. Average folks love, grieve, work, and party at a certain level, at a certain pitch. The Eight of Spades represents 80 percent of that output. Men and women represented by the card never get fully involved.

The man defined by the Eight craves a warm blanket of security. He likes teaching positions with tenure or he'll join a union and only accept union work. He takes his vitamins every day and finds a neutral haircut he can wear all his life. He's the kind of guy who wears a favorite baseball cap every day for ten years, owns ten suits cut from the same fabric in the same color, or buys one Ford truck after another.

Eight of Spades men often have abrupt speech patterns. They vacillate between blurting out and clamming up. The abruptness translates into their social life too. The new romantic prospect defined by the Eight will trot right through the early dating rituals with charm and style, but he'll shut down when the girl wants to take it to the next level. Men represented by the Eight don't make friends easily. It isn't that they're shy, it's that they don't completely open up. It's a lot of work to get to know them.

The bottom line reality is that the Eight of Spades man is an 80 percent person. He doesn't fully participate in relationships. What he needs is a partner who's respectful of his comfort levels. If you're crazy about one of these characters, expect to be underwhelmed by him. If your idea of romance is to exchange Shakespearean sonnets or X-rated e-mails, you won't feel 100 percent engaged by him. But you can take comfort in the knowledge that if the Eight of Spades man ever gets used to you he won't dissolve the relationship easily.

RELATIONSHIP: The marriage defined by the Upright Eight is dependable and conservative. There's something well established about it. The card is more likely to represent an ongoing alliance than a new one. The wedded couple represented by the Eight feels safe together because they know their partner's limits. Their marriage doesn't inspire them, but it doesn't disappoint them either.

The new romance described by the card won't motivate you because this guy isn't 100 percent available. He's not involved elsewhere (the Eight of Spades person is too conservative to fool around), but he might claim he works a lot of overtime or has family responsibilities. The truth is, he *chooses* to be too busy for a full relationship. In this way he sets a polite boundary against the relentlessness of a loving partnership.

CIRCUMSTANCES: As an outcome card, the Upright Eight foretells success within certain limits, probably in the 80 percent range.

How will you like the new job? It'll be okay. It'll be stable.

The apartment? Boring, but good. It's in a high-security building, is well constructed, and if not cutting edge modern, at least it's painted a safe, neutral color.

The car represented by the Eight might be the best one to buy. It's dependable, sound, and economically priced. It's reliable transportation, but far from a babe magnet.

REVERSED

The Eight of Spades stands for protective limits when Upright and a lack of boundaries when Reversed. When it falls upside down, the card of security becomes the card of insecurity.

INDIVIDUAL: The Reversed Eight of Spades defines the insecure person. Shy and easily overwhelmed, this one finds life painful and frightening.

If you pulled the card to describe a new love interest, he'll turn out to be so insecure that he isn't good relationship material. He'll need constant reassurance and accuse you of all kinds of insensitivities. He'll want to know why you didn't call, if he looks fat in his jeans, and what your friends think of him. The person described by the Reversed card will stand next to you at the office cocktail party and shiver with fear. These folks need extraordinary care and maintenance. You must dance only with them, hold their hand at all times, and remain by their side like a Seeing Eye dog.

Reversed Eight people don't have any boundaries of their own so they don't recognize them in others. These are the people who call you at 2 A.M. because they can't sleep and need to talk. (Forget that you have to get up at six!) These folks stand too close and their normal voices are either too loud or too quiet. They offer advice when you don't want any and *insist* on helping even when you've already said, "Please don't."

RELATIONSHIP: The union defined by the Reversed Eight is a neurotic, clingy alliance that will crumble when confronted with the smallest difficulty. Insecure people are completely self-consumed and incapable of being there for someone else.

In the beginning, these two will think they *finally* met someone as sensitive as they are. Initially, they'll be flattered by the dozens of messages on their answering machine or by their partner's tiny jealousies. They'll think it's cute the way their lover is convinced everybody who speaks to them is hitting on them. But eventually their relentless insecurities will chip away at their relationship.

"Where were you? Why didn't you call? Are you getting tired of me?"

"Do you think she's prettier than me? You like her big boobs, don't you?"

"I know you think he's better because he has more money. I'll never be enough for you, will I?"

Any coupling between two frightened, insecure people will forever stand on shaky ground.

CIRCUMSTANCES: The Reversed card says you'll feel so vulnerable and exposed that your teeth will rattle, so you'll probably say no. You'll never feel safe with any car, job, or apartment represented by the Reversed Eight.

NOTE

The Upright Eight of Spades is the card of appropriate boundaries. It represents the line we draw in the sand to say, "I'm honoring my own values and standards by not going any further than *this.*" It's the card of *not* loaning him the money, sleeping with him, or driving to his place for a nightcap unless you're comfortable doing it. Good boundaries are the mark of an emotionally healthy, self-confident person and we all need them if we're to feel sane and respected. Unfortunately, the boundaries represented by the Upright card can harden until they inhibit our participation in life and love.

The Reversed Eight doesn't have an accurate perception of boundaries. It can't tell where or when to set them. It's also the card of our insecurities, of the quivering, vulnerable bunny rabbit twitching inside each of us.

UPRIGHT: "Mmm . . . partially."
REVERSED: "Ohmigod, no."

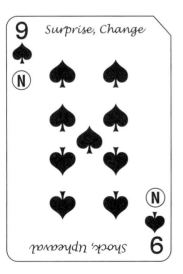

Nine of Spades

Nines: Culmination
Spades: Attitudes and Problems

**DISRUPTION,
DISTURBANCE,
UPHEAVAL**

UPRIGHT

The Nine of Spades is a card of frightening change and disturbing speed. It blows through your existence like a tornado to uproot your foundation with a careless wave of its hand. Once the storm has blown past, you'll find yourself standing in the rubble of your life, scratching your head in wonder.

INDIVIDUAL: The man portrayed by the Nine sees himself as EXCITING! CREATIVE! SPONTANEOUS! You may see him as a nut case. He won't be able to hold to a schedule no matter how hard he tries. He'll change jobs and move frequently. He'll be loud, disruptive, intense, and dress for effect. He won't understand the benefits of orderly conduct. In fact, he'll think he's plenty orderly and you're just a warden who ought to loosen up.

I once worked in an office with a young woman who was dating a Nine of Spades type of guy. He parked his cement mixer out front on Valentine's Day where he honked in the street until we clustered at the second-floor window. When he spotted his lady love, he turned on the mixer. The giant barrel rotated slowly until a sign painted on the side moved into view. It said, "Happy Valentine's Day. I Love You." She'd only known him a week and they'd only been on two dates. He stood on top of the truck grinning up at her, dressed from head to toe in bright red, waving a bouquet of roses. She giggled and blushed, blew kisses and waved back. We coworkers stood away from the window in silence with our arms folded across our chests. We watched her fall in love like a bird shot out of the sky.

The Nine of Spades person is a healer at heart. In his soul he seeks the truth and wants to use his truth to benefit mankind. Before he can bestow his gifts he must absorb the lesson of self-discipline. You'll find the mature Nine of Spades character working for the Peace Corps, in hospitals, and the Department of Social Services. But his basic nature will remain intact. He'll still be inappropriate and out of proportion. He'll still be flashy, the loudest guy at the water cooler, and the one to send the outlandish floral arrangement to your office when you discreetly have your face lifted.

RELATIONSHIP: How do we use this card to define a new relationship? Very carefully. The Nine of Spades describes the classic whirlwind romance. It will shock your friends by its speed, its flamboyance, and the sacrifices it will demand. At its best, this union will be a great departure from any you've known before. At its worst, it will tear you away from all you hold dear and destroy the structure of your life. The storm will end as suddenly as it began too. You could wind up alone, in another state, broke, and pregnant.

The established couple described by the Upright Nine subject one another to temperamental fits and explosive outbursts. The cops are familiar with them from cruising by every Christmas to break up their annual fight. They press charges against one another on Friday and fondly bail each other out on Monday. These two think their partnership is exciting, that they're a thrill-a-minute, dynamic, daredevil duo who's up for anything. Others see them as combustible and dangerous.

CIRCUMSTANCES: If the Nine has jolted into your spread it will predict an abrupt shift in circumstances. After the dust has settled, the task will be to sift through the debris of your old life. You must search the remains to sort what can be salvaged from what's been destroyed forever.

The employer represented by this card will be erratic, explosive, and unpredictable. This car will blow up on the freeway, this apartment will catch on fire, or your new roommate will turn out to be crazy. Draw a big red circle with a line through it around anything represented by the Nine of Spades.

REVERSED

The Nine is a naturally frightening card on its best day. But when you turn it upside down, things go from bad to worse.

INDIVIDUAL: The individual described by the Reversed Nine is a recent recipient of the card's negative impact. Angst, torment, and emotional devastation have fermented to the breaking point. This poor soul lies awake all night crying into his pillow, feverish with despair.

The new romantic prospect represented by the card is in the midst of a devastating breakup. He may look okay and he may race about the countryside to chat up the village maidens, but late at night, when he's home alone, he lines up bottles of sleeping pills on his dresser or fingers his revolver. Normally, he's just a drama queen. But right now, the combination of his explosive temperament and his genuine devastation makes using the pills or the gun a real possibility. Obviously, things aren't going to work out between the two of you.

RELATIONSHIP: This alliance can hardly call itself a marriage. In the process of separating or divorcing, the established union represented by the card is beyond repair.

If you want to understand why the new romance represented by the Reversed Nine won't work out, read the section above on the Reversed individual. If you insist on accepting a date with a new person defined by the Reversed card, expect to wake up in a motel on the outskirts of Las Vegas with the worst hangover of your life. You could find yourself lying next to a relative stranger who claims you're his new bride.

CIRCUMSTANCES: This situation is the most difficult in the deck. The Reversed Nine says your world has exploded. You're in shock, shattered, and can't believe you'll ever recover. When the Reversed card describes your condition you're coping with the trauma of an assault, a bankruptcy, or an automobile accident.

NOTE

Regardless of whether it represents a person, a relationship, or an external circumstance, the Nine of Spades is extreme. The card enjoys surprise attacks, but they could be terrifying to you. This lover could ask you to marry him on the first date or disappear so fast that he leaves tire tracks on your sheets. This relationship will challenge you to examine what you value and many of your convictions will be left behind. An encounter with the Nine of Spades, Upright or Reversed, could easily change your life forever.

UPRIGHT or REVERSED: This card is always an absolute "NO!"

Ten of Spades

Tens: Doorways
Spades: Attitudes and Problems

THE END

Tens are doors that bang open and shut and Spades are the cards of our problem-solving techniques. The Ten of Spades offers the ultimate solution: it walks out and slams the door.

When I see the rigid, absolute Ten of Spades, it reminds me of a Barbara Walters interview with Bing Crosby that I saw years ago. Bing wasn't embarrassed to tell Barbara on national television how he threw his beloved child out of the house because he disapproved of her relationship. He said his only daughter would never be welcome in his home again. When Barbara said, "Gee, Bing, isn't that a little harsh?" he just waved his hand in a farewell gesture and said as far as he was concerned, it was "aloha on the steel guitar."

The Reversed Ten is the card of final, unconditional endings.

The Upright card is more complicated. Like a traffic cop, it shoves its white-gloved hand in your face, toots on its whistle, and commands you to cease and desist. Then it waits patiently while you abandon your dreams. After a while, with a flick of white glove, it motions you forward into a brand-new life.

The Upright Ten is the card of transformation.

UPRIGHT

The Ten of Spades stands for the death and rebirth process. They say in order for something new to be born something old has to die. One of Christianity's basic tenets is that death leads to regeneration. Christians believe Christ died for them and then rose from the grave to give them everlasting life. Christ's crucifixion and resurrection are symbolic of the new, clean life Christians hope to live once they abandon their previous sinful life.

The Ten of Spades works the same way. If you release your current situation, the card says a door will open onto a new situation—except you can't open the second door until you close the first one. The Ten warns that the transition might be all-consuming, that the shift could become an obsession. The process may overwhelm your life or take you away from all that you hold dear.

INDIVIDUAL: A part of the Ten of Spades person is dying. Regardless of how positive and optimistic he is about it, there's no escaping the fact. This is a painful time for him and it requires great courage and spiritual strength. For now, this man is isolated and frightened. He waits, exposed and alone, while the Universe remakes him. Eventually, he'll be reborn as a different person with altered ideas but for now he has to endure the process.

The new romantic interest represented by the Upright Ten of

Spades will become a powerful presence in your life. Your connection to one another will be passionate and intense. Your lover's charisma and sexual magnetism will enchant you and his physical presence will intoxicate you. This connection could easily develop into an obsession.

RELATIONSHIP: The married couple portrayed by the Upright Ten has lost something they once had and they won't get it back. It's gone forever. If they can agree to accept a change in the fundamental nature of their relationship, they can go forward together in a new way. But if they no longer value their alliance, they will part forever.

Any union represented by the Upright Ten will go through many phases before it settles into a comfortable groove. These two will experience times of separation when nothing but perseverance will keep them going and times when their primary bond will be their mutual suffering. Their relationship will never be casual. Instead, it will be all-consuming and may threaten everything else in their lives.

You may not stay with the new romance represented by the Upright Ten of Spades, but the aftermath of this connection will resonate throughout your life and change your attitude toward love and sex forever.

CIRCUMSTANCES: You'll have to bulldoze the old house represented by the Ten and build a new one. You'll have to rebuild the engine before you can drive this car. You'll have to fire half the staff on your first day at this job. The Ten of Spades situation will require huge amounts of your time, energy, and emotional stamina. It'll suck everything out of you and leave nothing for your personal life.

REVERSED

When the Ten of Spades falls Reversed, it no longer contains an element of hope for a new beginning. Instead, it crystallizes into a resolute ending. There's no subtlety or nuance to the Reversed card and no hope for negotiation or modification. The Reversed Ten of Spades is probably the simplest card in the deck. When you pull the Ten, it's over, finished, kaput, and will never resume again under any circumstances.

INDIVIDUAL: This man's life is collapsing. He's caught smack in the middle of its demise. Fortunately, the Reversed Ten of Spades person has emotional and physical endurance. He'll resurrect himself the first chance he gets. For now, he's taking one step at a time. He's turning away from a life saturated with drugs or alcohol and going into rehab in the hope of finding a better way to exist. If physical addictions aren't destroying him, then something equally as intoxicating (a woman, power, money, or status) is taking him down. The Reversed Ten man is no stranger to loss and the recovery process. He has tremendous powers of regeneration and he's not afraid to use them.

The new romantic prospect represented by the Reversed Ten has a troubled disposition. If he's not in the transformation process, he'll be vulnerable to depression, grief, or rage. He'll have a secretive nature and be unwilling to let go of old habits. He'll be unable to accept his losses, so he'll obsess over them. As a result, he won't be able to reach out for the love and compassion he needs so desperately. His task is to look within and seize control of his future. Until he enters into the death and rebirth process, he won't be available for a full relationship with you.

The former lover represented by the Reversed Ten has left your life and won't be back. The Reversed Ten represents someone you can't forgive, who never forgave you. The recrimination you both feel and the new lives you have built since you separated will keep you apart forever.

RELATIONSHIP: This marriage is over. The papers are signed and the divorce is final. These two will never rekindle the passion. This couple was unable to make the transition from lovers to friends, from rich to poor, or from young to old. Somewhere along the line they lost the ability to adjust to life as a team. They will never reconcile.

The brand-new alliance represented by the card has also ended. This guy won't be back.

CIRCUMSTANCES: When you pull the Reversed Ten you're in the foreclosure or repossession process. You're going to lose the dream condo you bought with your tiny inheritance. You're going to lose your job or watch your precious Lexus be towed away on the back of the asset-recovery truck.

Give up your possessions and don't look back. Turn your attention to the future because you have nothing left to work with here.

NOTE

The Ten of Spades is the death card and a harsh message regardless of its Upright or Reversed position. The Upright Ten describes the concept of transformation. If you think you can survive the cleansing white heat of a scorched earth, a complete renovation of life as you know it, or a lonely, dark night of the soul, a rebirth is possible. But, when the big black Ten falls Reversed, the past is dead and you will never breathe life into it again.

UPRIGHT or REVERSED: The clearest "No" in the deck.

Jack of Spades

Jacks: Young People
Spades: Attitudes and Problems

A YOUTHFUL OUTLOOK

UPRIGHT

The Upright Jack of Spades says while you were out there living large and learning about life, the rest of us were elsewhere, absorbing other aspects of life. The card points out that over the years you skipped a few classes in life and love, and the time has come to enroll in the courses you missed.

I was divorced in the mid-nineties. I was fortunate enough to get the house in the settlement but that left me responsible for the yard work. Somehow, throughout my entire adult life, I had escaped ever pushing a lawnmower or mastering the art of screwing a sprinkler head onto a hose. I wound up at Home Depot chasing behind the nineteen-year-old nurseryman scribbling notes about pesticides and full sun versus partial shade. I had to get into shape physically, find a gardening wardrobe, squeeze the time into my busy schedule, and accumulate the tools and products.

All my life I'd had a terrible attitude toward my plants and sometimes they died of neglect. Once I opened up to the idea that I was the new gardener, I learned the truth about yard work. I discovered it paid dividends I hadn't expected. I once viewed gardening as labor, but I came to understand it's about nurturing, patience, and our natural human connection to the earth.

The passing over of some form of self-development early in life creates a need to develop that part of your self later on. The Jack is a cheery volunteer for the new experiences and procedures all around him.

INDIVIDUAL: When the Upright Jack describes a lover, it says he has come to a time of quiet hesitation. He stands perfectly still while he looks around. He's trying to remember where he went wrong the last time he fell in love and what it was he promised to memorize before opening the relationship door again. He acknowledges his role in past failures and seeks to learn from those failures. He knows he's taking tenuous little steps into very new and very different territory. Choosing to date you symbolizes a move forward for him and a big risk. You can nurture his new skills if you allow him to step slowly through the rituals of dating and give him plenty of space to process everything that happens.

RELATIONSHIP: This relationship will move slowly because these two are aware of how much they don't know. They've probably been married before and feel some degree of responsibility for the demise of those unions. As a result, they both question their ability to participate in an alliance in a healthy way. Therefore, they choose their words with care and proceed with caution as they inch through the dating process. They won't conduct their union at a fevered pitch because they refuse to get high on love or lust. They're best described as having an open mind about romance, but a cautious attitude toward relationships. I predict this couple will relax over time and develop a sturdy connection. How could any couple go wrong when their goal is to improve their relationship skills?

CIRCUMSTANCES: The Upright Jack defines a curious mind with an unguarded attitude and asks you to research fresh ways of doing things.

You wouldn't ordinarily consider renting the apartment represented by the Jack. This job isn't one you would normally apply for either. The card counsels you to keep an open mind and encourages you to explore. It says you'll find a job or house in an unusual field or neighborhood.

REVERSED

When turned upside down, the youngest and least mature of the characters who define the intellect slumps into a chair, folds his arms across his chest, and sneers, "So what if I don't wanna learn anything. I'm gonna do what I want and nobody is gonna tell me nuthin'!"

The Reversed Jack of Spades is belligerent, defensive, and irresponsible. This is the card of acting out. A lot of people don't understand the term "acting out." I'll explain it: Your husband makes you angry, so you run up the credit cards. Your boyfriend ignores you, so you sleep with his friend. Mom and Dad say, "Get a job," so you get loaded instead.

INDIVIDUAL: This is the "bad boy" of the deck. He's the sexy rock star in leather pants with elaborate tattoos and cool hair. He radiates counterculture charisma from the back of a motorcycle, where he easily defrosts the opposite sex with a shy scowl and the naughty lift of an eyebrow. But he's hard going for anyone, mainly because of his gender problems. He believes all women are bitches or men real assholes. It's not his fault he's an alcoholic, it's hers. He drinks, uses drugs, gambles, or has random sex because she's a bitch. It's not his fault he can't hold a job either. He may miss a day once in a while but he's good at what he does. His boss is the problem because he's an uptight jerk.

The Reversed Jack does better with an older lover who indulges him. He needs someone who will tolerate his tantrums, someone flattered by his appearance who doesn't require much from him. The Reversed Jack is always a taker and never a giver.

I've seen clients over the years who said, "No way!" upon hearing this description of their sweetheart. "My boyfriend's nothing like that!" they cry. "He has a good job, loves his mother, and treats me like a princess!" My response is a cryptic "Just wait." You pulled *this* card. It's only a matter of time.

Bad boys can be any age, but the Jack normally represents a young person between the ages of fifteen and twenty-five. When it does, this is the spoiled, angry child in the family and the one most likely to act out with alcohol, drugs, money, or sex.

If you pulled the Reversed Jack to describe yourself, well . . . you've let things get pretty sticky, haven't you? You're hostile and defensive and you're in the wrong. Just accept it and start to change. Pay back the money, give up the honey on the side, apologize, and quit complaining.

If the Reversed Jack describes your new lover, boy are you in for it. You need to examine him for his gender issues, his belligerence, and his bad puppy stance.

If the Reversed Jack describes your client, you'd better get payment in cash.

RELATIONSHIP: The established partnership described by the Reversed Jack is in trouble. One member is acting out and his defensive attitude, infidelities, or ruinous debt are destroying the marriage.

If you pulled the card to describe a budding alliance, it'll only have one redeeming quality: it will scare the hell out of your parents, which may be the whole point to the relationship anyway.

If you pulled the Reversed Jack to describe the connection between your fourteen-year-old daughter and her new boyfriend you can expect them to slouch through your front door and park it on your couch to watch *Jerry Springer*. They'll smoke pot in her bedroom and get matching piercings. Forget about school.

CIRCUMSTANCES: The primary attribute of this situation will be how strongly you defend it. If it represents a car, you'll justify your decision to own it. Or, you'll bristle when people ask about your living arrangement. A spoiled child with a chip on his shoulder governs any situation represented by the Reversed Jack of Spades.

NOTE

The Upright Jack of Spades describes an open mind and a new way of looking at life and love. The Reversed card has a narrow, childish perspective. It expects to be loved-at rather than to share in an open, thoughtful exchange of affection.

UPRIGHT: The card is a "Maybe."
REVERSED: "No, never . . . ever."

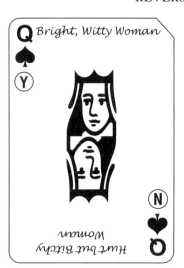

Queen of Spades

Queens: Women
Spades: Attitudes and Problems

OUR LADY OF IMMACULATE MENTAL HEALTH

Spades correspond to the element of Air. They rule our attitudes and ability to process information. The Queen is usually an Air sign woman: Gemini, Libra, or Aquarius.

UPRIGHT

INDIVIDUAL: The Upright Queen of Spades is bright, witty, funny, and risqué. She's loose yet refined; cool and detached, but rowdy and playful. She'll go anywhere and get along with anyone. There's no event too formal or too casual for her. She's adaptable, she turns on a dime, and she *loves* bright new shiny people.

Her home is noisy and busy. Traffic moves in and out all day long, and the phone rings constantly. Her decorating style is elegant but informal, comfortable but very pretty. She puts elaborate frames on colorful prints of people doing pleasant things. Landscapes are not to her taste; faces populate her living room. She has doll collections on shelves and teddy bears on the couch. She decorates with photos of her family and friends, including the hungry child she sponsors in El Salvador and the foreign-exchange student who stayed with her one summer. She likes smiling, accepting eyes that gaze out from warm, familiar faces.

The Queen of Spades is oriented to life through her head, not her heart. She's the woman who purchases those homely, countrified, wooden wall hangings with ducks and hearts that say "God Bless America" or "World's Best Mom." This is a Hallmark person who pays someone else to say what is so hard to find the words for in real life. She's more comfortable with homey platitudes. She goes with sentiment in lieu of real feeling.

Her wardrobe reflects her noisy, busy style. She chooses bright, laughing, colorful prints. She loves all colors, but she loves blue best of all—any variety from the palest tones of the sky to the electric zap of peacock. She's a sucker for things that sparkle too. Glitter corresponds to the electric impulses that shoot through her mind. She owns glitzy holiday sweaters and T-shirts with rhinestone kittens on them. Mickey and Minnie, Tweety and Pooh populate her wardrobe. The zany characters make her laugh and the innocence of the kitty touches her heart.

The Queen's insights are immediate and accurate. As your adviser, she'll sidestep the clutter of details and move straight to the heart of the issue. She'll give you her best, most thoughtful opinion, but allows for the soul. She knows everybody's other side is dark and murky, like hers. She'll say, "What!? Are you nuts? He's married!!... Ahh, but those strong, soft hands of his..." She won't advise you to go for it, but she won't blame you when you do either. She has a sage gift: she's able to sort out the disorganization in your heart and make sense of your feelings.

The Queen of Spades may appear to have moved very swiftly into her newest relationship, but the truth is, she began processing his merits the instant she laid eyes on the guy. She will have chosen him for his ideals. She doesn't care how much money he earns or if he just got done doing weekends at County, if he inspires that cosmic jolt in her heart, if he activates those electrical impulses that speak louder to her than the voice of sanity, well . . . she'll patch the details together later.

Once she decides her man shares her vision, the Queen of the Mind will defrost into a passionate, sensual hedonist. She'll persevere through shattering circumstances if she believes this is the partner destined to walk beside her into the valley of her dreams. When she falls in love, the Queen invests everything she's got into the union, which makes it almost impossible for her to acknowledge defeat when she has to, or to cut her losses and move on. She trusts her instincts. If her heart told her he was "the One!" she'll be devastated if they break up. When these light and airy girls finally fall, they fall harder than anyone else does. She's the one who never completely abandons her dream, the one who never totally gets over the man she loves and loses. She's very slow to cool off.

RELATIONSHIP: The Queen of Spades alliance is a meeting of the minds. It's the kind of union created by people who have spent years in therapy. These two analyze, debate, and examine every detail of their life together.

Their relationship may have seen many phases before it reached its current one. In the old days these two were more enmeshed. They've learned over time how to grant each other privacy and freedom and how to meet their individual time and space needs. They intellectualize their disputes and debate their issues instead of fighting or capitulating. Their lovemaking will be sincere but a bit detached until they get on the same page intellectually. Then pretty much anything goes.

If you pulled the Upright card to describe a new romance, it won't be a wild, passionate connection. But if you've been looking for a more rational, intellectual way to be involved, you've probably found it.

CIRCUMSTANCES: The best way to resolve this situation is to think it through, plan it out, do the math. The Queen favors objective reasoning and will not support choices based on sentiment.

Any environment described by the Queen of Spades is modern, uncluttered, and high-tech. This workplace is looking for someone bright and savvy with leadership qualities, a strong background in technology, and a relaxed, charming demeanor.

REVERSED

INDIVIDUAL: When the Queen of Spades falls Reversed, she's deeply hurt. This card more than any other will describe a woman in pain. But, this card, more than any other, will also describe a complete bitch. When the woman of the mind, the clearest thinker among us, turns her brilliance upside down and buries herself in grief, she can use her razor wit and skill with words to cut others to ribbons. She's formidable when she suffers, and she can remain in pain for years. When the Queen loses the objective use of her special gift, which is her cool, detached, big old brain, and surrenders to disappointment, or when she's unable to make the world fit her vision of life, she'll blame the boss, her man, or the kids. When she shuts down she becomes withholding, restrictive, bitter, and scary. I'd rather see her parked on the couch, sobbing her heart out, and gulping down ice cream. It's easier on the rest of us.

Spade girls need lots of air space in which to maneuver, and even the best of them fear vulnerability. In fact, when someone gets too close their skin begins to crawl. Relentless intimacy feels like bugs crawling all over their arms and legs. So they bolt! They withdraw to hose off the bugs. They'll return when their skin feels clean, once they can breathe again. The Reversed Queen acts remote and aloof or prissy and fussy as a defense against being overwhelmed by emotion. Upright or Reversed, she needs a lot of personal freedom in a relationship. The Reversed version has been known to remain single all her life or to bail out of romances early to avoid suffocation.

RELATIONSHIP: The connection represented by the Reversed Queen of Spades is best defined as a Porsche driving a hundred miles an hour toward a brick wall thirty yards away. This romance is ending at a breakneck pace. On top of the excruciating pain of your breakup will be the shock that you're the bad guy. Your boyfriend or husband will point an accusing finger at you and pronounce that not only are you the problem but you are also an absolute bitch of a human being.

Regardless of whether the Queen represents an established union or a new romance, it will be painful and bring out the worst in you.

CIRCUMSTANCES: Should the Reversed Queen of Spades describe an environment, a horrible shrew of a woman will dominate it. This is the workplace controlled by a mean-spirited Tiger Woman with a mouth full of criticism. It's the apartment building with the hateful landlady. Don't take the job or rent the dwelling represented by the Reversed Queen.

NOTE

When the Queen of Spades is functioning well, she's clever, sane, funny, bright, and a real treat of a friend. We can all use a wise counselor and witty sidekick like the discriminating Upright Queen. The Reversed Queen needs to lighten up and expose herself. It won't kill her to be vulnerable and kind, but it may take a lifetime to learn this one, simple lesson.

UPRIGHT: "Yes, because you've already thought it through."
REVERSED: "No way."

King of Spades

Kings: Men
Spades: Attitudes and Problems

STRICT MAN

UPRIGHT

The King of Spades is dispassionate and judicial. Sentiment and romantic ideals don't motivate him. He isn't open to individuals with their unique circumstances and biased points of view. Instead, he stands for government officials or institutions that hold power over others and hand down rulings based on conventions, procedures, and the law. The King of Spades is remote and impartial, and his goal is to be fair.

The King serves those occasions that require clearheaded evaluations. He represents the wisdom to step back, observe the field, and take a detached look at the situation. This card may represent your smartest move and can be very appropriate. The King of Spades is usually an Air sign man: Gemini, Libra, or Aquarius.

INDIVIDUAL: The man represented by the Upright King of Spades will be hard going for most women. As a husband he won't indulge in the small romantic pleasantries that girls live and breathe for. If he manages to pull off a lovely gesture, he will have accumulated the skill intellectually, like from watching TV. He won't understand the softer aspects of relationships, but he can adopt a working knowledge of them.

In fact, some of these guys can get positively flamboyant with their expressions of "Fabulous Love" when they put their minds to it. They'll drive you to the coast just to watch the sun set. They'll bring a bottle of Sauvignon Blanc and real crystal stemware in a wicker picnic basket. They'll park their sports car on a cliff overlooking the ocean and make a toast to love or recite a stanza of poetry *because that's how it's done in the movies!* These are the suave playboys who know how to set the stage with candlelight, champagne, and steamy jazzy music. But once they've seduced you with their smooth, elegant style, their act screeches to a halt. When they have to improvise, they don't know what to do. The movies don't show us how it's done fifteen years into the marriage.

Fortunately, you can buy the King a "how to" book. These men are intellectuals so they like to study up. On the first date you can tell how much they read about relationships by how familiar they are with wines or ballroom dance. If you slip your brainy King a copy of *How to Stay Lovers for Life*, the odds are excellent he'll read it.

The King of Spades can be an obsessive-compulsive personality. He often maintains a "his way or the highway" point of view and lacks real flexibility. Any effort by any woman to touch his heart or to coax open his mind is viewed as criticism.

The King of Spades needs to develop his compassionate side, to pray that vulnerability and tenderness will magically ooze from his pores. The King will shed a real tear when you hand him a mushy Valentine card, but when his parents die he'll freeze up and feel nothing. His challenge in life is to surrender to his woman, relinquish emotional control, and allow himself to experience his feelings, which may be too large a task for the stern King of Spades.

The King sees himself as jolly and clever, which he is, and he's bright beyond belief. He has an arsenal of hysterical jokes and puns, his career is brilliant, and he knows when to be quiet and polite. But eventually his partner will criticize him for his detachment and awkwardness in intimate moments. Most women need more emotional interaction, more shoulder to cry on, and more sentiment. The good Kings try to provide emotionally for the woman in their life, but their efforts are clumsy and stiff.

I advise you to acknowledge the King's attempts to be romantic. Never forget that poetry and flowers were bred out of his people generations ago. Judge him kindly and encourage him while he stumbles through the steps. And don't forget to praise him when he gets it right.

RELATIONSHIP: This is the union of two intellectuals united by their love of rules, standards, and procedures. They agree there's only one "right way" to live.

The following is a true story:

I know a devout Christian couple, but they aren't the charitable kind who help the poor and believe in a tolerant "we are all God's children" Christian ideology. They're the kind who use the Bible to control, not guide, their household.

This couple has a daughter who went to her Christian high school prom with a boy from her church. She bought a beautiful dress, had her nails done, and the afternoon before the prom her girlfriend came over to style her hair. The friend worked for an hour to create a half up, half down look with tiny fresh rosebuds tucked into the pile of pinned-up curls. When her hair was finished, she put on her gown and went downstairs to show her parents.

The parents were outraged by her hairdo. They said it was unbecoming and told her to go upstairs and comb it out. They wanted to see it neatly brushed and hanging down her back, without flowers. "When your hair looks likes this," said her father as he held up her senior picture, "you'll be ready for the dance."

The two girls retreated to the upstairs bathroom to cry in each other's arms. That night the daughter wore her hair the way her parents had insisted. The next morning, when she woke up, there was a letter propped against the lamp next to her bed. The letter was from her parents and contained a list of character traits they thought she should correct and try to improve.

The couple represented by the King of Spades is hard, harsh, unyielding, and self-righteous. They would rather be right than loving.

If you pulled the card to describe a new romance, ask yourself if you have an aptitude for an intellectualized alliance with a world-class stuffed shirt. Ask yourself if you're suited to be half of a sanctimonious whole.

CIRCUMSTANCES: Under these circumstances, use your judgment. Set aside your feelings and focus on the merits of the case. Don't take sides. Follow what you believe to be the proper procedures or the established rules. Make no apologies for your decision and trust that when you're in King of Spades mode, you'll choose correctly.

REVERSED

When the King of Spades falls Reversed things become extreme.

INDIVIDUAL: The Reversed King has a wall around him the length and breadth of the Great Wall of China. It's twelve feet thick, as old as dirt, and built to protect him from the barbarians on the other side. He'll seem cold, heartless, selfish, unreasonable, inaccessible, and insensitive. He'll tell you he wants you to leave him alone.

When he shuts down like this, the King of Spades is a real piece of work. He can't or won't share his inner life, not under any circumstances. Nothing, no gesture of love or affection, will thaw his frozen heart. Neither will counseling, because he's tougher than any shrink is. When his safety barometer tells him he's free from the threat of intrusion, he'll relax and return himself to his Upright position. He'll soften his heart at that time, but not a minute before.

If you pulled the Reversed King of Spades to describe your new love interest, you should abandon any hopes you may have for the relationship. This man won't give to you in any way, at any level; not emotionally, materially, or with his body. He may even go so far as to be cruel and abusive. The Reversed King is the meanest man in the deck. He's a stern, strict son of a bitch and an *impossible* romantic prospect.

Any woman who has been married to this man for any length of time can attest to how miserable he can be. Don't invest your tender heart here; the experience will be far too punishing.

RELATIONSHIP: The alliance defined by the Reversed King of Spades will be a frosty one. This couple doesn't share any aspect of their lives. They withhold all their feelings, every single one of them, everything from the trivial "I loved the soup" to the deeply significant "My mother died." They never hold hands. That would indicate that some flicker of warmth exists between them. This is the marriage of two stone-cold, indifferent partners who haven't slept together in years. They're held together by their fears, their anger, and their resentments.

If you pulled the Reversed King to describe a new courtship, this romance won't take off, primarily because the man won't call or won't have much to say if he does call. In no time, you'll begin to guard your feelings and withhold your opinions, too, because you'll be afraid to open up and expose your crazy goofball side. You two won't have anything to say to one another, you won't plan special evenings together, or enjoy long heart-to-heart conversations. There's nothing to work with here.

CIRCUMSTANCES: This situation is mean, spiteful, harsh, and unfair. You'll feel like a moth pinned to a fourth-grade science project. Expect to be poked, examined, and stashed in a desk next to a rotting apple. Expect to die of thirst and neglect while you struggle for freedom.

NOTE

The King of Spades is difficult under the best of circumstances. Upright, he's an intellectual and the woman interested in him must accept his nerdy ways and forgive his distant style while she feeds him a steady diet of romantic movies. But if he comes up Reversed, ditch him.

UPRIGHT or REVERSED: Either way, he's a huge "No."

In Conclusion

IT'S MY BELIEF THAT WE ARE ALL BORN WITH PSYCHIC ABILITY. IF YOU need evidence of our unspoken connection to one another, just think of babies. People say the baby has one cry for hunger, one for boredom, one for exhaustion, and one for a clean diaper. But I've listened to my own baby cry and I haven't heard such precise distinctions in the tone or intensity of each wail. I think the difference is in our response to the cry because our connection to our nonverbal child is a psychic one. When the baby cries, some part of us just knows what he or she needs. Sometimes we know because we haven't fed the little guy in three hours. Other times he's eaten, been changed, or just woken up. At those times, when he cries for no obvious reason, we know what to do intuitively.

I also believe our inborn ability to envision events and to sense the intentions of others has been acculturated out of us. The media, church, and the scientific community ridicule the notion that we can be connected at such a depth and by such a delicate thread. They don't understand how we could use our intuition and the tools that ground it, like astrology, Tarot, and the playing cards, to pick our way through the tangled jungle called life.

Sometimes, when people ask me about the phenomenon called psychic connection I respond by sharing a story. I tell about the time when my future husband and I were just dating, and I was asleep in his bed, sharing a pillow and dreaming. I dreamt that I was in a Hallmark store. I saw myself standing in front of a card rack stretched across the length of the room. In my search for the right card, I worked the entire rack. I selected a card, removed it, looked at the cover and opened it, read the message printed inside, closed it, returned it to its slot. Then I selected another. Halfway down the rack I entered the section for blank cards, those without messages printed inside. I continued to select cards at random, open them, look at the blank page, and replace the card in the rack. After I examined a few cards in this section, I thought, "One of these would be nice. I could write my own message."

Then I heard my future husband's voice cut through the night. Out loud he said, "I like the ones with something written in them."

♠ ♦ ♥ ♣

I'm not a New Age metaphysicist. I wish I were, but I'm not. I don't normally light candles, use aromatherapy in the house, or collect crystals, and my musical tastes run more toward Etta James than Enya. I live in my hometown, at the beach in southern California. I love to garden and dance. I'm a terrible gossip, but a great friend. I hate all sports except basketball and surfing, and I'm thinking about getting a dog. My ex-husband cuts my hair and I vacation at my sister's house in Idaho.

I'm normal.

I try to live my values every day, but I fail a lot. I succeed when I cook for my nephews, play card games with my daughter, pause to admire my brother's spiritual journey, and dip myself in the ocean.

When reading my book, try to remember that I'm not a prophet. I'm an average person, so I may be a tiny bit wrong sometimes. Though I take the art of card reading seriously, I have surely made mistakes.

I hope you have fun with this book and that through your exposure to the cards, you grow as a woman. Always remember your Prince Charming does indeed exist and that he's looking for you too.

Appendix

The Cheat Sheet

The purpose of providing a chart with a very brief description of each card is to trigger your memory of the longer essays contained in the text. Use the Cheat Sheet to mark your cards (as explained on pages 16–17) by writing these brief descriptions on them. Marking your cards will help you recall the details of the meanings when you're doing a reading. Or, you can tear out the Cheat Sheet, laminate it, and keep it with your cards for quick reference instead of marking your cards.

The Cheat Sheet

	HEARTS	Y/N	CLUBS	Y/N	DIAMONDS	Y/N	SPADES	Y/N
Joker	New, Original, Spontaneous	Y						
REVERSED	Unreliable, Fickle, Restless	N						
Ace	Permanent Love	Y	Talent	Y	Success	Y	Empowerment	Y
REVERSED	Unconventional Love	Y	Undeveloped Talent	Y	Education	Y	Powerless	N
Two	The Soul Mate Connection	Y	Will Call	Y	Physical Proximity & Travel	Y	Patience	?
REVERSED	Not a Match	N	Won't Call	N	No Proximity, Travel	N	Impatience	N
Three	Joy & Pleasure	Y	Gossip	N	Legal Marriage, Routines	Y	Interference	N
REVERSED	Faking the Pleasure	Y	Lies	N	Legal Divorce, Lack of Structure	N	Infidelity	N
Four	Young Child, Nurturing, Humanitarian	N	High Self-Esteem & Commitment	Y	Hard Work	Y	Healed	Y
REVERSED	Codependent	N	Low Self-Esteem & Won't Commit	N	Unemployed, Lazy, Overworked	N	Healing	Y
Five	Grief, Mourning	N	Competition	N	Conflict of Values	N	Separation	N
REVERSED	Repressed Grief	N	Jealousy	N	Full-Blown Fight	N	Abandonment	N
Six	Forever	Y	Faith, Trust	Y	The Natural Flow	Y	Anxiety	N
REVERSED	Temporary	Y	Lack of Faith, No Trust	Y	Not Flowing, Doesn't Feel Natural	Y	Panic Attack	N

	HEARTS	Y/N	CLUBS	Y/N	DIAMONDS	Y/N	SPADES	Y/N
Seven	Intimacy, Emotional Risk	Y	Meticulous Order	Y	Miscellaneous Stress	N	"How Can I Benefit?"	N
REVERSED	Unwilling to Be Vulnerable	N	Chaos & Confusion	N	Money Problems & Poor Health	N	Gold Digger, Failure	N
Eight	Second Marriage, Strength & Hope	Y	Happiness & Satisfaction	Y	The Art of Living, Balance & Equality	Y	Boundaries	?
REVERSED	Nothing to Give, Scorekeeping	N	Discontent	N	Unbalanced, Inequality	N	Insecurities	N
Nine	The Heart's Desire, True Love	Y	Ethics, Principles, Integrity	Y	Ambitious Expectations	Y	Surprise, Change	N
REVERSED	The One Who Got Away	N	Immorality	N	Expectations Too High, Ambitions Too Low	N	Shock, Upheaval	N
Ten	Home, Doorway to a New Romance	Y	The Future	Y	The Choice to Be Alone	Y	Transformation	N
REVERSED	Leaving a Home or Romance	Y	The Past	Y	Loneliness	N	The Final End	N
Jack	"Doing It"/ Immature Lover	Y	The Best Friend	Y	The Student, New Business	N	Open-Minded, Cautious Attitude	?
REVERSED	"Not Doing It," Favorite Child	Y	The Special Friend	Y	Identity Crisis	N	Defensive, Spoiled, Immature, Bad Boy	N
Queen	The Wife & Mother	Y	The Pretty Woman	Y	Mrs. Money, Physical Type	Y	Bright, Witty Woman	Y
REVERSED	Emotionally Unavailable	Y	Socially Incorrect Woman	Y	Broke, Disorganized, Unstable Finances	Y	Hurt but Bitchy Woman	N
King	The Marrying Man	Y	Mr. Right	Y	Healthy, Affluent Man, Physical Type	Y	Cool, Detached Man	N
REVERSED	Emotionally Unavailable	N	Mr. Almost Right	Y	Workaholic, Unhealthy, Financial Difficulties	?	Mean, Strict, Emotionally Shut Down Man	N

The Birth Card

The chart on the opposite page assigns one card to each day of the calendar year.

* ✳ The column on the left shows the days of the month.
* ✳ The months of the year are listed across the top of the table.
* ✳ In order to find the card that rules the day in question, read across to find the month you need, and down to find the day.
* ✳ Use the chart to look up an individual's date of birth.
* ✳ Then refer to the essay about the card. The copy under the subheading Individual will describe the character of the person born on that day. For example, the Queen of Spades represents a person born on October 15 and the Two of Hearts describes someone born on July 6.

The Birth Card will inform you of the motives and values of the new people who enter your life. But, it will also describe either their primary preoccupation or their destiny path. For example, the Two of Spades represents an individual born on May 28. When you read about the Two, you will learn that this person is meant to develop the virtue of patience. He must learn to drive slowly, make decisions slowly, and wait for opportunities to come to him. He must learn to allow others to take their time too. He will discover that the greatest treasures and his greatest happiness come to him slowly, over a long period of time.

Read the Reversed version of the card too. The Reversed description represents his character flaw, direction of disintegration, or his reaction under stress. The Reversed Two of Spades describes the way a character will dash through life—short tempered and exasperated with others.

When a Queen defines a man, or a King defines a woman, the description of the card will still be valid. The Queen of Diamonds represents the person born on January 14. A man born that day will be sensible and practical. In general, his life will be financially secure, but he's unlikely to generate great wealth in his lifetime. This man will be educated, enjoy a successful career, and establish financial stability, but he'll never be rich because the Queen represents middle management. She doesn't quite make it to the top, but she comes close.

When reading about your own Birth Card, substitute the word "she" for "he." And remember, being born under the domain of a "bold" card is nothing more than a challenge to function for the highest good.

	JAN.	FEB.	MAR.	APRIL	MAY	JUNE	JULY	AUG.	SEPT.	OCT.	NOV.	DEC.
1	Q♦	4♠	6♥	Joker	A♦	6♠	10♥	2♣	7♦	J♠	3♥	7♣
2	K♦	5♠	7♥	J♣	2♦	7♠	J♥	3♣	8♦	Q♠	4♥	8♣
3	A♦	6♠	8♥	Q♣	3♦	8♠	Q♥	4♣	9♦	K♠	5♥	9♣
4	2♦	7♠	9♥	K♣	4♦	9♠	K♥	5♣	10♦	A♠	6♥	10♣
5	3♦	8♠	10♥	A♣	5♦	10♠	A♥	6♣	J♦	2♠	7♥	J♣
6	4♦	9♠	J♥	2♣	6♦	J♠	2♥	7♣	Q♦	3♠	8♥	Q♣
7	5♦	10♠	Q♥	3♣	7♦	Q♠	3♥	8♣	K♦	4♠	9♥	K♣
8	6♦	J♠	K♥	4♣	8♦	K♠	4♥	9♣	A♦	5♠	10♥	A♣
9	7♦	Q♠	A♥	5♣	9♦	A♠	5♥	10♣	2♦	6♠	J♥	2♣
10	8♦	K♠	2♥	6♣	10♦	2♠	6♥	J♣	3♦	7♠	Q♥	3♣
11	9♦	A♠	3♥	7♣	J♦	3♠	7♥	Q♣	4♦	8♠	K♥	4♣
12	10♦	2♠	4♥	8♣	Q♦	4♠	8♥	K♣	5♦	9♠	A♥	5♣
13	J♦	3♠	5♥	9♣	K♦	5♠	9♥	A♣	6♦	10♠	2♥	6♣
14	Q♦	4♠	6♥	10♣	A♦	6♠	10♥	2♣	7♦	J♠	3♥	7♣
15	K♦	5♠	7♥	J♣	2♦	7♠	J♥	3♣	8♦	Q♠	4♥	8♣
16	A♦	6♥	8♥	Q♣	3♦	8♠	Q♥	4♣	9♦	K♠	5♥	9♣
17	2♦	7♠	9♥	K♣	4♦	9♠	K♥	5♣	10♦	A♠	6♥	10♣
18	3♦	8♠	10♥	A♣	5♦	10♠	A♥	6♣	J♦	2♠	7♥	J♣
19	4♦	9♥	J♥	2♣	6♦	J♠	2♥	7♣	Q♦	3♠	8♥	Q♣
20	5♦	10♥	Q♥	3♣	7♦	Q♠	3♥	8♣	K♦	4♠	9♥	K♣
21	6♠	J♥	K♥	4♦	8♠	K♠	4♥	9♣	A♠	5♠	10♥	A♦
22	7♠	Q♥	A♣	5♦	9♠	A♥	5♥	10♣	2♠	6♠	J♥	2♦
23	8♠	K♥	2♣	6♦	10♠	2♥	6♣	J♣	3♠	7♠	Q♣	3♦
24	9♠	A♥	3♣	7♦	J♠	3♥	7♣	Q♦	4♠	8♥	K♣	4♦
25	10♠	2♥	4♣	8♦	Q♠	4♥	8♣	K♦	5♠	9♥	A♣	5♦
26	J♠	3♥	5♣	9♦	K♠	5♥	9♣	A♦	6♠	10♥	2♣	6♦
27	Q♠	4♥	6♣	10♦	A♠	6♥	10♣	2♦	7♠	J♥	3♣	7♦
28	K♠	5♥	7♣	J♦	2♠	7♥	J♣	3♦	8♠	Q♥	4♣	8♦
29	A♠	Joker	8♣	Q♦	3♠	8♥	Q♣	4♦	9♠	K♥	5♣	9♦
30	2♠		9♣	K♦	4♠	9♥	K♣	5♦	10♠	A♥	6♣	10♦
31	3♠		10♣		5♠		A♣	6♦		2♥		J♦